ABOUT THIS PUBLICATION

FOR SERVICE ASSISTANCE

Customer Service
1.704.898.0770

North Carolina General Statues is published by The Muliti-Media Group of Greater Charlotte in Charlotte, North Carolina. Copyright 2015 by the Multi-Media Group of Greater Charlotte. This book or parts thereof may not be reproduced in any form, stored in a retrieval system, or transmitted in any form by any means—electronic, mechanical, photocopy, recording or otherwise—without prior written permission of the publisher, except as provided by United States of America copyright law.

The records required by U.S. Code 2257(a) through (c) and the pertinent regulations 28 C.F.R. Cli. 1, Part 75 with respect to this publication and all materials associated with such records are maintained by The Multi-Media Group of Greater Charlotte, Publisher and available for review by Attorney General.

www.visionbooks.org

Copyright © 2015 by MMGGC
All rights reserved!

TID: 5061744
ISBN (10) digit: 1502915480
ISBN (13) digit: 978-1502915481

123-4-56789-01239-Paperback
123-4-56789-01239-Hardback

First Edition

090520140547

Printed in the United States of America

2015 EDITION

North Carolina Criminal Law And Procedure-Pamphlet # 50

Printed In conjunction with the Administration of the Courts

North Carolina Criminal Law and Procedure
Pamphlet Reference Guide

Chapters	Pamphlet
Chapter 1 Civil Procedure	1
Chapter 1 Civil Procedure (Continue)	2
Chapter 1A Rules of Civil Procedure	2
Chapter 1B Contribution.	2
Chapter 1C Enforcement of Judgments.	2
Chapter 1D Punitive Damages.	2
Chapter 1E Eastern Band of Cherokee Indians.	2
Chapter 1F North Carolina Uniform Interstate Depositions and Discovery Act.	2
Chapter 2 - Clerk of Superior Court [Repealed and Transferred.]	3
Chapter 3 - Commissioners of Affidavits and Deeds [Repealed.]	3
Chapter 4 - Common Law	3
Chapter 5 - Contempt [Repealed.]	3
Chapter 5A - Contempt	3
Chapter 6 - Liability for Court Costs	3
Chapter 7 - Courts [Repealed and Transferred.]	3
Chapter 7A – Judicial Department	3
Chapter 7A – Continuation (Judicial Department)	4
Chapter 7A – Continuation (Judicial Department)	5
Chapter 7B - Juvenile Code	5
Chapter 8 - Evidence	6
Chapter 8A - Interpreters for Deaf Persons [Recodified.]	6
Chapter 8B - Interpreters for Deaf Persons	6
Chapter 8C - Evidence Code	6
Chapter 9 - Jurors	6
Chapter 10 - Notaries [Repealed.]	6
Chapter 10A - Notaries [Recodified.]	6
Chapter 10B - Notaries	6
Chapter 11 - Oaths	6
Chapter 12 - Statutory Construction	6
Chapter 13 - Citizenship Restored	6
Chapter 14 - Criminal Law	7
Chapter 14 –Criminal Law (Continuation)	8
Chapter 15 - Criminal Procedure	9
Chapter 15A - Criminal Procedure Act (Continuation)	10
Chapter 15A - Criminal Procedure Act (Continuation)	11
Chapter 15B - Victims Compensation	11
Chapter 15C - Address Confidentiality Program	11
Chapter 16 - Gaming Contracts and Futures	11
Chapter 17 - Habeas Corpus	11

Chapter 17A - Law-Enforcement Officers [Recodified.]	11
Chapter 17B - North Carolina Criminal Justice Education and Training System [Recodified.]	11
Chapter 17C - North Carolina Criminal Justice Education and Training Standards Commission	11
Chapter 17D - North Carolina Justice Academy	11
Chapter 17E - North Carolina Sheriffs' Education and Training Standards Commission	11
Chapter 18 - Regulation of Intoxicating Liquors [Repealed.]	12
Chapter 18A - Regulation of Intoxicating Liquors [Repealed.]	12
Chapter 18B - Regulation of Alcoholic Beverages	12
Chapter 18C - North Carolina State Lottery	12
Chapter 19 - Offenses against Public Morals	12
Chapter 19A - Protection of Animals	12
Chapter 20 - Motor Vehicles	13
Chapter 20 - Motor Vehicles (Continuation)	14
Chapter 20 - Motor Vehicles (Continuation)	15
Chapter 20 - Motor Vehicles (Continuation)	16
Chapter 21 - Bills of Lading	17
Chapter 22 - Contracts Requiring Writing	17
Chapter 22A - Signatures	17
Chapter 22B - Contracts Against Public Policy	17
Chapter 22C - Payments to Subcontractors	17
Chapter 23 - Debtor and Creditor	17
Chapter 24 – Interest	17
Chapter 25 – Uniform Commercial Code	18
Chapter 25 – Uniform Commercial Code (Continuation)	19
Chapter 25A – Retail Installment Sales Act	20
Chapter 25B - Credit	20
Chapter 25C - Sales of Artwork	20
Chapter 26 - Suretyship	20
Chapter 27 - Warehouse Receipts [Repealed.]	20
Chapter 28 - Administration [Repealed.]	20
Chapter 28A - Administration of Decedents' Estates	20
Chapter 28B - Estates of Absentees in Military Service	20
Chapter 28C - Estates of Missing Persons	20
Chapter 29 - Intestate Succession	21
Chapter 30 - Surviving Spouses	21
Chapter 31 - Wills	21
Chapter 31A - Acts Barring Property Rights	21
Chapter 31B - Renunciation of Property and Renunciation of Fiduciary Powers Act	21
Chapter 31C - Uniform Disposition of Community Property Rights at Death Act	21
Chapter 32 - Fiduciaries	21
Chapter 32A - Powers of Attorney	21
Chapter 33 - Guardian and Ward [Repealed and Recodified.]	21

Chapter 33A - North Carolina Uniform Transfers to Minors Act	21
Chapter 33B - North Carolina Uniform Custodial Trust Act	21
Chapter 34 - Veterans' Guardianship Act	22
Chapter 35 - Sterilization Procedures	22
Chapter 35A - Incompetency and Guardianship	22
Chapter 36 - Trusts and Trustees [Repealed.]	22
Chapter 36A - Trusts and Trustees	22
Chapter 36B - Uniform Management of Institutional Funds Act [Repealed.]	22
Chapter 36C - North Carolina Uniform Trust Code	22
Chapter 36D - North Carolina Community Third Party Trusts, Pooled Trusts	23
Chapter 36E - Uniform Prudent Management of Institutional Funds Act	23
Chapter 37 - Allocation of Principal and Income [Repealed.]	23
Chapter 37A - Uniform Principal and Income Act	23
Chapter 38 - Boundaries	23
Chapter 38A - Landowner Liability	23
Chapter 39 - Conveyances	23
Chapter 39A - Transfer Fee Covenants Prohibited	23
Chapter 40 - Eminent Domain [Repealed.]	23
Chapter 40A - Eminent Domain	23
Chapter 41 - Estates	23
Chapter 41A - State Fair Housing Act	23
Chapter 42 - Landlord and Tenant	23
Chapter 42A - Vacation Rental Act	23
Chapter 43 - Land Registration	23
Chapter 44 - Liens	24
Chapter 44A - Statutory Liens and Charges	24
Chapter 45 - Mortgages and Deeds of Trust	24
Chapter 45A - Good Funds Settlement Act	24
Chapter 46 - Partition	24
Chapter 47 - Probate and Registration	25
Chapter 47A - Unit Ownership	25
Chapter 47B - Real Property Marketable Title Act	25
Chapter 47C - North Carolina Condominium Act	25
Chapter 47D - Notice of Settlement Act [Expired.]	25
Chapter 47E - Residential Property Disclosure Act	25
Chapter 47F - North Carolina Planned Community Act	25
Chapter 47G - Option to Purchase Contracts	25
Chapter 47H - Contracts for Deed	25
Chapter 48 - Adoptions +	26
Chapter 48A - Minors	26
Chapter 49 - Bastardy	26
Chapter 49A - Rights of Children	26
Chapter 50 - Divorce and Alimony	26
Chapter 50A - Uniform Child-Custody Jurisdiction and	

Enforcement Act	26
Chapter 50B - Domestic Violence	26
Chapter 50C - Civil No-Contact Orders	26
Chapter 51 - Marriage	26
Chapter 52 - Powers and Liabilities of Married Persons	27
Chapter 52A - Uniform Reciprocal Enforcement of Support Act [Repealed.]	27
Chapter 52B - Uniform Premarital Agreement Act	27
Chapter 52C - Uniform Interstate Family Support Act	27
Chapter 53 - Banks	27
Chapter 53A - Business Development Corporations and North Carolina Capital Resource Corporations	28
Chapter 53B - Financial Privacy Act	28
Chapter 54 - Cooperative Organizations	28
Chapter 54A - Capital Stock Savings and Loan Associations [Repealed.]	28
Chapter 54B - Savings and Loan Associations	29
Chapter 54C - Savings Banks	29
Chapter 55 - North Carolina Business Corporation Act	30
Chapter 55A - North Carolina Nonprofit Corporation Act	31
Chapter 55B - Professional Corporation Act	31
Chapter 55C - Foreign Trade Zones	31
Chapter 55D - Filings, Names, and Registered Agents for Corporations, Nonprofit Corporations, and Partnerships	31
Chapter 56 - Electric, Telegraph and Power Companies [Repealed.]	31
Chapter 57 - Hospital, Medical and Dental Service Corporations [Recodified.]	31
Chapter 57A - Health Maintenance Organization Act [Recodified.]	31
Chapter 57B - Health Maintenance Organization Act [Recodified.]	31
Chapter 57C - North Carolina Limited Liability Company Act.	31
Chapter 58 - Insurance.	32
Chapter 58 - Insurance (Continuation)	33
Chapter 58 - Insurance (Continuation)	34
Chapter 58 - Insurance (Continuation)	35
Chapter 58 - Insurance (Continuation)	36
Chapter 58 - Insurance (Continuation)	37
Chapter 58 - Insurance (Continuation)	38
Chapter 58A - North Carolina Health Insurance Trust Commission [Recodified.]	38
Chapter 59 - Partnership.	39
Chapter 59B - Uniform Unincorporated Nonprofit Association Act.	39
Chapter 60 - Railroads and Other Carriers [Repealed and Transferred.]	39
Chapter 61 - Religious Societies	39
Chapter 62 - Public Utilities	39

Chapter 62 - Public Utilities (Continuation)	40
Chapter 62A - Public Safety Telephone Service And Wireless Telephone Service	40
Chapter 63 - Aeronautics	40
Chapter 63A - North Carolina Global TransPark Authority	40
Chapter 64 - Aliens	40
Chapter 65 – Cemeteries	40
Chapter 66 - Commerce and Business	41
Chapter 67 - Dogs	41
Chapter 68 - Fences and Stock Law	41
Chapter 69 - Fire Protection	41
Chapter 70 - Indian Antiquities, Archaeological Resources and Unmarked Human Skeletal Remains Protection	42
Chapter 71 - Indians [Repealed.]	42
Chapter 71A - Indians	42
Chapter 72 - Inns, Hotels and Restaurants	42
Chapter 73 - Mills	42
Chapter 74 - Mines and Quarries	42
Chapter 74A - Company Police [Repealed.]	42
Chapter 74B - Private Protective Services Act [Repealed.]	42
Chapter 74C - Private Protective Services	42
Chapter 74D - Alarm Systems	42
Chapter 74E - Company Police Act	42
Chapter 74F - Locksmith Licensing Act	42
Chapter 74G - Campus Police Act	42
Chapter 75 - Monopolies, Trusts and Consumer Protection	42
Chapter 75A - Boating and Water Safety	43
Chapter 75B - Discrimination in Business	43
Chapter 75C - Motion Picture Fair Competition Act	43
Chapter 75D - Racketeer Influenced and Corrupt Organizations	43
Chapter 75E - Unlawful Activities in Connection With Certain Corporate Transactions	43
Chapter 76 - Navigation	43
Chapter 76A - Navigation and Pilotage Commissions	43
Chapter 77 - Rivers, Creeks, and Coastal Waters	43
Chapter 78 - Securities Law [Repealed.]	43
Chapter 78A - North Carolina Securities Act	43
Chapter 78B - Tender Offer Disclosure Act [Repealed.]	43
Chapter 78C - Investment Advisers	43
Chapter 78D - Commodities Act	43
Chapter 79 - Strays [Repealed.]	43
Chapter 80 - Trademarks, Brands, etc.	44
Chapter 81 - Weights and Measures [Recodified.]	44
Chapter 81A - Weights and Measures Act of 1975.	44
Chapter 82 - Wrecks [Repealed.]	44
Chapter 83 - Architects [Recodified.]	44

Chapter 83A - Architects	44
Chapter 84 - Attorneys-at-Law	44
Chapter 84A - Foreign Legal Consultants	44
Chapter 85 - Auctions and Auctioneers [Repealed.]	44
Chapter 85A - Bail Bondsmen and Runners [Recodified.]	44
Chapter 85B - Auctions and Auctioneers	44
Chapter 85C - Bail Bondsmen and Runners [Recodified.]	44
Chapter 86 - Barbers [Recodified.]	44
Chapter 86A - Barbers	44
Chapter 87 - Contractors	44
Chapter 88 - Cosmetic Art [Repealed.]	44
Chapter 88A - Electrolysis Practice Act	44
Chapter 88B - Cosmetic Art	45
Chapter 89 - Engineering and Land Surveying [Recodified.]	45
Chapter 89A - Landscape Architects	45
Chapter 89B - Foresters	45
Chapter 89C - Engineering and Land Surveying	45
Chapter 89D - Landscape Contractors	45
Chapter 89E - Geologists Licensing Act	45
Chapter 89F - North Carolina Soil Scientist Licensing Act	45
Chapter 89G - Irrigation Contractors	45
Chapter 90 - Medicine and Allied Occupations	45
Chapter 90 - Medicine and Allied Occupations (Continuation)	46
Chapter 90 - Medicine and Allied Occupations (Continuation)	47
Chapter 90 - Medicine and Allied Occupations (Continuation)	48
Chapter 90A - Sanitarians and Water and Wastewater Treatment Facility Operators	48
Chapter 90B - Social Worker Certification and Licensure Act	48
Chapter 90C - North Carolina Recreational Therapy Licensure Act	48
Chapter 90D - Interpreters and Transliterators	48
Chapter 91 - Pawnbrokers [Repealed.]	48
Chapter 91A - Pawnbrokers Modernization Act of 1989	48
Chapter 92 - Photographers [Deleted.]	48
Chapter 93 - Certified Public Accountants	48
Chapter 93A - Real Estate License Law	49
Chapter 93B - Occupational Licensing Boards	49
Chapter 93C - Watchmakers [Repealed.]	49
Chapter 93D - North Carolina State Hearing Aid Dealers and Fitters Board.	49
Chapter 93E - North Carolina Appraisers Act	49
Chapter 94 - Apprenticeship	49
Chapter 95 - Department of Labor and Labor Regulations	49
Chapter 95 - Department of Labor and Labor Regulations (Continuation)	50
Chapter 96 - Employment Security	50
Chapter 97 - Workers' Compensation Act	50
Chapter 97 - Workers' Compensation Act (Continuation)	51

Chapter 98 - Burnt and Lost Records	51
Chapter 99 - Libel and Slander	51
Chapter 99A - Civil Remedies for Criminal Actions	51
Chapter 99B - Products Liability	51
Chapter 99C - Actions Relating to Winter Sports Safety and Accidents	51
Chapter 99D - Civil Rights	51
Chapter 99E - Special Liability Provisions	51
Chapter 100 - Monuments, Memorials and Parks	51
Chapter 101 - Names of Persons	51
Chapter 102 - Official Survey Base	51
Chapter 103 - Sundays, Holidays and Special Days	51
Chapter 104 - United States Lands	51
Chapter 104A - Degrees of Kinship	51
Chapter 104B - Hurricanes or Other Acts of Nature	51
Chapter 104C - Atomic Energy, Radioactivity and Ionizing Radiation [Repealed and Recodified.]	51
Chapter 104D - Southern States Energy Compact	51
Chapter 104E - North Carolina Radiation Protection Act	51
Chapter 104F - Southeast Interstate Low-Level Radioactive Waste Management Compact [Repealed]	51
Chapter 104G - North Carolina Low-Level Radioactive Waste Management Authority Act of 1987 [Repealed]	51
Chapter 105 - Taxation	51
Chapter 105 - Taxation (Continuation)	52
Chapter 105 - Taxation (Continuation)	53
Chapter 105 - Taxation (Continuation)	54
Chapter 105A - Setoff Debt Collection Act	55
Chapter 105B - Defaulted Student Loan Recovery Act	55
Chapter 106 - Agriculture	55
Chapter 106 - Agriculture (Continue)	56
Chapter 106 - Agriculture (Continue)	57
Chapter 107 - Agricultural Development Districts [Repealed.]	57
Chapter 108 - Social Services [Repealed and Recodified.]	57
Chapter 108A - Social Services	57
Chapter 108B - Community Action Programs	58
Chapter 108C Medicaid and Health Choice Provider Requirements.	58
Chapter 108D Medicaid Managed Care for Behavioral Health Services.	58
Chapter 109 - Bonds [Recodified.]	58
Chapter 110 - Child Welfare	58
Chapter 111 - Aid to the Blind	58
Chapter 112 - Confederate Homes and Pensions [Repealed.]	58
Chapter 113 - Conservation and Development	58
Chapter 113 - Conservation and Development (Continuation)	59

Chapter 113A - Pollution Control and Environment	59
Chapter 113A - Pollution Control and Environment (Continuation)	60
Chapter 113B - North Carolina Energy Policy Act of 1975	60
Chapter 114 - Department of Justice	60
Chapter 115 - Elementary and Secondary Education [Repealed.]	60
Chapter 115A - Community Colleges, Technical Institutes, and Industrial Education Centers [Repealed.]	60
Chapter 115B - Tuition and Fee Waivers	60
Chapter 115C - Elementary and Secondary Education	60
Chapter 115C - Elementary and Secondary Education (Continuation)	61
Chapter 115C - Elementary and Secondary Education (Continuation)	62
Chapter 115C - Elementary and Secondary Education (Continuation)	63
Chapter 115D - Community Colleges	63
Chapter 115E - Private Educational Facilities Finance Act [Recodified]	63
Chapter 116 - Higher Education	63
Chapter 116 - Higher Education (Continuation)	63
Chapter 116A - Escheats and Abandoned Property [Repealed.]	64
Chapter 116B - Escheats and Abandoned Property	64
Chapter 116C - Continuum of Education Programs	64
Chapter 116D - Higher Education Bonds	64
Chapter 117 - Electrification	64
Chapter 118 - Firemen's and Rescue Squad Workers' Relief and Pension Funds [Recodified]	64
Chapter 118A - Firemen's Death Benefit Act [Repealed.]	64
Chapter 118B - Members of a Rescue Squad Death Benefit Act [Repealed.]	64
Chapter 119 - Gasoline and Oil Inspection and Regulation	64
Chapter 120 - General Assembly	65
Chapter 120 - General Assembly (Continuation)	66
Chapter 120 - General Assembly (Continuation)	67
Chapter 120C - Lobbying	67
Chapter 121 - Archives and History	67
Chapter 122 - Hospitals for the Mentally Disordered [Repealed.]	67
Chapter 122A - North Carolina Housing Finance Agency	67
Chapter 122B - North Carolina Agricultural Facilities Finance Act [Repealed.]	67
Chapter 122C - Mental Health, Developmental Disabilities, and Substance Abuse Act of 1985	67
Chapter 122C - Mental Health, Developmental Disabilities, and Substance Abuse Act of 1985 (Continuation)	68
Chapter 122D - North Carolina Agricultural Finance Act	68

Chapter 122E - North Carolina Housing Trust and Oil Overcharge Act	68
Chapter 123 - Impeachment	69
Chapter 123A - Industrial Development [Repealed.]	69
Chapter 124 - Internal Improvements	69
Chapter 125 - Libraries	69
Chapter 126 - State Personnel System	69
Chapter 127 - Militia [Repealed.]	69
Chapter 127A - Militia	69
Chapter 127B - Military Affairs	69
Chapter 127C - Advisory Commission on Military Affairs	69
Chapter 128 - Offices and Public Officers	69
Chapter 128 - Offices and Public Officers (Continuation)	70
Chapter 129 - Public Buildings and Grounds	70
Chapter 130 - Public Health [Repealed.]	70
Chapter 130A - Public Health	70
Chapter 130A - Public Health (Continuation)	71
Chapter 130A - Public Health (Continuation)	72
Chapter 130B - Hazardous Waste Management Commission [Repealed.]	72
Chapter 131 - Public Hospitals [Repealed.]	72
Chapter 131A - Health Care Facilities Finance Act	72
Chapter 131B - Licensing of Ambulatory Surgical Facilities [Repealed.]	72
Chapter 131C - Charitable Solicitation Licensure Act [Repealed.]	72
Chapter 131D - Inspection and Licensing of Facilities	72
Chapter 131E - Health Care Facilities and Services	72
Chapter 131E - Health Care Facilities and Services (Continuation)	73
Chapter 131F - Solicitation of Contributions	73
Chapter 132 - Public Records	73
Chapter 133 - Public Works	74
Chapter 134 - Youth Development [Recodified.]	74
Chapter 134A - Youth Services [Repealed.]	74
Chapter 135 - Retirement System for Teachers and State Employees; Social Security; Health Insurance Program for Children	74
Chapter 135 - Retirement System for Teachers and State Employees; Social Security; Health Insurance Program for Children	75
Chapter 136 - Transportation	75
Chapter 136 - Transportation (Continuation)	76
Chapter 137 - Rural Rehabilitation [Repealed.]	76
Chapter 138 - Salaries, Fees and Allowances	76
Chapter 138A - State Government Ethics Act	76
Chapter 139 - Soil and Water Conservation Districts	76

Chapter 140 - State Art Museum; Symphony and Art Societies	76
Chapter 140A - State Awards System	76
Chapter 141 - State Boundaries	76
Chapter 142 - State Debt	76
Chapter 143 - State Departments, Institutions, and Commissions	77
Chapter 143 - State Departments, Institutions, and Commissions (Continuation)	78
Chapter 143 - State Departments, Institutions, and Commissions (Continuation)	79
Chapter 143 - State Departments, Institutions, and Commissions (Continuation)	80
Chapter 143A - State Government Reorganization	80
Chapter 143B - Executive Organization Act of 1973	80
Chapter 143B - Executive Organization Act of 1973 (Continuation)	81
Chapter 143B - Executive Organization Act of 1973 (Continuation)	82
Chapter 143C - State Budget Act	83
Chapter 143D - The State Governmental Accountability and Internal Control Act	83
Chapter 144 - State Flag, Official Governmental Flags, Motto, and Colors	83
Chapter 145 - State Symbols and Other Official Adoptions.	83
Chapter 146 - State Lands	83
Chapter 147 - State Officers	83
Chapter 148 - State Prison System	84
Chapter 149 - State Song and Toast	84
Chapter 150 - Uniform Revocation of Licenses [Repealed.]	84
Chapter 150A - Administrative Procedure Act [Recodified.]	84
Chapter 150B - Administrative Procedure Act	84
Chapter 151 - Constables [Repealed.]	84
Chapter 152 - Coroners	84
Chapter 152A - County Medical Examiner [Repealed.]	84
Chapter 152A - County Medical Examiner [Repealed.] (Continuation)	85
Chapter 153 - Counties and County Commissioners [Repealed.]	85
Chapter 153A - Counties	85
Chapter 153B - Mountain Resources Planning Act	85
Chapter 153C - Uwharrie Regional Resources Act	85
Chapter 154 - County Surveyor [Repealed.]	85
Chapter 155 - County Treasurer [Repealed.]	85
Chapter 156 - Drainage	85
Chapter 156 – Drainage (Continuation)	86

Chapter 157 - Housing Authorities and Projects	86
Chapter 157A - Historic Properties Commissions [Transferred.]	86
Chapter 158 - Local Development	86
Chapter 159 - Local Government Finance	86
Chapter 159 - Local Government Finance (Continuation)	87
Chapter 159A - Pollution Abatement and Industrial Facilities Financing Act [Unconstitutional.]	87
Chapter 159B - Joint Municipal Electric Power and Energy Act	87
Chapter 159C - Industrial and Pollution Control Facilities Financing Act	87
Chapter 159D - The North Carolina Capital Facilities Financing Act	87
Chapter 159E - Registered Public Obligations Act	87
Chapter 159F - North Carolina Energy Development Authority [Repealed.]	87
Chapter 159G - Water Infrastructure	87
Chapter 159H - [Reserved.]	87
Chapter 159I - Solid Waste Management Loan Program and Local Government Special Obligation Bonds	87
Chapter 160 - Municipal Corporations [Repealed And Transferred.]	87
Chapter 160A - Cities and Towns	88
Chapter 160A - Cities and Towns (Continuation)	89
Chapter 160B - Consolidated City-County Act	89
Chapter 160C - Baseball Park Districts [Repealed.]	90
Chapter 161 - Register of Deeds	90
Chapter 162 - Sheriff	90
Chapter 162A - Water and Sewer Systems	90
Chapter 162B Continuity of Local Government in Emergency.	90
Chapter 163 Elections and Election Laws.	90
Chapter 163 Elections and Election Laws. (Continuation)	91
Chapter 164 Concerning the General Statutes of North Carolina.	92
Chapter 165 Veterans.	92
Chapter 166 Civil Preparedness Agencies [Repealed.]	92
Chapter 166A North Carolina Emergency Management Act.	92
Chapter 167 State Civil Air Patrol [Repealed.]	92
Chapter 168 Persons with Disabilities.	92
Chapter 168A Persons With Disabilities Protection Act.	92

§ 95-151. Discrimination.

No employer, employee, or any other person related to the administration of this Article shall be discriminated against in any work, procedure, or employment by reason of sex, race, ethnic origin, or by reason of religious affiliation. (1973, c. 295, s. 26.)

§ 95-152. Confidentiality of trade secrets.

All information reported to or otherwise obtained by the Commissioner or his agents or representatives in connection with any inspection or proceeding under this Article which contains or which might reveal a trade secret shall be considered confidential, as provided by section 1905 of Title 18 of U.S.C., except as to carrying out this Article or when it is relevant in any proceeding under this Article. In any such proceeding the Commissioner, the Commission, or the court shall issue such orders as may be appropriate to protect the confidentiality of trade secrets. (1973, c. 295, s. 27; 2005-133, s. 9.)

§ 95-153. Reserved for future codification purposes.

§ 95-154. Authorization for similar safety and health federal-state programs.

Consistent with the requirements and conditions provided in this Article the State, upon the recommendation of the Commissioner of Labor and approval of the Governor, may enter into agreements or arrangements with other federal agencies for the purpose of administering occupational safety and health measures for such employees and employers within the State of North Carolina as may be covered by such federal safety and health statutes. (1973, c. 295, s. 29.)

§ 95-155. Construction of Article and severability.

This Article shall receive a liberal construction to the end that the safety and health of the employees of the State may be effectuated and protected. If any provision of this Article or the application thereof to any person or circumstance is held to be invalid, such invalidity shall not affect other provisions or applications of the Article which can be given effect without the invalid provision or application, and to this end the provisions of this Article are severable. (1973, c. 295, s. 30.)

§§ 95-156 through 95-160. Reserved for future codification purposes.

Article 17.

The Uniform Wage Payment Law of North Carolina.

§§ 95-161 through 95-172. Repealed by Session Laws 1979, c. 839, s. 2.

Article 18.

Identification of Toxic or Hazardous Substances.

Part 1. General Provisions.

§ 95-173. Short title.

This Article shall be cited as the Hazardous Chemicals Right to Know Act. (1985, c. 775, s. 1.)

§ 95-174. Definitions.

(a) "Chemical manufacturer" shall mean a manufacturing facility classified in Standard Industrial Classification (SIC) Codes 20 through 39 where chemicals are produced for use or distribution in North Carolina.

(b) "Chemical name" shall mean the scientific designation of a chemical in accordance with the nomenclature system developed by the International Union of Pure and Applied Chemistry (IUPAC), or the Chemical Abstracts Service (CAS) rules of nomenclature or a name which will clearly identify the chemical for the purpose of conducting a hazard evaluation.

(c) "Common name" shall mean any designation or identification such as a code name, code number, trade name, brand name or generic name used to identify a chemical other than by its chemical name.

(d) "Distributor" shall mean any business, other than a chemical manufacturer or importer, which supplies hazardous chemicals to other distributors or to purchasers.

(e) "Employee" shall mean any person who is employed by an employer under normal operating conditions.

(f) "Employer" means a person engaged in business who has employees, including the State and its political subdivisions but excluding an individual whose only employees are domestic workers or casual laborers who are hired to work at the individual's residence.

(g) "Facility" shall mean one or more establishments, factories, or buildings located at one contiguous site in North Carolina.

(h) "Fire Chief" shall mean Fire Chief or Fire Marshall, or Emergency Response Coordinator in the absence of a Fire Chief or Fire Marshall for the appropriate local fire department.

(i) Repealed by Session Laws 1987, c. 489, s. 1.

(j) "Fire Department" shall mean the fire department having jurisdiction over the facility.

(k) "Hazardous chemical" shall mean any element, chemical compound or mixture of elements and/or compounds which is a physical hazard or health hazard as defined in subsection (c) of the OSHNC Standard or a hazardous substance as defined in standards adopted by the Occupational Safety and Health Division of the North Carolina Department of Labor in Title 13, Chapter 7 of the North Carolina Administrative Code (13 NCAC 7).

(l) "Hazardous Substance List" shall mean the list required by G.S. 95-191.

(m) "Hazardous substance trade secret" means any formula, plan, pattern, device, process, production information, or compilation of information, which is not patented, which is known only to the employer, the employer's licensees, the employer's employees, and certain other individuals, and which is used or developed for use in the employer's business, and which gives the employer possessing it the opportunity to obtain a competitive advantage over businesses who do not possess it, or the secrecy of which is certified by an appropriate official of the federal government as necessary for national defense purposes. The chemical name and Chemical Abstracts Service number of a substance shall be considered a trade secret only if the employer can establish that the identity or composition of the substance cannot be readily ascertained without undue expense by analytical techniques, laboratory procedures, or other lawful means available to a competitor.

(n) "Label" shall mean any written, printed, or graphic material displayed on or affixed to containers of hazardous chemicals.

(o) "Manufacturing facility" shall mean a facility classified in SIC Codes 20 through 39 which manufactures or uses a hazardous chemical or chemicals in North Carolina.

(p) "Material Safety Data Sheets" or "MSDS" shall mean chemical information sheets adopted by the Occupational Safety and Health Division of the North Carolina Department of Labor in Title 13, Chapter 7 of the North Carolina Administrative Code (13 NCAC 7).

(q) "Nonmanufacturing facility" shall mean any facility in North Carolina other than a facility in SIC Code 20 through 39, the State of North Carolina (and its political subdivisions) and volunteer emergency service organizations whose members may be exposed to chemical hazards during emergency situations.

(r) "OSHNC Standard" shall mean the current Hazard Communication Standard adopted by the Occupational Safety and Health Division of North Carolina Department of Labor in Title 13, Chapter 7 of the North Carolina Administrative Code (13 NCAC 7).

(s) "Storage and Container" shall have the ordinary meaning however it does not include pipes used in the transfer of substances or the fuel tanks of self propelled internal combustion vehicles. (1985, c. 775, s. 1; 1987, c. 489, ss. 1, 2; 1998-217, ss. 28-30.)

§§ 95-175 through 95-190. Reserved for future codification purposes.

Part 2. Public Safety and Emergency Response Right to Know.

§ 95-191. Hazardous Substance List.

(a) All employers who manufacture, process, use, store, or produce hazardous chemicals, shall compile and maintain a Hazardous Substance List which shall contain the following information for each hazardous chemical stored in the facility in quantities of 55 gallons or 500 pounds, whichever is greater:

(1) The chemical name or the common name used on the MSDS or container label;

(2) The maximum amount of the chemical stored at the facility at any time during a year, using the following ranges:

Class A, which shall include quantities of less than 55 gallons or 500 pounds;

Class B, which shall include quantities of between 55 gallons to 550 gallons, and quantities of between 500 pounds and 5,000 pounds; and

Class C, which shall include quantities of between 550 gallons and 5500 gallons, and quantities between 5,000 pounds and 50,000 pounds; and

Class D, which shall include quantities of greater than 5500 gallons or 50,000 pounds; and

(3) The area in the facility in which the hazardous chemical is normally stored and to what extent the chemical may be stored at altered temperature or pressure.

(b) The Hazardous Substance List shall be updated quarterly if necessary, but not less often than annually; however, if a chemical is deleted from, or added to, the Hazardous Substance List, or if the quantity changes sufficiently to cause the chemical to be in a different class as defined in subsection (a) of this section, the employer shall update the Hazardous Substance List to reflect those changes as soon as practicable, but in any event within 30 days of such change.

(b1) In lieu of the information required by subdivisions (a)(1) through (a)(3), employers may substitute the information specified in section 312(d)(2) of the Superfund Amendments and Reauthorization Act of 1986, P.L. 99-499.

(c) The Hazardous Substance List may be prepared for the facility as a whole, or for each area in a facility where hazardous chemicals are stored, at the option of the employer but shall include only chemicals used or stored in North Carolina. (1985, c. 775, s. 1; 1987, c. 489, s. 3.)

§ 95-192. Material safety data sheets.

(a) Chemical manufacturers and distributors shall provide material safety data sheets (MSDS's) to manufacturing and nonmanufacturing purchasers of hazardous chemicals in North Carolina for each hazardous chemical purchased.

(b) Employers shall maintain the most current MSDS received from manufacturers or distributors for each hazardous chemical purchased. If an MSDS has not been provided by the manufacturer or distributor for chemicals on the Hazardous Substance List at the time the chemicals are received at the facility, the employer shall request one in writing from the manufacturer or distributor within 30 days after receipt of the chemical. If the employer does not receive an MSDS within 30 days after his written request, he shall notify the Commissioner of Labor of the failure by manufacturer or distributor to provide the MSDS. (1985, c. 775, s. 1.)

§ 95-193. Labels.

Existing labels on incoming containers of hazardous chemicals shall not be removed or defaced. All containers of hazardous substances must be clearly designated as hazardous. (1985, c. 775, s. 1.)

§ 95-194. Emergency information.

(a)   An employer who normally stores at a facility any hazardous chemical in an amount of at least 55 gallons or 500 pounds, whichever is greater, shall provide the Fire Chief of the Fire Department having jurisdiction over the facility, in writing, (i) the name(s) and telephone number(s) of knowledgeable representative(s) of the employer who can be contacted for further information or in case of an emergency and (ii) a copy of the Hazardous Substance List.

(b)   Each employer shall provide a copy of the Hazardous Substance List to the Fire Chief. The employer shall notify the Fire Chief in writing of any updates that occur in the previously submitted Hazardous Substance List as provided in G.S. 95-191(b).

(c)   The Fire Chief or his representative, upon request, shall be permitted on-site inspections at reasonable times of the chemicals located at the facility on the Hazardous Substance List for the sole purpose of preplanning Fire Department activities in the case of an emergency and insuring by inspection the usefulness and accuracy of the Hazardous Substance List and labels.

(d)   Employers shall provide to the Fire Chief, upon written request of the Fire Chief, a copy of the MSDS for any chemical on the Hazardous Substance List.

(e)   Upon written request of the Fire Chief, an employer shall prepare an emergency response plan for the facility that includes facility evacuation procedures, a list of emergency equipment available at the facility, and copies of other emergency response plans, such as the contingency plan required under rules governing the management of hazardous waste adopted pursuant to Article 9 of Chapter 130A of the General Statutes. A copy of the emergency response plan or any prefire plan or emergency response plan required under applicable North Carolina or federal statute or rule or regulation shall, upon written request by the Fire Chief, be given to the Fire Chief.

(f) The Fire Chief shall make information from the Hazardous Substance List, the emergency response plan, and MSDS's available to members of the Fire Department having jurisdiction over the facility and to personnel responsible for preplanning emergency response, police, medical or fire activities, but shall not otherwise distribute or disclose (or allow the disclosure of) information not available to the public under G.S. 95-208. Such persons receiving such information shall not disclose the information received and shall use such information only for the purpose of preplanning emergency response, police, medical or fire activities.

(g) Any knowing distribution or disclosure (or permitted disclosure) of any information referred to in subsection (f) of this section in any manner except as specifically permitted under that subsection (f) shall be punishable as a Class 1 misdemeanor. Restrictions concerning confidentiality or nondisclosure of information under this Article 18 shall be exemptions from the Public Records Act contained in Chapter 132 of the General Statutes, and such information shall not be disclosed notwithstanding the provisions of Chapter 132 of the General Statutes. (1985, c. 775, s. 1; 1987, c. 489, ss. 4-6; 1993, c. 539, s. 672; 1994, Ex. Sess., c. 24, s. 14(c); 2002-165, s. 1.2.)

§ 95-195. Complaints, investigations, penalties.

(a) Complaints of violations of this Part shall be filed in writing with the Commissioner of Labor. Such complaints received in writing from any Fire Chief relating to alleged violations of this Part shall be investigated in a timely manner by the Commissioner of Labor or his designated representative.

(b) Duly designated representatives of the Commissioner of Labor, upon presentation of appropriate credentials to the employer, shall have the right of entry into any facility at reasonable times to inspect and investigate complaints within reasonable limits, and in a reasonable manner. Following the investigation, the Commissioner shall make appropriate findings. Either the employer or the person complaining of a violation may request an administrative hearing pursuant to Chapter 150B of the General Statutes. This request for an administrative hearing shall be submitted to the Commissioner of Labor within 14 days following the Commissioner making his findings. The Commissioner shall within 30 days of receiving the request hold an administrative hearing in accordance with Article 3 of Chapter 150B of the General Statutes.

(c) If the Commissioner of Labor finds that the employer violated this Article, the Commissioner shall order the employer to comply within 14 days following receipt of written notification of the violation. Employers not complying within 14 days following receipt of written notification of a violation shall be subject to civil penalties of not more than one thousand dollars ($1,000) per violation imposed by the Commissioner of Labor. There shall be a separate offense for each day the violation continues. The clear proceeds of civil penalties provided for in this section shall be remitted to the Civil Penalty and Forfeiture Fund in accordance with G.S. 115C-457.2.

(d) Any order by the Commissioner under subsection (b) or (c) of this section shall be subject to judicial review as provided under Article 4 of Chapter 150B of the General Statutes. (1985, c. 775, s. 1; 1987, c. 489, s. 7; 1998-215, s. 112.)

§ 95-196. Employee rights.

No employer shall discharge, or cause to be discharged, or otherwise discipline or in any manner discriminate against an employee at the facility because the employee has assisted the Commissioner of Labor or his representative or the Fire Chief or his representative who may make or is making an inspection under G.S. 95-194(c) or G.S. 95-195(b), or has testified or is about to testify in any proceeding under this Article, or has used the provisions of G.S. 95-208. (1985, c. 775, s. 1.)

§ 95-197. Withholding hazardous substance trade secret information.

(a) An employer who believes that all or any part of the information required under G.S. 95-191, 95-192, 95-194(b) or 95-194(d) is a hazardous substance trade secret may withhold the information, provided that (i) hazard information on chemicals the identity of which is claimed as a hazardous substance trade secret is provided to the Fire Chief who shall hold it in confidence and (ii) the employer claims that the information is a hazardous substance trade secret.

(b) Any person in North Carolina may request in writing that the Commissioner of Labor review in camera an employer's hazardous substance trade secret claim. If the Commissioner of Labor finds that the claim is other than completely valid, this finding shall be appealable under subsection (d) of this section. If the Commissioner of Labor finds that the claim is valid, he shall then determine whether the nonconfidential information is sufficient for the Fire Chief to fulfill the responsibilities of his office. If the Commissioner of Labor finds that the information is not sufficient, he shall direct the employer to supplement the information with such other information as will provide the Fire Chief with sufficient information to fulfill the responsibilities of his office, but this finding shall be appealable under subsection (d) of this section.

(c) The Commissioner of Labor and the Fire Chief shall protect from disclosure any or all information coming into either or both of their possession when such information is marked by the employer as confidential, and they shall return all information so marked to the employer at the conclusion of their determination by the Commissioner of Labor. Any person who has access to any hazardous substance trade secret solely pursuant to this section and who discloses it knowing it to be a hazardous substance trade secret to any person not authorized to receive it shall be guilty of a Class I felony, and if knowingly or negligently disclosed to any person not authorized, shall be subject to civil action for damages and injunction by the owner of the hazardous substance trade secret, including, without limitation, actions under Article 24 of Chapter 66 of the General Statutes.

(d) The employer, Fire Chief, or person making the original request who is an aggrieved party shall have 30 days after receipt of notification by the Commissioner of his findings under subsection (b) to request an administrative hearing on the determination. Any such hearing shall be held in a manner similar to that provided for in G.S. Chapter 150B, Article 3 and the decision upon the request of any aggrieved party shall be subject to the judicial review provided for by G.S. Chapter 150B, Article 4, provided that these administrative and judicial hearings shall be conducted in camera to assure the confidentiality of the information being reviewed. (1985, c. 775, s. 1; 1987, c. 827, s. 1; 1993, c. 539, s. 1290; 1994, Ex. Sess., c. 24, s. 14(c).)

§ 95-198. Medical emergency and nonemergency situations.

(a) Where a treating health care provider determines that a medical emergency exists and the specific chemical identity of a hazardous chemical is necessary for emergency or first-aid treatment, the chemical manufacturer, importer, or employer shall immediately disclose the specific chemical identity of a hazardous substance trade secret substance to that treating physician or nurse, regardless of the existence of written statement of need or a confidentiality agreement. The chemical manufacturer, importer, or employer may require a written statement of need and a confidentiality agreement as soon as circumstances permit. The confidentiality agreement (i) may restrict the use of the information to the health purposes indicated in a written statement of need; (ii) may provide for appropriate legal remedies in the event of a breach of the agreement, including stipulation of a reasonable pre-estimate of likely damages; and (iii) may not include requirements for the posting of a penalty bond. The parties are not precluded from pursuing noncontractual remedies to the extent permitted by law.

(b) In nonemergency situations, a chemical manufacturer, importer, or employer shall, upon request, disclose a specific chemical identity, otherwise permitted to be withheld under this section, to a responsible party, as defined in the standards adopted in Title 13, Subchapter 7F of the North Carolina Administrative Code (13 NCAC 7F), providing medical or other occupational health services to exposed persons if the request is in writing and states the medical need for the information. The employer may require that the responsible party sign a confidentiality agreement prior to release of the information. The parties are not precluded from pursuing noncontractual remedies to the extent permitted by law.

(c) If the chemical manufacturer, importer or employer denies a written request for hazardous substance trade secret release, or does not provide this information within 30 days, the Department of Labor shall initiate the trade secret claim determination process under G.S. 95-197. (1985, c. 775, s. 1; 1998-217, s. 31.)

§§ 95-199 through 95-207. Reserved for future codification purposes.

Part 3. Community Right to Know.

§ 95-208. Community information on hazardous chemicals.

(a) Any person in North Carolina may request in writing from the employer a list of chemicals used or stored at the facility. The request shall include the name and address of the person making the request and a statement of the purpose for the request. If the person is requesting the list on behalf of or for the use of an organization, partnership, or corporation, he shall also disclose the name and business address of such organization, partnership, or corporation. The request may include, at the option of the employer, a statement to the effect that the information will be used only for the purpose stated. The employer shall furnish to the person making the request a list containing, at a minimum, all chemicals included on the Hazardous Substance List, the class of each chemical as defined in G.S. 95-191(a)(2), and an MSDS for each chemical for which an MSDS is available and is requested. Whenever an employer has withheld a chemical under the provisions of G.S. 95-197 from the information provided under G.S. 95-208, the employer must state that the information is being withheld and, upon request, must provide the MSDS for the chemical. Additional information may be furnished to the person making the request at the option of the employer. The employer shall provide, at a fee not to exceed the cost of reproducing the materials, the materials requested within 10 working days of the date the employer receives the written request for information.

(b) If the employer fails or refuses to provide the information required under subsection (a) of this section, the person requesting the information may request in writing that the Commissioner of Labor review the request. The Commissioner of Labor may conduct an investigation in the same manner as provided in G.S. 95-195(b). Following the investigation, the Commissioner shall make appropriate findings. Either the employer or the person making the initial request may request an administrative hearing pursuant to Chapter 150B of the General Statutes. This request for an administrative hearing shall be submitted to the Commissioner of Labor within 30 days following the Commissioner making his findings. The Commissioner of Labor shall within 30 days of receiving the request hold an administrative hearing to consider the request for information under subsection (a) of this section. This hearing shall be held as provided for in G.S. Chapter 150B, Article 3. If the Commissioner of Labor finds that the request complies with the requirements of subsection (a) of this section, the Commissioner of Labor shall direct that the employer provide to the person making the request a list containing, at a minimum, all chemicals used or stored at the facility included on the Hazardous Substance List, the class of each chemical as defined in G.S. 95-191(a)(2), and an MSDS for each chemical for which an MSDS is available and is requested and may in his discretion assess civil penalties as provided in G.S. 95-195(c); provided that it shall be a defense to such disclosure if the employer proves that the information has been requested directly or indirectly by, or in behalf of, a competitor of the employer, or that such information is a Hazardous Substance Trade Secret, or that the request did not comply with the requirements of subsection (a) of this section.

(c)   Any order by the Commissioner of Labor under subsection (b) of this section shall be subject to judicial review as provided under G.S. Chapter 150B, Article 4. (1985, c. 775, s. 1; 1987, c. 827, s. 1.)

§§ 95-209 through 95-215. Reserved for future codification purposes.

Part 4. Implementation.

§ 95-216. Exemptions.

Notwithstanding any language to the contrary, the provisions of this Article shall not apply to chemicals in or on the following:

(1)   Hazardous substances while being transported in interstate commerce into or through this State;

(2)   Products intended for personal consumption by employees in the facilities;

(3)   Retail food sale establishments and all other retail trade establishments in Standard Industrial Classification Codes 53 through 59, exclusive of processing and repair areas, except that the employer must comply with the provisions of G.S. 95-194(a)(i);

(4)   Any food, food additive, color additive, drug or cosmetic as such terms are defined in the Federal Food, Drug and Cosmetic Act (21 U.S.C. 301 et seq.);

(5)   A laboratory under the direct supervision or guidance of a technically qualified individual provided that:

a.   Labels on containers of incoming chemicals shall not be removed or defaced;

b. MSDS's received by the laboratory shall be maintained and made accessible to employees and students;

c. The laboratory is not used primarily to produce hazardous chemicals in bulk for commercial purposes; and

d. The laboratory operator complies with the provisions of G.S. 95-194(a)(i);

(6) Any farming operation which employs 10 or fewer full-time employees, except that if any hazardous chemical in an amount in excess of 55 gallons or 500 pounds, whichever is greater, is normally stored at the farming operation, the employer must comply with the provisions of G.S. 95-194(a)(i); and

(7) Any distilled spirits, tobacco, and untreated wood products; and

(8) Medicines used directly in patient care in health care facilities and health care facility laboratories. (1985, c. 775, s. 1; 1987, c. 489, s. 8.)

§ 95-217. Preemption of local regulations.

It is the intent of the General Assembly to prescribe this uniform system for the disclosure of information regarding the use or storage of hazardous chemicals. To that end, all units of local government in the State are preempted from exercising their powers to require disclosure, directly or indirectly, of information regarding the use or storage of hazardous chemicals by employers to any members of the public, or to any branch or agent of State or local government in any manner other than as provided for in this Article. This section does not preempt the enforcement of the provisions of any nationally recognized fire code that may be adopted by a unit of local government. (1985, c. 775, s. 1; 1987, c. 489, s. 9.)

§ 95-218. Severability.

The provisions of this Article are severable, and if any phrase, clause, sentence, or provision of this Article, or the application of any such phrase, clause, sentence or provision to any person, business entity or circumstances, other than those to which it was held invalid shall not be affected thereby. (1985, c. 775, s. 1.)

§ 95-219. Reserved for future codification purposes.

§ 95-220. Reserved for future codification purposes.

§ 95-221. Reserved for future codification purposes.

Article 19.

Migrant Housing Act of North Carolina.

§ 95-222. Short title; legislative purpose.

(a) This Article may be cited as the "Migrant Housing Act of North Carolina."

(b) It is the purpose and policy of the General Assembly to conform migrant housing standards to, as much as reasonably possible, the Occupational Safety and Health Act of North Carolina, and to ensure safe and healthy migrant housing conditions. The General Assembly finds that the general welfare of the State requires the enactment of this law under the police power of the State. (1989, c. 91, s. 2.)

§ 95-223. Definitions.

As used in this Article, unless the context requires otherwise:

(1) "Agricultural employment" means employment in any service or activity included within the provisions of Section 3(f) of the Fair Labor Standards Act of 1938, or section 3121(g) of the Internal Revenue Code of 1986; and the handling, planting, drying, packing, packaging, processing, freezing, or grading prior to delivery for storage of any agricultural or horticultural commodity in its unmanufactured state and including the harvesting of Christmas trees, and the harvesting of saltwater crabs;

(2) "Commissioner" means the Commissioner of Labor of North Carolina;

(3) "Day" means a calendar day;

(3a) "Director" means the Director of the Agricultural Safety and Health Bureau, who is the agent designated by the Commissioner to assist in the administration of this Article.

(4) "Established federal standard" means those standards as set out in, and interpretations issued by, the Secretary of the United States Department of Labor in 29 C.F.R. 1910.142, as amended;

(5) "Migrant" means an individual, and his dependents, who is employed in agricultural employment of a seasonal or other temporary nature, and who is required to be absent overnight from his permanent place of residence;

(6) "Migrant housing" means any facility, structure, real property, or other unit that is established, operated, or used as living quarters for migrants;

(7) "Operator" means any person who owns or controls migrant housing; and

(8) "Person" means an individual, partnership, association, joint stock company, corporation, trust, or legal representative;

(9) "Substantive violation" means a violation of a safety and health standard, including those that provide fire prevention, and adequate and sanitary supply of water, plumbing maintenance, structurally sound construction of buildings, effective maintenance of those buildings, provision of adequate heat as weather conditions require, and reasonable protection for inhabitants from insects and rodents. A substantive violation does not include technical or procedural violations of safety and health standards. (1989, c. 91, s. 2; 1993, c. 300, s. 3; 2007-548, s. 1.)

§ 95-224. Scope; powers and duties.

(a) The provisions of this Article shall apply to all operators and migrants except:

(1) Any person who, in the ordinary course of that person's business, regularly provides housing on a commercial basis to the general public; and who provides housing to migrants of the same character and on the same or comparable terms and conditions as those provided to the general public; or

(2) A housing unit owned by one or more of the occupants and occupied solely by a family unit.

(b) The Commissioner shall have the following powers and duties under this Article:

(1) To delegate to the Director the powers, duties, and responsibilities necessary to ensure safe and healthy migrant housing conditions.

(2) To supervise the Director.

(3) To issue preoccupancy certificates to certify that housing for migrant workers has been found to be in compliance with this Article.

(4) To conduct postoccupancy inspections of migrant housing in accordance with the provisions of G.S. 95-226(g). (1989, c. 91, s. 2; 2007-548, s. 2.)

§ 95-225. Adoption of standards and interpretations.

(a) Unless otherwise provided, all established federal standards are adopted and shall be enforced by the Department of Labor of North Carolina.

(b) The Commissioner shall provide for publication in the North Carolina Register any modification by the federal government of the established federal standards within 30 days of their adoption.

(c) For the protection of the public health, the Commission for Public Health shall adopt and the Department of Environment and Natural Resources shall enforce rules that establish water quality and water sanitation standards for migrant housing under this Article.

(d)   The requirements for the collection, treatment, and disposal of sewage, as provided in Article 11 of Chapter 130A, and the rules adopted pursuant to that Article shall apply to migrant housing.

(e)   Whenever the outside temperature falls below 50 degrees Fahrenheit and the migrant housing is occupied, heating equipment shall be provided and operable. Regardless of outside temperature, this equipment must be capable of maintaining living areas of 65 degrees Fahrenheit. If housing is to be occupied from May 15 until September 1 only, no heating equipment shall be required at the time of preoccupancy inspection.

(f)   All migrant housing shall comply with the standards regarding fire safety for migrant housing as adopted by the Commission for Public Health and in effect on January 1, 1989.

(g)   For purposes of this Article, the established federal standard provided in 29 C.F.R. 1910.142(i) does not apply. The following standards shall apply to migrant housing:

(1)   Food preparation facilities and eating areas shall be provided and maintained in a clean and sanitary manner;

(2)   A kitchen facility shall be provided with an operable stove with at least one burner per five people, and in no event with less than two burners; an operable refrigerator with .75 cubic feet per person minimum; a table; and a sink with running hot and cold water;

(3)   Surfaces with which food or drink come in contact shall be easily accessible for cleaning, and shall be nontoxic, resistant to corrosion, nonabsorbent, and free of open crevices;

(4)   Acceptable storage facilities shall be provided and shall be kept clean and free of vermin; and

(5)   All food service facilities, other than those where migrants procure and prepare food for their own or their family's consumption, shall comply with the standards regarding kitchen and dining room facilities for migrant housing, as adopted by the Commission for Public Health and in effect on January 1, 1989.

(h)   Each migrant shall be provided with a bed that shall include a mattress in good repair with a clean cover. The Department of Labor of North Carolina inspector shall determine the condition of the mattress and cover during the preoccupancy inspection. If the mattress or cover is damaged beyond normal wear and tear during the migrant's occupancy of the housing, the operator may charge the migrant the reasonable cost of replacing the mattress or cover. (1989, c. 91, s. 2; c. 727, s. 220; 1997-443, s. 11A.36; 2007-182, s. 2; 2007-548, s. 3.)

§ 95-226. Application for inspection.

(a) Except as provided in subsection (f) of this section, every operator shall request a preoccupancy inspection at least 45 days prior to the anticipated date of occupancy by applying directly to the Department of Labor of North Carolina or to the local health department. Upon receipt of an application by the Department of Labor of North Carolina, the Department of Labor of North Carolina shall immediately notify, in writing, the appropriate local health department; and the local health department shall inspect the migrant housing for compliance with G.S. 95-225(c) and (d). Upon receipt of the application by the local health department, the local health department shall immediately notify, in writing, the Department of Labor of North Carolina and shall inspect the migrant housing for compliance with G.S. 95-225(c) and (d).

The local health department shall forward the results of its inspection to the Department of Labor of North Carolina and to the operator. The Department of Labor of North Carolina shall inspect the migrant housing and certify to the operator the results of the inspection.

At the time the Department of Labor of North Carolina conducts a preoccupancy inspection, the Department of Labor of North Carolina shall provide the operator with a copy of the guide for employers on compliance with the Immigration and Nationality Act, 8 U.S.C. § 1101, et seq., as amended, prepared by the United States Department of Justice.

(b) The Department of Labor of North Carolina shall provide local health departments and Agricultural Extension offices with blank copies of forms for applying for preoccupancy inspections.

(c) The application for inspection shall include:

(1) The name, address, and telephone number of the operator;

(2) The location of the migrant housing;

(3) The anticipated number of migrants to be housed in the migrant housing; and

(4) The anticipated dates of occupancy of the migrant housing.

(d) Except as provided in subsections (e) and (f) of this section, an operator may allow the migrant housing to be occupied only if the migrant housing has been certified by the Department of Labor of North Carolina or the United States Department of Labor to be in compliance with all of the standards under this Article, except that an operator may allow migrant housing to be occupied on a provisional basis if the operator applied for a preoccupancy inspection at least 45 days prior to occupancy and the preoccupancy inspection was not conducted by the Department of Labor of North Carolina at least four days prior to the anticipated occupancy. Upon subsequent inspection by the Department of Labor of North Carolina, the provisional occupancy shall be revoked if any deficiencies have not been corrected within the period of time specified by the Department of Labor of North Carolina, or within two days after receipt of written notice provided on-site to the operator. No penalties may be assessed for any violation of this Article which are found during the preoccupancy inspection, unless substantive violations exist during provisional occupancy.

(e) If an operator has applied for an inspection pursuant to this Article and one or more migrants arrives in advance of the arrival date stated in the application, the operator shall notify the Department of Labor of North Carolina within two working days of the occupancy of the migrant housing.

(f) If an operator receives a preoccupancy inspection rating from the Department of Labor of North Carolina of one hundred percent (100%) compliance for a particular migrant housing unit for two consecutive years, in the third year the operator shall have the right to conduct the preoccupancy inspection for that particular migrant housing unit himself or herself. Operators conducting their own preoccupancy inspections pursuant to this subsection shall, at least 45 days prior to occupancy, register the migrant housing with the Department of Labor of North Carolina and notify in writing the appropriate local health department. The local health department shall inspect the migrant housing for compliance with G.S. 95-225(c) and (d). The operator shall request a preoccupancy inspection under subsection (a) of this section in the year following a year when the operator conducted a self-inspection under this subsection.

(g) In addition to any other applicable federal or State law or regulation, the Department may only conduct a postoccupancy inspection of operators:

(1) Who were subject to an annual preoccupancy inspection by the Department of Labor of North Carolina and found not to be in one hundred percent (100%) compliance at that inspection.

(2) Who were assessed a civil penalty by the Department of Labor of North Carolina during the previous calendar year for violations of this Article or pursuant to G.S. 95-136(a)(3).

(3) Who did not undergo a preoccupancy inspection, unless the operator conducted a self-inspection pursuant to subsection (f) of this section.

(4) In response to a referral from a federal, State, county, or local government official or any person with firsthand knowledge of an alleged violation of this Article or of an alleged safety or health hazard whom the Department of Labor of North Carolina deems to have provided a credible referral. (1989, c. 91, s. 2; 2007-548, ss. 3.1, 3.2, 4.)

§ 95-227. Enforcement.

(a) For the purpose of enforcing the standards provided by this Article, the provisions of G.S. 95-129, G.S. 95-130 and G.S. 95-136 through G.S. 95-142 shall apply under this Article in a similar manner as they apply to places of employment under OSHANC; however, G.S. 95-129(4), 95-130(2), and 95-130(6) do not apply to migrant housing. For the purposes of this Article, the term:

(1) "Employer" in G.S. 95-129, G.S. 95-130 and G.S. 95-136 through G.S. 95-142 shall be construed to mean an operator.

(2) "Employee" shall be construed to mean a migrant.

(3) Repealed by Session Laws 2007-548, s. 5, effective August 31, 2007.

(b)   The Commissioner may establish a new division to enforce this Article.

(c)   The Department of Labor of North Carolina shall maintain a list of operators and the physical address of their migrant housing units, number of beds, and the date of the annual preoccupancy inspection and certification.

(d)   The Department of Labor of North Carolina shall maintain a summary of any inspections filed annually with the Division that enforce this Article, including the number and type of citations issued and the violations found, if any.

(e)   The Commissioner shall report no later than May 1 of each year to the Chairpersons of the Senate Appropriations Committee on Natural and Economic Resources and the Chairpersons of the House of Representatives Appropriations Subcommittee on Natural and Economic Resources regarding the number of annual preoccupancy certifications issued, the number of operators with one hundred percent (100%) compliance at the preoccupancy inspection, the number of postoccupancy inspections conducted by the Department of Labor of North Carolina, the number and type of citations and fines issued, the total number of migrant worker beds in the State, and the identification of operators who fail to apply for or obtain permits to operate migrant housing pursuant to this Article. (1989, c. 91, s. 2; 1997-35, s. 1; 2007-548, s. 5.)

§ 95-228. Waiver of rights.

Agreements entered into by migrants to waive or to modify their rights under this Article shall be deemed void as contrary to public policy. A waiver or modification of rights by the Department of Labor of North Carolina shall be valid under this Article. (1989, c. 91, s. 2.)

§ 95-229. Construction of Article; severability.

This Article shall be liberally construed to the end that the safety and health of the migrants of this State may be effectuated and protected.

The provisions of this Article are severable, and if any provision of this Article is held invalid by a court of competent jurisdiction, the invalidity may not affect other provisions of the Article, which can be given effect without the invalid provision. (1989, c. 91, s. 2.)

§ 95-229.1. Actions upon finding uninhabitable migrant housing.

If the Department of Labor of North Carolina determines that housing provided to migrants under this Article is uninhabitable, but is not reasonably expected to cause death or serious physical harm, the migrants shall be allowed to remain in the housing for a reasonable period, not to exceed 14 days, while the operator locates alternative housing or makes necessary repairs to make the housing habitable. No additional civil penalties arising from the condition of the housing shall be levied against the operator during the 14-day period after the housing has been determined to be uninhabitable in which the migrants are allowed to remain in the housing. The alternative housing shall be provided at the same rate or less than the rate paid by the migrants for the uninhabitable housing. If the Director determines, after recommendation by an inspector, that housing provided to migrants could reasonably be expected to cause death or serious physical harm immediately or before the imminence of such danger can be eliminated, the migrants shall not be allowed to stay in the housing, and alternative housing shall be provided by the operator at the same rate or less than the rate paid by the migrants for the uninhabitable housing. (2007-548, s. 5.1.)

§ 95-229.2. Reserved for future codification purposes.

§ 95-229.3. Reserved for future codification purposes.

§ 95-229.4. Reserved for future codification purposes.

Article 19A.

Overhead High-Voltage Line Safety Act.

§ 95-229.5. Purpose; scope.

The purpose of this Article is to promote the safety and protection of persons engaged in work in the vicinity of high-voltage overhead lines. This Article defines the conditions under which work may be carried on safely and provides for the precautionary safety arrangements to be taken when any person engages in work in proximity to overhead high-voltage lines. (1995 (Reg. Sess., 1996), c. 587, s. 1.)

§ 95-229.6. Definitions.

As used in this Article, unless the context requires otherwise:

(1) "Covered equipment" or "covered items" means any mechanical equipment, hoisting equipment, antenna, or rigging; any part of which is capable of vertical, lateral, or swinging motion that could cause any portion of the equipment or item to come closer than 10 feet to a high-voltage line during erection, construction, operation, or maintenance; including, but not limited to, equipment such as cranes, derricks, power shovels, backhoes, dump trucks, drilling rigs, pile drivers, excavating equipment, hay-loaders, haystackers, combines, irrigation equipment, portable grain augers or elevators, and mechanical cotton pickers. These terms also include items such as handheld tools, ladders, scaffolds, antennas, and outriggers, houses or other structures in transport, and gutters, siding, and other construction materials, the motion or manipulation of which could cause them to come closer than 10 feet to a high-voltage line.

(2) "High-voltage line" means all aboveground electrical conductors of voltage in excess of 600 volts measured between conductor and ground.

(3) "Person" means natural person, firm, business association, company, partnership, corporation, or other legal entity.

(4) "Person responsible for the work to be done" means the person performing or controlling the work that necessitates the precautionary safety measures required by this Article, unless the person performing or controlling the work is under contract or agreement with a governmental entity, in which case "person responsible for the work to be done" means that governmental entity.

(5) "Warning sign" means a weather-resistant sign of not less than five inches by seven inches with at least two panels: a signal panel and a message panel. The signal panel shall contain the signal word "WARNING" in black

lettering and a safety alert symbol consisting of a black triangle with an orange exclamation point, all on an orange background. The message panel shall contain the following words, either in black letters on a white background or white letters on a black background: "UNLAWFUL TO OPERATE THIS EQUIPMENT WITHIN TEN FEET OF OVERHEAD HIGH-VOLTAGE LINES - Contact with power lines can result in death or serious burns." A symbol or pictorial panel may also be added. Such warning sign language, lettering, style, colors, size, and format shall meet the requirements of the American National Standard ANSI Z535.4-1991, Product Safety Signs and Labels, or its successor or such equally effective standard as may be approved for use by the Commissioner of Labor. In the event of a conflict with regard to the appearance or content of the warning sign, the standard approved by the Commissioner of Labor shall take precedence over any description or standard set out in this subdivision. (1995 (Reg. Sess., 1996), c. 587, s. 1; 1998-193, s. 2.)

§ 95-229.7. Prohibited activities.

(a) Unless danger of contact with high-voltage lines has been guarded against as provided by G.S. 95-229.8, 95-229.9, and 95-229.10, the following actions are prohibited:

(1) No person shall, individually or through an agent or employee, perform, or require any other person to perform, any work upon any land, building, highway, or other premises that will cause:

a. Such individual, agent, employee, or other person to be placed within six feet of any overhead high-voltage line; or any part of any tool or material used by the agent, employee, or other person to be brought within six feet of any overhead high-voltage line, or

b. Any part of any covered equipment or covered item used by the individual, agent, employee, or other person to be brought within 10 feet of any high-voltage line.

(2) No person shall, individually or through an agent or employee or as an agent or employee, erect, construct, operate, maintain, transport, or store any covered equipment or covered item within 10 feet of any high-voltage line, or such greater clearance as may be required under the circumstances by OSHA, except as provided herein. This prohibition shall not apply, however, to covered

equipment as defined herein when lawfully driven or transported on public streets and highways in compliance with applicable height restrictions. The required clearance from high-voltage lines shall be not less than four feet when:

a. Covered equipment as defined herein is lawfully driven or transported on public streets and highways in compliance with the height restriction applicable thereto,

b. Refuse collection equipment is operating, or

c. Agricultural equipment is operating.

(3) No person shall, individually or through an agent or employee or as an agent or employee, operate or cause to be operated an airplane or helicopter within 20 feet of a high-voltage line, except that no clearance is specified for licensed aerial applicators that may incidentally pass within the 20-foot limitation during normal operation.

(4) No person shall, individually or through an agent or employee or as an agent or employee, store or cause to be stored any materials that are expected to be moved or handled by covered equipment or any covered item within 10 feet of a high-voltage line.

(5) No person shall, individually or through an agent or employee or as an agent or employee, provide or cause to be provided additional clearance by either (i) raising, moving, or displacing any overhead utility electric lines or (ii) pulling or pushing any pole, guy, or other structural appurtenance.

(6) No person shall, individually or through an agent or employee or as an agent or employee, excavate or cause to be excavated any portion of any foundations of structures, including guy anchors or other structural appurtenances, which support any overhead utility electric lines.

(b) If the high-voltage line has been insulated or de-energized and grounded, in accordance with G.S. 95-229.10, the required clearances specified in subdivisions (1), (2), and (4) of subsection (a) of this section may be reduced to not less than two feet. Under no circumstances shall the line or its covering be contacted. If the line is temporarily raised or moved to accommodate the expected work, without also being insulated or de-energized and grounded, the required clearances from the line, specified in subsection (a) of this section, shall not be reduced. (1995 (Reg. Sess., 1996), c. 587, s. 1; 1998-193, s. 3.)

§ 95-229.8. Warning signs.

(a)   No person shall, individually or through an agent or employee or as an agent or employee, operate any covered equipment in the proximity of a high-voltage line unless warning signs are posted and maintained as follows:

(1)   A sign shall be located within the equipment and readily visible and legible to the operator of such equipment when at the controls of such equipment; and

(2)   Signs shall be located on the outside of equipment so as to be readily visible and legible at 12 feet to other persons engaged in the work operations.

This subsection shall not apply to handheld tools, handheld equipment, and other items which by their size or configuration cannot accommodate the warning signs specified in G.S. 95-229.6(5).

(b)   If the Commissioner of Labor determines that a successor, substitute, or additional sign standard may or shall be used in place of the requirements listed in G.S. 95-229.6, a period of not less than 18 months from such determination shall be allowed for any required replacement of signs. (1995 (Reg. Sess., 1996), c. 587, s. 1; 1998-193, s. 4.)

§ 95-229.9. Notification.

(a)   When any person desires to carry on any work in closer proximity to any high-voltage line than permitted by G.S. 95-229.7(a), the person responsible for the work to be done shall notify the owner or operator of the high-voltage line prior to the time the work is to be commenced. Such notification shall occur at the earliest practical time; however, such notification shall occur not less than 48 hours, excluding Saturday, Sunday, and legal State and federal holidays, prior to the intended work. In emergency situations, including police, fire, and rescue emergencies, such notification shall occur as soon as possible under the circumstances. In cases where the person or business entity responsible for doing the work is doing so under contract or agreement with a government entity, and the government entity and the owner or operator of the lines have already made satisfactory mutual arrangements, further arrangements for that particular work are not required.

(b) Every notice served by any person on an owner or operator of a high-voltage line shall contain the following information:

(1) The name, address, and telephone number of the individual serving such notice;

(2) The location of the proposed work;

(3) The name, address, and telephone number of the person responsible for the work;

(4) The field telephone number of the site of such work, if one is available;

(5) The type, duration, and extent of the proposed work;

(6) The name of the person for whom the proposed work is being performed;

(7) The time and date of the notice; and

(8) The approximate date and time when the work is to begin.

(c) If the notification required by this Article is made by telephone, a record of the information in subsection (b) of this section shall be maintained by the owner or operator notified and the person giving the notice to document compliance with the requirements of this Article.

(d) Owners or operators of high-voltage lines may form and operate an association providing for mutual receipt of notification of activities close to high-voltage lines in a specified area. In areas where an association is formed, the following shall occur:

(1) Notification to the association shall be effected as set forth in this section.

(2) Owners or operators of high-voltage lines in the area:

a. May become members of the association;

b. May participate in and receive the services furnished by the association; and

c.   Shall pay their proportionate share of the cost for the services furnished.

(3)   The association whose members or participants have high-voltage lines within a county shall file a list containing the name, address, and telephone number of every member and participating owner or operator of high-voltage lines with the clerk of superior court.

(4)   If notification is made by telephone, an adequate record of the information required by subsection (b) of this section shall be maintained by the association to document compliance with the requirements of this Article. (1995 (Reg. Sess., 1996), c. 587, s. 1.)

§ 95-229.10. Precautionary safety arrangements.

(a)   Installation or performance of precautionary safety arrangements shall be performed by the owner or operator of high-voltage lines only after mutually satisfactory arrangements have been negotiated between the owner or the operator of the lines, or both, and the person responsible for the work to be done. The negotiations shall proceed promptly and in good faith with the goal of accommodating the requested work consistent with the owner's or operator's service needs and the intent to protect the public from the danger of contact with high-voltage lines as far as is reasonable and cost-effective. The person responsible for the work may perform the work only after satisfactory mutual arrangements, including coordination of work and construction schedules, have been made between the owner or operator of the high-voltage lines and the person responsible for the work. The owners or operators of high-voltage lines shall make the final determination as to which arrangements are most feasible and appropriate under the circumstances; provided, however, that the utility may determine that no arrangements can be made that would allow the proposed work to be carried out in a reasonably safe manner or at reasonable cost taking into account the cost to its customers, and the owner or operator of high-voltage lines may refuse to enter into an agreement on that basis.

(b)   The precautionary safety measures shall be appropriate, reasonable, and cost-effective for the work of which the owner or operator of high-voltage lines has received notification. During mutual negotiations, the person responsible for the work may change the notification of intended work to include different or limited work so as to reduce the precautionary safety measures required to accommodate such work. The precautionary safety measures shall not violate the requirements of the current edition of the National Electrical Safety Code.

(c)   The owner or operator of the high-voltage lines is not required to provide the precautionary safety arrangements until an agreement for payment has been made; except that, if the amount of payment is in dispute, the owner or operator shall commence with providing precautionary safety measures as if agreement had then been reached and the undisputed amount shall be paid according to the agreement reached as to that amount. If agreement for payment of the disputed amount has not been reached within 14 days from completion of precautionary safety measures, the owner or operator and the person or business entity responsible for doing the work may resolve the dispute by arbitration or other legal means.

(d)   Unless otherwise agreed, the owner or operator of the high-voltage lines shall initiate the precautionary safety arrangements agreed upon within five working days after the agreement for payment has been reached as required in subsection (c) of this section, but no earlier than the agreed construction date coordinated between the parties. Once initiated, the owner or operator shall complete the work promptly and without interruption, consistent with the owner's or operator's service needs. Should the owner or operator of the high-voltage lines fail to provide the precautionary safety measures agreed upon in a timely manner, the owner or operator of the high-voltage lines shall be liable for costs or loss of production of the person or business entity requesting assistance to work in close proximity to high-voltage lines, except that no such liability shall exist during times of emergency, such as storm repair and the like.

(e)   Precautionary safety arrangements may include:

(1)   Placement of temporary mechanical barriers separating and preventing contact between material, equipment, other objects, or persons and high-voltage lines;

(2)   Temporary de-energization and grounding;

(3)   Temporary relocation or raising of the high-voltage lines; or

(4)   Other such measures found to be appropriate in the judgment of the owner or operator of the high-voltage lines.

(f)   The actual expense incurred by any owner or operator of high-voltage lines in taking precautionary measures as set out in subsections (a) through (e) of this section, including the wages of its workers involved in making safety arrangements, shall be paid by the person responsible for the work to be done, except if:

(1)   Any owner or operator of an overhead high-voltage line has located its facilities within a public highway or street right-of-way and the work is performed by or for the Department of Transportation or a city, county, or town, the actual expenses shall be the responsibility of the owner or operator of the overhead high-voltage lines, unless the owner or operator can provide evidence of prior rights or there is a prior written agreement specifying cost responsibility. However, if it is determined by the Department of Transportation or a city, county, or town that the temporary safety arrangements are for the sole convenience of its contractor, the actual expense shall be the responsibility of the contractor;

(2)   The owner or operator of the high-voltage lines has not installed the line in conformance with an applicable edition of the National Electrical Safety Code. In that case, the liability of the person responsible for the work shall be limited to the amount required to accommodate the work over and above the amount required to bring the installation into compliance with the National Electrical Safety Code; or

(3)   In the case of property used for residential purposes, such actual expenses shall be limited to those in excess of one thousand dollars ($1,000). (1995 (Reg. Sess., 1996), c. 587, s. 1.)

§ 95-229.11. Exemptions.

(a)   This Article shall not apply to the construction, reconstruction, operation, and maintenance of overhead electrical or communication circuits or conductors and their supporting structures and associated equipment of the following systems, provided that such work on any of the following systems is performed by the employees of the owner or operator of the systems or independent contractors engaged on behalf of the owner or operator of the systems to perform the work, and the owner of the system has a valid joint-use contract or agreement with the owner of the high-voltage lines:

(1) Rail transportation systems;

(2) Electrical generating, transmission, or distribution systems;

(3) Communications systems, including cable television; or

(4) Any other publicly or privately owned system, including traffic signals.

(b) This Article also shall not apply to electrical or communications circuits or conductors on the premises of coal or other mines which are subject to the provisions of the Federal Mine Safety and Health Act of 1977 (30 U.S.C. § 801, et seq.) and regulations adopted pursuant to that Act by the Mine Safety and Health Administration. (1995 (Reg. Sess., 1996), c. 587, s. 1.)

§ 95-229.12. Application.

Nothing in this Article shall relieve any person from complying with any safety rule, regulation, or statute not imposed by this Article. A violation of this Article shall not constitute negligence or contributory negligence, nor give rise to any cause of action based upon injury to persons or property. An action may be brought by an owner or operator of a high-voltage line to recover the cost of precautionary safety arrangements or for damage to its facilities. Nothing contained in this Article shall be construed to alter, amend, restrict, or limit the liability of any person for violation of that person's duty under law; nor shall any person be relieved from liability as a result of violations of standards under existing law where such violations of existing standards of care are found to be a cause of damage to property, personal injury, or death. (1995 (Reg. Sess., 1996), c. 587, s. 1.)

§ 95-229.13. Severability.

The provisions of this Article are severable. If any part of this Article is declared invalid or unconstitutional, such declaration shall not affect the remainder. (1995 (Reg. Sess., 1996), c. 587, s. 1.)

Article 20.

Controlled Substance Examination Regulation.

§ 95-230. Purpose.

The General Assembly finds that individuals should be protected from unreliable and inadequate examinations and screening for controlled substances. The General Assembly also finds that employers who test employees for controlled substances shall use reliable and minimally invasive examinations and screenings and be afforded the opportunity to select from a range of cost-effective and advanced drug testing technologies. The purpose of this Article is to establish procedural and other requirements for the administration of controlled substance examinations. (1991, c. 687, s. 1; 2001-487, s. 66(a).)

§ 95-231. Definitions.

As used in this Article, unless the context clearly requires otherwise:

(1) "Approved laboratory" means a clinical chemistry laboratory which performs controlled substances testing and which has demonstrated satisfactory performance in the forensic urine drug testing programs of the United States Department of Health and Human Services or the College of American Pathologists for the type of tests and controlled substances being evaluated.

(1a) "Controlled substance" is as defined in G.S. 90-87(5) or a metabolite thereof.

(1b) "Controlled substance examination" means all actions related to drug testing for the purpose of determining if an examinee has used controlled substances.

(2) "Examiner" means a person, firm, or corporation, doing business in the State, including State, county, and municipal employers, who is the employer or prospective employer of the examinee and who performs or has performed by an approved laboratory a controlled substance examination.

(3) "Examinee" means an individual who is an employee of the examiner or an applicant for employment with the examiner and who is requested or required by an examiner to submit to a controlled substance examination.

(4) "Screening" means initial controlled substance examination performed for the purpose of determining use of controlled substances by an examinee. (1991, c. 687; 1993, c. 213, s. 1.)

§ 95-232. Procedural requirements for the administration of controlled substance examinations.

(a) An examiner who requests or requires an examinee to submit to a controlled substance examination shall comply with the procedural requirements set forth in this section.

(b) Collection of samples: the collection of samples for examination or screening shall be performed under reasonable and sanitary conditions. Individual dignity shall be preserved to the extent practicable. Samples shall be collected in a manner reasonably calculated to prevent substitution of samples and interference with the collection, examination, or screening of samples. Samples for prospective or current employees may be collected on-site or at an approved laboratory.

(c) Screening test of samples:

(1) Prospective employees: a preliminary screening procedure that utilizes a single-use test device may be used for prospective employees.

(2) Current employees: the screening test of samples for current employees shall only be performed by an approved laboratory.

(c1) Confirmation test of samples: if a screening test for a prospective employee produces a positive result, an approved laboratory shall confirm that result by a second examination of the sample utilizing gas chromatography with mass spectrometry or an equivalent scientifically accepted method, unless the examinee signs a written waiver at the time or after they receive the preliminary test result. All screening tests for current employees that produce a positive result shall be confirmed by a second examination of the sample utilizing gas chromatography with mass spectrometry or an equivalent scientifically accepted method.

(d)   Retention of samples: a portion of every sample that produces a confirmed positive examination result shall be preserved by the laboratory that conducts the confirmatory examination for a period of at least 90 days from the time the results of the confirmed positive examination are mailed or otherwise delivered to the examiner.

(e)   Chain of custody: the examiner or his agent shall establish procedures regarding chain of custody for sample collection and examination to ensure proper record keeping, handling, labeling, and identification of examination samples.

(f)   Retesting of positive samples: the examinee shall have the right to retest a confirmed positive sample at the same or another approved laboratory. The examiner, through the approved laboratory, shall make confirmed positive samples available to the affected examinee, or a designated agent, during the time which the sample is required to be retained. The examinee must request release of the sample in writing specifying to which approved laboratory the sample is to be sent. The examinee incurs all reasonable expenses for chain of custody procedures, shipping, and retesting of positive samples related to this request. (1991, c. 687, s. 1; 1993, c. 213, s. 2; 1995, c. 383, s. 1; 2006-264, s. 52(a); 2009-535, s. 1.)

§ 95-233. No duty to examine.

Nothing in this Article shall be construed to place a duty on examiners to conduct controlled substance examinations. (1991, c. 687.)

§ 95-234. Violation of controlled substance examination regulations; civil penalty.

(a)   Any examiner who violates the provisions of this Article shall be subject to a civil penalty of up to two hundred fifty dollars ($250.00) per affected examinee with the maximum not to exceed one thousand dollars ($1,000) per investigation by the Commissioner of Labor or his authorized representative. In determining the amount of the penalty, the Commissioner shall consider:

(1)   The appropriateness of the penalty for the size of the business of the employer charged; and

(2)   The gravity of the violation.

The determination by the Commissioner shall be final, unless within 15 days after receipt of notice thereof by certified mail with return receipt, by signature confirmation as provided by the U.S. Postal Service, by a designated delivery service authorized pursuant to 26 U.S.C. § 7502(f)(2) with delivery receipt, or via hand delivery, the person charged with the violation takes exception to the determination, in which event final determination of the penalty shall be made in an administrative proceeding pursuant to Article 3 of Chapter 150B and which final determination shall be subject to judicial review in a judicial proceeding pursuant to Article 4 of Chapter 150B.

(b)   The amount of the penalty when finally determined may be recovered in a civil action brought by the Commissioner in the General Court of Justice.

(c)   The clear proceeds of civil penalties provided for in this section shall be remitted to the Civil Penalty and Forfeiture Fund in accordance with G.S. 115C-457.2.

(d)   Assessment of penalties under this section shall be subject to a two-year statute of limitations commencing at the time of the occurrence of the violation.

(e)   The Commissioner of Labor may adopt, modify, or revoke such rules as are necessary for carrying out the provisions of this Article. The rules adopted shall promote individual dignity and privacy while not posing an undue burden on employers. (1991, c. 687, s. 1; 1993, c. 213, s. 3; 1998-215, s. 113; 2003-308, s. 7; 2007-231, s. 11.)

§ 95-235. Certain federal agencies exempted.

The provisions of this Article shall not apply to a controlled substance examination required by the United States Department of Transportation or the United States Nuclear Regulatory Commission. (1993, c. 213, s. 4.)

§§ 95-236 through 95-239. Reserved for future codification purposes.

Article 21.

Retaliatory Employment Discrimination.

§ 95-240. Definitions.

The following definitions apply in this Article:

(1) "Person" means any individual, partnership, association, corporation, business trust, legal representative, the State, a city, town, county, municipality, local agency, or other entity of government.

(2) "Retaliatory action" means the discharge, suspension, demotion, retaliatory relocation of an employee, or other adverse employment action taken against an employee in the terms, conditions, privileges, and benefits of employment. (1991 (Reg. Sess., 1992), c. 1021, s. 1.)

§ 95-241. Discrimination prohibited.

(a) No person shall discriminate or take any retaliatory action against an employee because the employee in good faith does or threatens to do any of the following:

(1) File a claim or complaint, initiate any inquiry, investigation, inspection, proceeding or other action, or testify or provide information to any person with respect to any of the following:

a. Chapter 97 of the General Statutes.

b. Article 2A or Article 16 of this Chapter.

c. Article 2A of Chapter 74 of the General Statutes.

d. G.S. 95-28.1.

e. Article 16 of Chapter 127A of the General Statutes.

f. G.S. 95-28.1A.

g. Article 52 of Chapter 143 of the General Statutes.

h. Article 5F of Chapter 90 of the General Statutes.

(2) Cause any of the activities listed in subdivision (1) of this subsection to be initiated on an employee's behalf.

(3) Exercise any right on behalf of the employee or any other employee afforded by Article 2A or Article 16 of this Chapter, by Article 2A of Chapter 74 of the General Statutes, or by Article 52 of Chapter 143 of the General Statutes.

(4) Comply with the provisions of Article 27 of Chapter 7B of the General Statutes.

(5) Exercise rights under Chapter 50B. Actions brought under this subdivision shall be in accordance with the provisions of G.S. 50B-5.5.

(b) It shall not be a violation of this Article for a person to discharge or take any other unfavorable action with respect to an employee who has engaged in protected activity as set forth under this Article if the person proves by the greater weight of the evidence that it would have taken the same unfavorable action in the absence of the protected activity of the employee. (1991 (Reg. Sess., 1992), c. 1021, s. 1; 1993, c. 423, s. 1; 1997-153, s. 7; 1997-350, s. 3; 1998-202, s. 7; 1999-423, s. 4; 2004-186, s. 18.2; 2008-212, s. 1; 2009-205, s. 2.)

§ 95-242. Complaint; investigation; conciliation.

(a) An employee allegedly aggrieved by a violation of G.S. 95-241 may file a written complaint with the Commissioner of Labor alleging the violation. The complaint shall be filed within 180 days of the alleged violation. Within 20 days following receipt of the complaint, the Commissioner shall forward a copy of the complaint to the person alleged to have committed the violation and shall initiate an investigation. If the Commissioner determines after the investigation that there is not reasonable cause to believe that the allegation is true, the Commissioner shall dismiss the complaint, promptly notify the employee and the respondent, and issue a right-to-sue letter to the employee that will enable the employee to bring a civil action pursuant to G.S. 95-243. If the Commissioner determines after investigation that there is reasonable cause to believe that the allegation is true, the Commissioner shall attempt to eliminate the alleged violation by informal methods which may consist of conference, conciliation, and persuasion. The Commissioner shall make a determination as soon as possible and, in any event, not later than 90 days after the filing of the complaint.

(b)   If the Commissioner is unable to resolve the alleged violation through the informal methods, the Commissioner shall notify the parties in writing that conciliation efforts have failed. The Commissioner shall then either file a civil action on behalf of the employee pursuant to G.S. 95-243 or issue a right-to-sue letter to the employee enabling the employee to bring a civil action pursuant to G.S. 95-243.

(b1)   The Commissioner may reopen an investigation under this Article for good cause shown within 30 days of receipt of the right-to-sue letter. If an investigation is reopened pursuant to this section, the 90-day time limit set forth in G.S. 95-243(b) shall not commence until the new investigation is complete and either a new right-to-sue letter is issued or the Commissioner notifies the parties in writing that conciliation efforts have failed.

(c)   An employee may make a written request to the Commissioner for a right-to-sue letter after 90 days following the filing of a complaint if the Commissioner has not issued a notice of conciliation failure and has not commenced an action pursuant to G.S. 95-242.

(d)   Nothing said or done during the use of the informal methods described in subsection (a) of this section may be made public by the Commissioner or used as evidence in a subsequent proceeding under this Article without the written consent of the persons concerned.

(e)   The Commissioner's files and the Commissioner's other records relating to investigations and enforcement proceedings pursuant to this Article shall not be subject to inspection and examination as authorized by G.S. 132-6 while such investigations and proceedings are open or pending in the trial court division.

(f)   In making inspections and investigations under this Article, the Commissioner or his duly authorized agents may, in addition to exercising the authority granted in G.S. 95-4, issue subpoenas to require the attendance and testimony of witnesses and the production of evidence under oath. Witnesses shall be reimbursed for all travel and other necessary expenses which shall be claimed and paid in accordance with the prevailing travel reimbursement requirements of the State. In the case of failure or refusal of any person to obey a subpoena under this Article, the district court judge or superior court judge of the county in which the inspection or investigation is conducted shall, upon the application of the Commissioner, have jurisdiction to issue an order requiring compliance. (1991 (Reg. Sess., 1992), c. 1021, s. 1; 1993, c. 423, s. 2; 2011-366, ss. 9, 10.)

§ 95-243. Civil action.

(a) An employee who has been issued a right-to-sue letter or the Commissioner of Labor may commence a civil action in the superior court of the county where the violation occurred, where the complainant resides, or where the respondent resides or has his principal place of business.

(b) A civil action under this section shall be commenced by an employee within 90 days of the date upon which the right-to-sue letter was issued or by the Commissioner within 90 days of the date on which the Commissioner notifies the parties in writing that conciliation efforts have failed.

(c) The employee or the Commissioner may seek and the court may award any or all of the following types of relief:

(1) An injunction to enjoin continued violation of this Article.

(2) Reinstatement of the employee to the same position held before the retaliatory action or discrimination or to an equivalent position.

(3) Reinstatement of full fringe benefits and seniority rights.

(4) Compensation for lost wages, lost benefits, and other economic losses that were proximately caused by the retaliatory action or discrimination.

If in an action under this Article the court finds that the employee was injured by a willful violation of G.S. 95-241, the court shall treble the amount awarded under subdivision (4) of this subsection.

The court may award to the plaintiff and assess against the defendant the reasonable costs and expenses, including attorneys' fees, of the plaintiff in bringing an action pursuant to this section. If the court determines that the plaintiff's action is frivolous, it may award to the defendant and assess against the plaintiff the reasonable costs and expenses, including attorneys' fees, of the defendant in defending the action brought pursuant to this section.

(d)   Parties to a civil action brought pursuant to this section shall have the right to a jury trial as provided under G.S. 1A-1, Rules of Civil Procedure.

(e)   An employee may only bring an action under this section when he has been issued a right-to-sue letter by the Commissioner. (1991 (Reg. Sess., 1992), c. 1021, s. 1.)

§ 95-244. Effect of Article on other rights.

Nothing in this Article shall be deemed to diminish the rights or remedies of any employee under any collective bargaining agreement, employment contract, other statutory rights or remedies, or at common law. (1991 (Reg. Sess., 1992), c. 1021, s. 1.)

§ 95-245. Rules.

The Commissioner may adopt rules needed to implement this Article pursuant to the provisions of Chapter 150B of the General Statutes. (1993, c. 423, s. 3.)

§§ 95-246 through 95-249. Reserved for future codification purposes.

Article 22.

Safety and Health Programs and Committees.

§ 95-250. Definitions.

The following definitions shall apply in this Article:

(1)   "Experience rate modifier" means the numerical modification applied by the Rate Bureau to an experience rating for use in determining workers' compensation premiums.

(2)   "Worksite" means a single physical location where business is conducted or where operations are performed by employees of an employer.

The definitions of Article 16 of this Chapter shall also apply to this Article, except that "employee" for the purposes of G.S. 95-252(a), 95-252(c)(1)b., 95-255, and 95-256 means an employee employed for some portion of a working day in each of 20 or more calendar weeks in the current or preceding calendar year. (1991 (Reg. Sess., 1992), c. 962, s. 1.)

§ 95-251. Safety and health programs.

(a)   Establishment of safety and health programs.

(1)   Except as provided in subdivision (2) of this subsection, each employer with an experience rate modifier of 1.5 or greater shall, in accordance with this section, establish and carry out a safety and health program to reduce or eliminate hazards and to prevent injuries and illnesses to employees.

(2)   Employers with an experience rate modifier of 1.5 or greater which provide temporary help services shall, in accordance with this section, establish and implement a safety and health program to reduce or eliminate hazards and to prevent injuries and illnesses to its full-time employees permanently located at the employer's worksite. Employers which provide temporary help services shall not be required to establish and implement a safety and health program under this section for its employees assigned to a client's worksite. This subdivision shall not apply to employee leasing companies.

(3)   The Commissioner may modify the application of the requirements of this section to classes of employers where the Commissioner determines that, in light of the nature of the risks faced by the employees of these employers, such a modification would not reduce the employees' safety and health protection.

(b) Safety and health program requirements. A safety and health program established and implemented under this section shall be a written program that shall include at least all of the following:

(1) Methods and procedures for identifying, evaluating, and documenting safety and health hazards.

(2) Methods and procedures for correcting the safety and health hazards identified under subdivision (1) of this subsection.

(3) Methods and procedures for investigating work-related fatalities, injuries, and illnesses.

(4) Methods and procedures for providing occupational safety and health services, including emergency response and first aid procedures.

(5) Methods and procedures for employee participation in the implementation of the safety and health program.

(6) Methods and procedures for responding to the recommendations of the safety and health committee, where applicable.

(7) Methods and procedures for providing safety and health training and education to employees and to members of any safety and health committee established under G.S. 95-252.

(8) The designation of a representative of the employer who has the qualifications and responsibility to identify safety and health hazards and the authority to initiate corrective action where appropriate.

(9) In the case of a worksite where employees of two or more employers work, procedures for each employer to protect employees at the worksite from hazards under the employer's control, including procedures to provide information on safety and health hazards to other employers and employees at the worksite.

(10) Any other provisions as the Commissioner requires to effectuate the purposes of this section.

(c) No loss of pay. The time during which employees are participating in training and education activities under this section shall be considered as hours worked for purposes of wages, benefits, and other terms and conditions of employment. The training and education shall be provided by an employer at no cost to the employees of the employer. (1991 (Reg. Sess., 1992), c. 962, s. 1.)

§ 95-252. Safety and health committees required.

(a) Establishment of safety and health committees. Except as provided in subsection (b) of this section, each employer with 11 or more employees and an experience rate modifier of 1.5 or greater shall provide for the establishment of safety and health committees and the selection of employee safety and health representatives in accordance with this section.

(b) Temporary help services. Temporary employees of employers which provide temporary help services shall not be counted as part of the 11 or more employees needed to establish a safety and health committee under this section, and employers which provide temporary help services shall not be required to establish a safety and health committee under this section for its employees assigned to a client's worksite. This subsection shall not apply to employee leasing companies.

(c) Safety and health committee requirements.

(1) In general. Each employer covered by this section shall establish a safety and health committee at each worksite of the employer, except as provided as follows:

a. An employer covered by this section whose employees do not primarily report to or work at a fixed location is required to have only one safety and health committee to represent all employees.

b. A safety and health committee is not required at a covered employer's worksite with less than 11 employees.

c. The Commissioner may, by rule, modify the application of this subdivision to worksites where employees of more than one employer are employed.

(2) Membership. Each safety and health committee shall consist of:

a. The employee safety and health representatives selected or appointed under subsection (d) of this section.

b. As determined appropriate by the employer, employer representatives, the number of which may not exceed the number of employee representatives.

(3) Chairpersons. Each safety and health committee shall be cochaired by:

a. A representative selected by the employer.

b. A representative selected by the employee members of the committee.

(4) Rights. Each safety and health committee shall, within reasonable limits and in a reasonable manner, exercise the following rights:

a. Review any safety and health program established by the employer under G.S. 95-251.

b. Review incidents involving work-related fatalities, injuries and illnesses, and complaints by employees regarding safety or health hazards.

c. Review, upon the request of the committee or upon the request of the employer representatives or employee representatives of the committee, the employer's work injury and illness records, other than personally identifiable medical information, and other reports or documents relating to occupational safety and health.

d. Conduct inspections of the worksite at least once every three months and in response to complaints by employees or committee members regarding safety or health hazards.

e. Conduct interviews with employees in conjunction with inspections of the worksite.

f. Conduct meetings, at least once every three months, and maintain written minutes of the meetings.

g. Observe the measurement of employee exposure to toxic materials and harmful physical agents.

h. Establish procedures for exercising the rights of the committee.

i. Make recommendations on behalf of the committee, and in making recommendations, permit any members of the committee to submit separate views to the employer for improvements in the employer's safety and health program and for the correction of hazards to employee safety or health, except that recommendations shall be advisory only and the employer shall retain full authority to manage the worksite.

j. Accompany, upon request, the Commissioner or the Commissioner's representative during any physical inspection of the worksite.

(5) Time for committee activities. The employer shall permit members of the committee established under this section to take the time from work reasonably necessary to exercise the rights of the committee without suffering any loss of pay or benefits for time spent on duties of the committee.

(d) Employee safety and health representatives.

(1) In general. Safety and health committees established under this section shall include:

a. One employee safety and health representative where the average number of nonmanagerial employees of the employer at the worksite during the preceding year was more than 10, but less than 50.

b. Two employee safety and health representatives where the average number of nonmanagerial employees of the employer at the worksite during the preceding year was 50 or more, but less than 100.

c. An additional employee safety and health representative for each additional 100 such employees at the worksite, up to a maximum of six employee safety and health representatives.

d. Where an employer's employees do not primarily report to or work at a fixed location or at worksites where employees of more than one employer are employed, a number of employee safety and health representatives as determined by the Commissioner by rule.

(2) Selection. Employee safety and health representatives shall be selected by and from among the employer's nonmanagerial employees in accordance with rules adopted by the Commissioner. The rules adopted by the Commissioner may provide for different methods of selection of employee

safety and health representatives at worksites with no bargaining representative, worksites with one bargaining representative, and worksites with more than one bargaining representative. (1991 (Reg. Sess., 1992), c. 962, s. 1.)

§ 95-253. Additional rights.

The rights and remedies provided to employees and employee safety and health representatives under this Article are in addition to, and not in lieu of, any other rights and remedies provided by contract or by other applicable law and are not intended to alter or affect those other rights and remedies. (1991 (Reg. Sess., 1992), c. 962, s. 1.)

§ 95-254. Rules.

(a) Safety and health programs. Not later than one year after July 15, 1992, the Commissioner shall adopt final rules concerning the establishment and implementation of employer safety and health programs under G.S. 95-251. Rules adopted shall include provisions for the training and education of employees and safety and health committee members. These rules shall include at least all of the following:

(1) Provision for the training and education of employees, including safety and health committee members, in a manner that is readily understandable by the employees, concerning safety and health hazards, control measures, the employer's safety and health program, employee rights, and applicable laws and regulations.

(2) Provision for the training and education of the safety and health committee concerning methods and procedures for hazard recognition and control, the conduct of worksite safety and health inspections, the rights of the safety and health committee, and other information necessary to enable the members to carry out the activities of the committee under G.S. 95-252.

(3) Requirement that training and education be provided to new employees at the time of employment and to safety and health committee members at the time of selection.

(4) Requirement that refresher training be provided on at least an annual basis and that additional training be provided to employees and to safety and health committee members when there are changes in conditions or operations that may expose employees to new or different safety or health hazards or when there are changes in safety and health rules or standards under Article 16 of this Chapter that apply to the employer.

(b) Safety and health committees. Not later than one year after July 15, 1992, the Commissioner shall adopt final rules for the establishment and operation of safety and health committees under G.S. 95-252. The rules shall include provisions concerning at least the following:

(1) The establishment of such committees by an employer whose employees do not primarily report to or work at a fixed location.

(2) The establishment of committees at worksites where employees of more than one employer are employed.

(3) The employer's obligation to enable the committee to function properly and effectively, including the provision of facilities and materials necessary for the committee to conduct its activities, and the maintenance of records and minutes developed by the committee.

(4) The provision for different methods of selection of employee safety and health representatives at worksites with no bargaining representative, worksites with one bargaining representative, and worksites with more than one bargaining representative. (1991 (Reg. Sess., 1992), c. 962, s. 1.)

§ 95-255. Reports.

(a) Upon the final adoption of all rules required to be adopted by the Commissioner under this Article, the Commissioner shall determine, based on information provided by the North Carolina Rate Bureau, the employers with an experience rate modifier of 1.5 or greater and shall notify these employers of the applicability of G.S. 95-251 and the potential applicability of G.S. 95-252.

(b) Within 60 days of notification by the Commissioner, the employer shall certify on forms provided by the Commissioner that he meets the requirements of G.S. 95-251 and, if applicable, the requirements of G.S. 95-252.

(c) The Commissioner shall notify an employer when his experience rate modifier falls below 1.5. An employer subject to the provisions of G.S. 95-252 shall notify the Commissioner if he no longer employs 11 or more employees and has discontinued or will discontinue the safety and health committee. (1991 (Reg. Sess., 1992), c. 962, s. 1.)

§ 95-255.1. Technical assistance.

Employers notified pursuant to G.S. 95-255(a) shall be offered technical assistance from the Division of Occupational Safety and Health to reduce injuries and illnesses in their workplaces. (1997-443, s. 17(a).)

§ 95-256. Penalties.

(a) The Commissioner may levy a civil penalty, not to exceed the amounts listed as follows, for a violation of this Article:

Employers with 10 or less employees $ 2,000

Employers with 11-50 employees $ 5,000

Employers with 51-100 employees $10,000

Employers with more than 100 employees $25,000.

(b) The Commissioner, in determining the amount of the penalty, shall consider the nature of the violation, whether it is a first or subsequent violation, and the steps taken by the employer to remedy the violation upon discovery of the violation.

(c) An employer may appeal a penalty levied by the Commissioner pursuant to this section to the North Carolina Occupational Safety and Health Review Commission subject to the procedures and requirements applicable to contested penalties under Article 16 of this Chapter. The determination of the Commission shall be final unless further appeal is made to the courts under the provisions of Chapter 150B of the General Statutes.

(d) All civil penalties and interest recovered by the Commissioner, together with any costs, shall be paid into the General Fund of the State. (1991 (Reg. Sess., 1992), c. 962, s. 1; 2005-133, s. 1; 2006-226, s. 30.)

§ 95-257: Reserved for future codification purposes.

§ 95-258: Reserved for future codification purposes.

§ 95-259: Reserved for future codification purposes.

Article 23.

Workplace Violence Prevention.

§ 95-260. Definitions.

The following definitions apply in this Article:

(1) Civil no-contact order. - An order granted under this Article, which includes a remedy authorized by G.S. 95-264.

(2) Employer. - Any person or entity that employs one or more employees. Employer also includes the State of North Carolina and its political subdivisions.

(3) Unlawful conduct. - Unlawful conduct means the commission of one or more of the following acts upon an employee, but does not include acts of self-defense or defense of others:

a. Attempting to cause bodily injury or intentionally causing bodily injury.

b. Willfully, and on more than one occasion, following, being in the presence of, or otherwise harassing, as defined in G.S. 14-277.3A, without legal purpose and with the intent to place the employee in reasonable fear for the employee's safety.

c. Willfully threatening, orally, in writing, or by any other means, to physically injure the employee in a manner and under circumstances that would cause a reasonable person to believe that the threat is likely to be carried out and that actually causes the employee to believe that the threat will be carried out. (2004-165, s. 1; 2009-58, s. 7.)

§ 95-261. Civil no-contact orders; persons protected.

An action for a civil no-contact order may be filed as a civil action in district court by an employer on behalf of an employee who has suffered unlawful conduct from any individual that can reasonably be construed to be carried out, or to have been carried out, at the employee's workplace. The employee that is the subject of unlawful conduct shall be consulted prior to seeking an injunction under this Article in order to determine whether any safety concerns exist in relation to the employee's participation in the process. Employees who are targets of unlawful conduct who are unwilling to participate in the process under this Article shall not face disciplinary action based on their level of participation or cooperation. (2004-165, s. 1.)

§ 95-262. Commencement of action; venue.

(a) An action for a civil no-contact order is commenced by filing a verified complaint for a civil no-contact order in any civil district court or by filing a motion in any existing civil action.

(b) A complaint or motion for a civil no-contact order shall be filed in the county where the unlawful conduct took place. (2004-165, s. 1.)

§ 95-263. Process for action for no-contact order.

(a) Any action for a civil no-contact order requires that a separate summons be issued and served. The summons issued pursuant to this Article shall require the respondent to answer within 10 days of the date of service. Attachments to the summons shall include the verified complaint for the civil no-contact order and any temporary civil no-contact order that has been issued and the notice of hearing on the temporary civil no-contact order.

(b) Service of the summons and attachments shall be by the sheriff by personal delivery in accordance with Rule 4 of the Rules of Civil Procedure, and if the respondent cannot with due diligence be served by the sheriff by personal delivery, the respondent may be served by publication by the complainant in accordance with Rule 4(j1) of the Rules of Civil Procedure.

(c) The court may enter a civil no-contact order by default for the remedy sought in the complaint if the respondent has been served in accordance with this section and fails to answer as directed, or fails to appear on any subsequent appearance or hearing date agreed to by the parties or set by the court. (2004-165, s. 1.)

§ 95-264. Civil no-contact order; remedy.

(a) Upon a finding that the employee has suffered unlawful conduct committed by the respondent, the court may issue a temporary or permanent civil no-contact order. In determining whether or not to issue a civil no-contact order, the court shall not require physical injury to the employee or injury to the employer's property.

(b) The court may grant one or more of the following forms of relief in its orders under this Article:

(1) Order the respondent not to visit, assault, molest, or otherwise interfere with the employer or the employer's employee at the employer's workplace, or otherwise interfere with the employer's operations.

(2) Order the respondent to cease stalking the employer's employee at the employer's workplace.

(3) Order the respondent to cease harassment of the employer or the employer's employee at the employer's workplace.

(4) Order the respondent not to abuse or injure the employer, including the employer's property, or the employer's employee at the employer's workplace.

(5)   Order the respondent not to contact by telephone, written communication, or electronic means the employer or the employer's employee at the employer's workplace.

(6)   Order other relief deemed necessary and appropriate by the court.

(c)   A civil no-contact order shall include the following notice, printed in conspicuous type: "A knowing violation of a civil no-contact order shall be punishable as contempt of court which may result in a fine or imprisonment." (2004-165, s. 1.)

§ 95-265. Temporary civil no-contact order; court holidays and evenings.

(a)   A temporary civil no-contact order may be granted ex parte, without written or oral notice to the respondent, only if both of the following are shown:

(1)   It clearly appears from specific facts shown by a verified complaint or affidavit that immediate injury, loss, or damage will result to the complainant, or the complainant's employee before the respondent can be heard in opposition.

(2)   Either one of the following:

a.   The complainant certifies to the court in writing the efforts, if any, that have been made to give the notice and the reasons supporting the claim that notice should not be required.

b.   The complainant certified to the court that there is good cause to grant the remedy because the harm that the remedy is intended to prevent would likely occur if the respondent were given any prior notice of the complainant's efforts to obtain judicial relief.

(b)   Every temporary civil no-contact order granted without notice shall:

(1)   Be endorsed with the date and hour of issuance.

(2)   Be filed immediately in the clerk's office and entered of record.

(3)   Define the injury, state why it is irreparable and why the order was granted without notice.

(4) Expire by its terms within such time after entry, not to exceed 10 days.

(5) Give notice of the date of hearing on the temporary order as provided in G.S. 95-267(a).

(c) If the respondent appears in court for the hearing for a temporary order, the respondent may elect to file a general appearance and testify. Any resulting order may be a temporary order, governed by this section. Notwithstanding the requirements of this section, if all requirements of G.S. 95-266 have been met, the court may issue a permanent order.

(d) When the court is not in session, the complainant may file a complaint for a temporary order before any judge or magistrate designated to grant relief under this Article. If the judge or magistrate finds that there is an immediate and present danger of abuse against the complainant or employee of the complainant and that the complainant has satisfied the prerequisites set forth in subsection (a) of this section, the judge or magistrate may issue a temporary civil no-contact order. The chief district court judge may designate for each county at least one judge or magistrate to be reasonably available to issue temporary civil no-contact orders when the court is not in session. (2004-165, s. 1; 2006-264, s. 9.)

§ 95-266. Permanent civil no-contact order.

Upon a finding that the employee has suffered unlawful conduct committed by the respondent, a permanent civil no-contact order may issue if the court additionally finds that process was properly served on the respondent, the respondent has answered the complaint and notice of hearing was given, or the respondent is in default. No permanent civil no-contact order shall be issued without notice to the respondent. (2004-165, s. 1.)

§ 95-267. Duration; extension of orders.

(a) A temporary civil no-contact order shall be effective for not more than 10 days as the court fixes, unless within the time so fixed the temporary civil no-contact order, for good cause shown, is extended for a like period or a longer period if the respondent consents. The reasons for the extension shall be stated in the temporary order. In case a temporary civil no-contact order is granted without notice and a motion for a permanent civil no-contact order is made, it shall be set down for hearing at the earliest possible time and takes precedence over all matters except older matters of the same character. When the motion for a permanent civil no-contact order comes on for hearing, the complainant may proceed with a motion for a permanent civil no-contact order, and, if the complainant fails to do so, the judge shall dissolve the temporary civil no-contact order. On two days' notice to the complainant or on such shorter notice to that party as the judge may prescribe, the respondent may appear and move its dissolution or modification. In that event the judge shall proceed to hear and determine such motion as expeditiously as the ends of justice require.

(b) A permanent civil no-contact order shall be effective for a fixed period of time not to exceed one year.

(c) Any temporary or permanent order may be extended one or more times, as required, provided that the requirements of G.S. 95-265 or G.S. 95-266, as appropriate, are satisfied. The court may renew a temporary or permanent order, including an order that previously has been renewed, upon a motion by the complainant filed before the expiration of the current order. The court may renew the order for good cause. The commission of an act of unlawful conduct by the respondent after entry of the current order is not required for an order to be renewed. If the motion for extension is uncontested and the complainant seeks no modification of the order, the order may be extended if the complainant's motion or affidavit states that there has been no material change in relevant circumstances since entry of the order and states the reason for the requested extension. Extensions may be granted only in open court and not under the provisions of G.S. 95-265(d).

(d) Any civil no-contact order expiring on a court holiday shall expire at the close of the next court business day. (2004-165, s. 1.)

§ 95-268. Notice of orders.

(a) The clerk of court shall deliver on the same day that a civil no-contact order is issued a certified copy of that order to the sheriff.

(b) Unless the respondent was present in court when the order was issued, the sheriff shall serve that order upon the respondent and file proof of service in the manner provided for service of process in civil proceedings. If process has not yet been served upon the respondent, it shall be served with the order.

(c) A copy of the order shall be issued promptly to and retained by the police department of the municipality of the employer's workplace. If the employer's workplace is not located in a municipality or in a municipality with no police department, copies shall be issued promptly to and retained by the sheriff and the county police department, if any, of the county in which the employer's workplace is located.

(d) Any order extending, modifying, or revoking any civil no-contact order shall be recorded, issued, and served in accordance with the provisions of this Article. (2004-165, s. 1.)

§ 95-269. Violation of valid order.

A violation of an order entered pursuant to this Article is punishable as contempt of court. (2004-165, s. 1.)

§ 95-270. Employment discrimination unlawful.

(a) No employer shall discharge, demote, deny a promotion, or discipline an employee because the employee took reasonable time off from work to obtain or attempt to obtain relief under Chapter 50B or Chapter 50C. An employee who is absent from the workplace shall follow the employer's usual time-off policy or procedure, including advance notice to the employer, when required by the employer's usual procedures, unless an emergency prevents the employee from doing so. An employer may require documentation of any emergency that prevented the employee from complying in advance with the employer's usual time-off policy or procedure, or any other information available to the employee which supports the employee's reason for being absent from the workplace.

(b) The Commissioner of Labor shall enforce the provisions of this section according to Article 21 of Chapter 95 of the General Statutes, including the rules and regulations issued pursuant to the Article. (2004-165, s. 1.)

§ 95-271. Scope of Article; other remedies available.

This Article does not expand, diminish, alter, or modify any duty of any employer to provide a safe workplace for employees and other persons. This Article does not limit the ability of an employer, employee, or victim to pursue any other civil or criminal remedy provided by law. This Article does not apply in circumstances where an employee or representative of employees is engaged in union organizing, union activity, a labor dispute, or any activity or action protected by the National Labor Relations Act, 29 U.S.C. § 151, et seq. Nothing in this Article is intended to change the National Labor Relations Act's preemptive regulation of legally protected activities, nor to change the right of the State and its courts to regulate activities not protected by the National Labor Relations Act. (2004-165, s. 1; 2004-199, s. 58.)

Chapter 96.

Employment Security.

Article 1.

Definitions and Funds.

§ 96-1. Title and definitions.

(a) Title. - This Chapter shall be known and may be cited as the "Employment Security Law."

(b) Definitions. - The following definitions apply in this Chapter:

(1) Agricultural labor. - Defined in section 3306 of the Code.

(2) Average weekly insured wage. - The weekly rate obtained by dividing the total wages reported by all insured employers for a calendar year by the average monthly number of individuals in insured employment during that year and then dividing that quotient by 52.

(3) Base period. - The first four of the last five completed calendar quarters immediately preceding the first day of an individual's benefit year.

(4) Benefit. - Compensation payable to an individual with respect to the individual's unemployment.

(5) Benefit year. - The fifty-two-week period beginning with the first day of a week with respect to which an individual first files a valid claim for benefits and registers for work. If the individual is payroll attached, the benefit year begins on the Sunday preceding the payroll week ending date. If the individual is not payroll attached, the benefit year begins on the Sunday of the calendar week with respect to which the individual filed a valid claim for benefits and registered for work.

(6) Code. - Defined in G.S. 105-228.90.

(7) Computation date. - August 1 of each year.

(8) Department. - The North Carolina Department of Commerce.

(9) Division. - The Department's Division of Employment Security.

(10) Employee. - Defined in section 3306 of the Code.

(11) Employer or employing unit. - Any of the following:

a. An employer as defined in section 3306 of the Code.

b. A State or local governmental unit required to provide unemployment compensation coverage to its employees under section 3309 of the Code.

c. A nonprofit organization required to provide unemployment compensation coverage to its employees under section 3309 of the Code.

d. An Indian tribe required to provide unemployment compensation coverage to its employees under section 3309 of the Code.

(12) Employment. - Defined in section 3306 of the Code, with the following additions and exclusions:

a. Additions. - The term includes service to a governmental unit, a nonprofit organization, or an Indian tribe as described in 3306(c)(7) and 3306(c)(8) of the Code.

b. Exclusions. - The term excludes all of the following:

1. Service performed by an independent contractor.

2. Service performed for a governmental entity or nonprofit organization under 3309(b) and 3309(c) of the Code.

3. Service by one or more of the following individuals if the individual is authorized to exercise independent judgment and control over the performance of the work and is compensated solely by way of commission:

A. A real estate broker, as defined in G.S. 93A-2.

B. A securities salesman, as defined in G.S. 78A-2.

(13) Employment security law. - A law enacted by this State or any other state or territory or by the federal government providing for the payment of unemployment insurance benefits.

(14) Employment service company. - A person that contracts with a client or customer to supply an individual to perform employment services for the client or customer and that both under contract and in fact meets all of the following conditions:

a. Negotiates with the client or customer on such matters as time, place, and type of work, working conditions, quality, and price of the employment services.

b. Determines the assignment of an individual to the client or customer, even if the individual retains the right to refuse a specific assignment.

c. Hires and terminates an individual supplied.

d. Sets the rate of pay for the individual supplied.

e. Pays the individual supplied.

(15) Federal Unemployment Tax Act (FUTA). - Chapter 23 of the Code.

(16) Full-time student. - Defined in section 3306 of the Code.

(17) Governmental unit. - The term includes all of the following:

a. The State, a county, or a municipality, or any department, agency, or other instrumentality of one of these entities.

b. The State Board of Education, the Board of Trustees of The University of North Carolina, the board of trustees of other institutions and agencies supported and under the control of the State, a local board of education, or another entity that pays a teacher at a public school or educational institution.

c. A special district, an authority, or another entity exercising governmental authority.

d. An alcoholic beverage control board, an airport authority, a housing authority, a regional authority, or another governmental authority created pursuant to an act of the General Assembly.

(18) Immediate family. - An individual's spouse, child, grandchild, parent, and grandparent, whether the relationship is a biological, step-, half-, or in-law relationship.

(19) Independent contractor. - An individual who contracts to do work for a person and is not subject to that person's control or direction with respect to the manner in which the details of the work are to be performed or what the individual must do as the work progresses.

(20) Indian tribe. - Defined in section 3306 of the Code.

(21) Nonprofit organization. - A religious, charitable, educational, or other organization that is exempt from federal income tax and described in section 501(c)(3) of the Code.

(22) Person. - An individual, a firm, a partnership, an association, a corporation, whether foreign or domestic, a limited liability company, or any other organization or group acting as a unit.

(23) Secretary. - The Secretary of the Department of Commerce or the Secretary's designee.

(24) Taxable wages. - The amount determined under G.S. 96-9.3.

(25) Unemployed. - Defined in G.S. 96-15.01.

(26) Unemployment Trust Fund. - The federal fund established pursuant to section 904 of the Social Security Act, as amended.

(27) United States. - Defined in section 3306 of the Code.

(28) Wages. - Defined in section 3306 of the Code, except that no amount is excluded as provided under subdivision (b)(1) of that section. (Ex. Sess., 1936, c. 1, s. 1; 1947, c. 598, s. 1; 1977, c. 727, s. 1; 2011-401, s. 2.1; 2013-2, s. 1(b); 2013-224, s. 19.)

§§ 96-1.1 through 96-1.5. Repealed by Session Laws 1977, c. 727, ss. 2-6.

§ 96-2. Declaration of State public policy.

As a guide to the interpretation and application of this Chapter, the public policy of this State is declared to be as follows: Economic insecurity due to unemployment is a serious menace to the health, morals, and welfare of the people of this State. Involuntary unemployment is therefore a subject of general interest and concern which requires appropriate action by the legislature to prevent its spread and to lighten its burden which now so often falls with crushing force upon the unemployed worker and his family. The achievement of social security requires protection against this greatest hazard of our economic life. This can be provided by encouraging employers to provide more stable employment and by the systematic accumulation of funds during periods of employment to provide benefits for periods of unemployment, thus maintaining purchasing power and limiting the serious social consequences of poor relief assistance. The legislature, therefore, declares that in its considered judgment the public good and the general welfare of the citizens of this State require the enactment of this measure, under the police powers of the State, for the compulsory setting aside of unemployment reserves to be used for the benefit of persons unemployed through no fault of their own. (Ex. Sess. 1936, c. 1, s. 2.)

§ 96-3. Division of Employment Security.

The Division of Employment Security (DES) is created within the Department of Commerce and shall administer the provisions of this Chapter under the supervision of the Assistant Secretary of Commerce through two coordinate sections: the Employment Security Section and the Employment Insurance Section. The Employment Security Section shall administer the employment services functions of the Division. The Employment Insurance Section shall administer the unemployment taxation and assessment functions of the Division. (Ex. Sess. 1936, c. 1, s. 10; 1941, c. 108, s. 10; c. 279, ss. 1-3; 1943, c. 377, s. 15; 1947, c. 598, s. 1; 1953, c. 401, s. 1; 1957, c. 541, s. 5; 1965, c. 795, s. 1; 1977, c. 727, s. 7; 1979, c. 660, s. 1; 1981, c. 354; 1983, c. 717, s. 19; 1983 (Reg. Sess., 1984), c. 1034, s. 164; 1987, c. 103, s. 1; 1996, 2nd Ex. Sess., c. 18, s. 28.2(c); 1997-443, s. 33.3; 2005-276, ss. 29.20A(a), 29.20A(b); 2011-401, s. 2.2.)

§ 96-4. Administration; powers and duties of the Assistant Secretary; Board of Review.

(a) Duties and Powers of the Secretary and Assistant Secretary. - It shall be the duty of the Secretary of the Department of Commerce to administer this Chapter. The Secretary shall appoint an Assistant Secretary to assist in the implementation of the Employment Security Laws and the oversight of the Division of Employment Security.

(b) Board of Review. - The Governor shall appoint a three-person Board of Review to determine appeals policies and procedures and to hear appeals arising from the decisions and determinations of the Division. The Board of Review shall be comprised of one member representing employers, one member representing employees, and one member representing the general public. Members of the Board of Review are subject to confirmation by the General Assembly and shall serve four-year terms. The member appointed to represent the general public shall serve as chair of the Board of Review and shall be a licensed attorney. The annual salaries of the Board of Review shall be set by the General Assembly in the current Operations Appropriations Act. The Board of Review shall exercise its decision-making processes independent of the Governor, the General Assembly, the Department, and the Division.

(c) Procedures. - The Secretary of the Department of Commerce shall determine the organization and methods of procedure of the Division, in accordance with the provisions of this Chapter, and shall have an official seal which shall be judicially noticed. The Assistant Secretary shall, except as otherwise provided by the Secretary, be vested with all authority of the Secretary under this Chapter, including the authority to conduct hearings and make decisions and determinations, and shall execute all orders, rules and regulations established by the Secretary. Not later than November 20 preceding the meeting of the General Assembly, the Secretary shall submit to the Governor a report covering the administration and operation of this Chapter during the preceding biennium, and shall make such recommendation for amendments to this Chapter as the Secretary deems proper. The report shall include a balance sheet of the monies in the fund in which there shall be provided, if possible, a reserve against the liability in future years to pay benefits in excess of the then current contributions, which reserve shall be set up by the Secretary in accordance with accepted actuarial principles on the basis of statistics of employment, business activity, and other relevant factors for the longest possible period. Whenever the Secretary believes that a change in contribution or benefit rates will become necessary to protect the solvency of the fund, the Secretary shall promptly so inform the Governor and the legislature, and make recommendations with respect thereto.

(d) Rule Making. - Rules adopted to implement the Employment Security Laws in accordance with this Chapter shall be made pursuant to Article 2A of Chapter 150B of the General Statutes, the Administrative Procedures Act.

(e) Publication. - The Division shall cause to be printed for distribution to the public the text of this Chapter, the Division's rules, and any other material the Division deems relevant and suitable, and shall furnish the same to any person upon application therefor. All publications printed shall comply with the requirements of G.S. 143-170.1.

(f) Personnel. - Subject to other provisions of this Chapter, the Assistant Secretary is authorized to appoint, fix the compensation, and prescribe the duties and powers of such officers, accountants, attorneys, experts, and other persons as may be necessary in the performance of the Division's duties under this Chapter. The Assistant Secretary shall provide for the holding of examinations to determine the qualifications of applicants for the positions so classified, and except for temporary appointments not to exceed six months in duration, shall appoint its personnel on the basis of efficiency and fitness as determined in such examinations. All positions shall be filled by persons selected and appointed on a nonpartisan merit basis. The Secretary of Commerce may delegate to any such person so appointed such power and authority as the Secretary deems reasonable and proper for the effective administration of this Chapter, and may, in his or her discretion, bond any person handling monies or signing checks hereunder.

(g) Advisory Councils. - The State Advisory Council shall be composed of the Assistant Secretary and 15 persons representing employers, employees, and the general public, to be appointed as follows:

(1) Five members appointed by the Governor.

(2) Five members appointed by the President Pro Tempore of the Senate.

(3) Five members appointed by the Speaker of the House of Representatives.

Each member shall be appointed for a term of four years. Vacancies on the State Advisory Council shall be filled by the appointing authority. The Assistant Secretary shall serve as chair. A quorum of the State Advisory Council shall consist of the chairman, or such appointed member as he may designate, plus one half of the total appointed members. The function of the Council shall be to aid the Division in formulating policies and discussing problems related to the administration of this Chapter. Each member of the State Advisory Council attending meetings of the Council shall be paid the same amount per diem for his or her services as is provided for the members of other State boards, commissions, and committees who receive compensation for their services, including necessary time spent in traveling to and from his place of residence within the State to the place of meeting while engaged in the discharge of the duties of his office, and his actual mileage and subsistence at the same rate allowed to State officials.

(h) Employment Stabilization. - The Secretary of Commerce, in consultation with the Assistant Secretary and with the advice and aid of the advisory councils, shall take all appropriate steps to reduce and prevent unemployment; to encourage and assist in the adoption of practical methods of vocational training, retraining and vocational guidance; to investigate, recommend, advise, and assist in the establishment and operation, by municipalities, counties, school districts, and the State, of reserves for public works to be used in times of business depression and unemployment; to promote the reemployment of unemployed workers throughout the State in every other way that may be feasible; and to these ends to carry on and publish the results of investigations and research studies.

(i) Records and Reports. -

(1) Each employer shall keep true and accurate employment records, containing such information as the Division may prescribe. The records shall be open to inspection and be subject to being copied by the Division or its authorized representatives at any reasonable time and as often as may be necessary. An employer doing business in North Carolina shall make available in this State to the Division, such information with respect to persons performing services for it which the Secretary deems necessary in connection with the administration of this Chapter. The Division may require from an employer any sworn or unsworn reports, with respect to persons employed by it, which the Secretary deems necessary for the effective administration of this Chapter, including the employer's quarterly tax and wage report containing the name, social security number, and gross wages of persons employed during that quarter.

(2) If the Division finds that any employer has failed to file any report or return required by this Chapter or any regulation made pursuant hereto, or has filed a report which the Division finds incorrect or insufficient, the Division may make an estimate of the information required from such employer on the basis of the best evidence reasonably available to it at the time, and make, upon the basis of such estimate, a report or return on behalf of such employer, and the report or return so made shall be deemed to be prima facie correct, and the Division may make an assessment based upon such report and proceed to collect contributions due thereon in the manner as set forth in G.S. 96-10(b) of this Chapter: Provided, however, that no such report or return shall be made until the employer has first been given at least 10 days' notice by registered mail to the last known address of such employer: Provided further, that no such report or return shall be used as a basis in determining whether a person is an employer within the meaning of this Chapter.

(j) Hearings. - The Assistant Secretary shall appoint hearing officers or appeals referees to hear contested matters arising from the Employment Security Section and the Employment Insurance Section. Appeals from the decisions of the hearing officers or appeals referees shall be heard by the Board of Review.

(k) Oaths and Witnesses. - In the discharge of the duties imposed by this Chapter, the Assistant Secretary, the Chair of the Board of Review, and any duly authorized representative of the Division shall have power to administer oaths and affirmations, take depositions, certify to official acts, and issue subpoenas to compel the attendance of witnesses and the production of books, papers, correspondence, memoranda, and other records deemed necessary as evidence in connection with a disputed claim or the administration of this Chapter. Upon a motion, the Assistant Secretary, the Chair of the Board of Review, and any duly authorized representative of the Division may quash a subpoena if, after a hearing, any of the following findings are made:

(1)   The subpoena requires the production of evidence that does not relate to a matter in issue.

(2)   The subpoena fails to describe with sufficient particularity the evidence required to be produced.

(3)   The subpoena is subject to being quashed for any other reason sufficient in law.

(l)   Hearing on Motion to Quash Subpoena; Appeal. - A hearing on a motion to quash a subpoena pursuant to subsection (k) of this section shall be heard at least 20 days prior to the hearing for which the subpoena was issued. The denial of a motion to quash a subpoena is subject to immediate judicial review in the Superior Court of Wake County or in the superior court of the county where the person subject to the subpoena resides.

(m)   Subpoenas. - In case of contumacy by, or refusal to obey a subpoena issued to any person by the Secretary, the Assistant Secretary, the Board of Review, or the Division's authorized representative, any clerk of a superior court of this State within the jurisdiction of which the inquiry is carried on or within the jurisdiction of which said person guilty of contumacy or refusal to obey is found or resides or transacts business, upon application by the Division, or its duly authorized representatives, shall have jurisdiction to issue to such person an order requiring such person to appear before the Division, or its duly authorized representatives, there to produce evidence if so ordered, or there to give testimony touching upon the matter under investigation or in question; and any failure to obey such order of the said clerk of superior court may be punished by any Superior Court judge as a contempt of said court. Any person who shall, without just cause, fail or refuse to attend and testify or to answer any lawful inquiry or to produce books, papers, correspondence, memoranda, or other records in obedience to a subpoena of the Division, shall be punished by a fine of not more than fifty dollars ($50.00).

(n)   Protection against Self-Incrimination. - No person shall be excused from attending and testifying or from producing books, papers, correspondence, memoranda, and other records before the Division, Board of Review, or in obedience to the subpoena of the Division, Board of Review, or any member thereof, or any duly authorized representative of the Division, or Board of Review in any cause or proceeding before the Division, on the ground that the testimony or evidence, documentary or otherwise, required of him may tend to incriminate him or subject him to a penalty or forfeiture; but no individual shall be prosecuted or subjected to any penalty or forfeiture for or on account of any transaction, matter, or thing concerning which he is compelled, after having claimed his privilege against self-incrimination, to testify or produce evidence, documentary or otherwise, except that such individual so testifying shall not be exempt from prosecution and punishment for perjury committed in so testifying.

(o)   State-Federal Cooperation. - In the administration of this Chapter, the Board of Review or Division shall cooperate, to the fullest extent consistent with the provisions of this Chapter, with the federal agency, official, or bureau fully authorized and empowered to administer the provisions of the Social Security Act approved August 14, 1935, as amended, shall make such reports, in such form and containing such information as such federal agency, official, or bureau may from time to time require, and shall comply with such provisions as such federal agency, official, or bureau may from time to time find necessary to assure the correctness and verification of such reports; and shall comply with the regulations prescribed by such agency, official, or bureau governing the expenditures of such sums as may be allotted and paid to this State under Title III of the Social Security Act for the purpose of assisting in the administration of this Chapter. The Board of Review or Division shall further make its records available to the Railroad Retirement Board, created by the Railroad Retirement Act and the Railroad Unemployment Insurance Act, and shall furnish to the Railroad Retirement Board at the expense of the Railroad Retirement Board, such copies thereof as the Board shall deem necessary for its purposes in accordance with the provisions of section 303(c) of the Social Security Act as amended.

Upon request therefor, the Division shall furnish to any agency of the United States charged with the administration of public works or assistance through public employment, the name, address, ordinary occupation, and employment status of each recipient of benefits, and such recipient's rights to further benefits under this Chapter.

The Division is authorized to make such investigations, secure and transmit such information, make available such services and facilities and exercise such of the other powers provided herein with respect to the administration of this Chapter as it deems necessary or appropriate to facilitate the administration of any employment security or public employment service law, and in like manner, to accept and utilize information, services and facilities made available to this State by the agency charged with the administration of such other employment security or public employment service law.

The Division shall fully cooperate with the agencies of other states and shall make every proper effort within its means to oppose and prevent any further action which would, in its judgment, tend to effect complete or substantial federalization of State unemployment insurance funds or State employment security programs.

(p) Reciprocal Arrangements. -

(1) The Secretary is hereby authorized to enter into reciprocal arrangements with appropriate and duly authorized agencies of other states or of the federal government, or both, whereby:

a. Services performed by an individual for an employer for which services are customarily performed in more than one state shall be deemed to be services performed entirely within any one of the states

1. In which any part of such individual's service is performed or

2. In which such individual has his residence or

3. In which the employer maintains a place of business, provided there is in effect, as to such services, an election by the employer, approved by the agency charged with the administration of such state's employment security law, pursuant to which the services performed by such individual for the employer are deemed to be performed entirely within such state.

b. Combining wage credits. - The Division shall participate in any arrangements for the payment of compensation on the basis of combining an individual's wages and employment covered under this Chapter with his wages and employment covered under one or more laws of the federal government and the unemployment compensation laws of other states which are approved by the United States Secretary of Labor in consultation with the state unemployment compensation agencies as reasonably calculated to assure the prompt and full payment of compensation in such situations and which include provisions for (1) applying the base period of a single state law to a claim involving the combining of an individual's wages and employment covered under two or more state unemployment compensation laws, and (2) avoiding the duplicate use of wages and employment by reason of such combining.

 c. The services of the Division as agent may be made available to other states in taking interstate claims for such states.

 d. Contributions due under this Chapter with respect to wages for insured work shall for the purposes of G.S. 96-10 be deemed to have been paid to the fund as of the date payment was made as contributions therefor under another state or federal employment security law, but no such arrangement shall be entered into unless it contains provisions for such reimbursement to the fund of such contributions as the Division finds will be fair and reasonable as to all affected interests.

 e. The services of the Division may be made available to such other agencies to assist in the enforcement and collection of judgments of such other agencies.

 f. The services on vessels engaged in interstate or foreign commerce for a single employer, wherever performed, shall be deemed performed within this State or within such other state.

 g. Benefits paid by agencies of other states may be reimbursed to such agencies in cases where services of the claimant were "employment" under this Chapter and contributions have been paid by the employer to this agency on remuneration paid for such services; provided the amount of such reimbursement shall not exceed the amount of benefits such claimant would have been entitled to receive under the provisions of this Chapter.

(2) Reimbursements paid from the fund pursuant to subparagraphs b and c of subdivision (1) of this subsection shall be deemed to be benefits. The Division is authorized to make to other states or federal agencies and to receive from such other state or federal agencies, reimbursements from or to the fund, in accordance with arrangements entered into pursuant to subdivision (1) of this subsection.

(3) To the extent permissible under the laws and Constitution of the United States, the Division is authorized to enter into or cooperate in arrangements whereby facilities and services provided under this Chapter and facilities and services provided under the employment security law of any foreign government, may be utilized for the taking of claims and the payment of benefits under the Employment Security Law of this State or under a similar law of such government.

(q) The Board of Review after due notice shall have the right and power to hold and conduct hearings for the purpose of determining the rights, status and liabilities of an employer. The Board of Review shall have the power and authority to determine any and all questions and issues of fact or questions of law that may arise under the Employment Security Law that may affect the rights, liabilities and status of an employer including the right to determine the amount of contributions, if any, which may be due the Division by any employer. Hearings may be before the Board of Review and shall be held in the central office of the Board of Review or at any other designated place within the State. They shall be open to the public and shall consist of a review of the evidence taken by a hearing officer designated by the Board of Review and a determination of the law applicable to that evidence. The Board of Review shall provide for the taking of evidence by a hearing officer employed in the capacity of an attorney by the Department. Such hearing officer shall have the same power to issue subpoenas, administer oaths, conduct hearings and take evidence as is possessed by the Board of Review and such hearings shall be recorded, and he shall transmit all testimony and records of such hearings to the Board for its determination. All such hearings conducted by such hearing officer shall be scheduled and held in any county in this State in which the employer resides, maintains a place of business, or conducts business; however, the Board of Review may require additional testimony at any hearings held by it at its office. From all decisions or determinations made by the Board of Review, any party affected thereby shall be entitled to an appeal to the superior court. Before a party shall be allowed to appeal, the party shall within 10 days after notice of such decision or determination, file with the Board of Review exceptions to the decision or the determination, which exceptions will state the grounds of objection to the decision or determination. If any one of the exceptions shall be overruled then the party may appeal from the order overruling the exceptions, and shall, within 10 days after the decision overruling the exceptions, give notice of his appeal. When an exception is made to the facts as found by the Board of Review, the appeal shall be to the superior court in term time but the decision or determination of the Board of Review upon such review in the superior court shall be conclusive and binding as to all questions of fact supported by any competent evidence. When an exception is made to any rulings of law, as determined by the Board of Review, the appeal shall be to the judge of the superior court at chambers. The party appealing shall, within 10 days after the notice of appeal has been served, file with the Board of Review exceptions to the decision or determination overruling the exception which statement shall assign the errors complained of and the grounds of the appeal. Upon the filing of such statement the Board of Review shall, within 30 days, transmit all the papers and evidence considered by it, together with the assignments of errors filed by the appellant to a judge of the superior court holding court or residing in some district in which such appellant either resides, maintains a place of business or conducts business, or, unless the appellant objects after being given reasonable opportunity to object, to a judge of the Superior Court of Wake County: Provided, however, the 30-day period specified herein may be extended by agreement of parties.

(r)   The cause shall be entitled "State of North Carolina on Relationship of the Board of Review, Department of Commerce, of North Carolina against (here insert name of appellant)," and if there are exceptions to any facts found by the Board of Review, it shall be placed on the civil issue docket of such court and shall have precedence over other civil actions except those described in G.S. 96-10(b), and such cause shall be tried under such rules and regulations as are prescribed for the trial of other civil causes. By consent of all parties the appeal may be held and determined at chambers before any judge of a district in which the appellant either resides, maintains a place of business or conducts business, or said appeal may be heard before any judge holding court therein, or in any district in which the appellant either resides, maintains a place of business or conducts business. Either party may appeal to the appellate division from the judgment of the superior court under the same rules and regulations as are prescribed by law for appeals, except that if an appeal shall be taken on behalf of the Department of Commerce, it shall not be required to give any undertaking or make any deposit to secure the cost of such appeal and such court may advance the cause on its docket so as to give the same a speedy hearing.

(s)   The decision or determination of the Board of Review when docketed in the office of the clerk of the superior court of any county and when properly indexed and cross-indexed shall have the same force and effect as a judgment rendered by the superior court, and if it shall be adjudged in the decision or determination of the Board of Review that any employer is indebted to the Division for contributions, penalties and interest or either of the same, then said judgment shall constitute a lien upon any realty owned by said employer in the county only from the date of docketing of such decision or determination in the office of the clerk of the superior court and upon personalty owned by said employer in said county only from the date of levy on such personalty, and upon the execution thereon no homestead or personal property exemptions shall be allowed; provided, that nothing herein shall affect any rights accruing to the Division under G.S. 96-10. The provisions of this section, however, shall not have the effect of releasing any liens for contributions, penalties or interest, or either of the same, imposed by other law, nor shall they have the effect of postponing the payment of said contributions, penalties or interest, or depriving the Division of Employment Security of any priority in order of payment provided in any other statute under which payment of the said contributions, penalties and interest or either of the same may be required. The superior court or any appellate court shall have full power and authority to issue any and all executions, orders, decrees, or writs that may be necessary to carry out the terms of said decision or determination of the Division or to collect any amount of contribution, penalty or interest adjudged to be due the Division by said decision or determination. In case of an appeal from any decision or determination of the Division to the superior court or from any judgment of the superior court to the appellate division all proceedings to enforce said judgment, decision, or determination shall be stayed until final determination of such appeal but no proceedings for the collection of any amount of contribution, penalty or interest due on same shall be suspended or stayed unless the employer or party adjudged to pay the same shall file with the clerk of the superior court a bond in such amount not exceeding double the amount of contribution, penalty, interest or amount due and with such sureties as the clerk of the superior court deems necessary conditioned upon the payment of the contribution, penalty, interest or amount due when the appeal shall be finally decided or terminated.

(t) The conduct of hearings shall be governed by suitable rules and regulations established by the Secretary of Commerce. The manner in which appeals and hearings shall be presented and conducted before the Division shall be governed by suitable rules and regulations established by the Secretary. The Division shall not be bound by common-law or statutory rules of evidence or by technical or formal rules of procedure but shall conduct hearings in such manner as to ascertain the substantial rights of the parties.

(u) Notices of hearing shall be issued by the Board of Review or its authorized representative and sent by registered mail, return receipt requested, to the last known address of employer, employers, persons, or firms involved. The notice shall be sent at least 15 days prior to the hearing date and shall contain notification of the place, date, hour, and purpose of the hearing. Subpoenas for witnesses to appear at any hearing shall be issued by the Division or its authorized representative and shall order the witness to appear at the time, date and place shown thereon. Any bond or other undertaking required to be given in order to suspend or stay any execution shall be given payable to the Department of Commerce. Any such bond or other undertaking may be forfeited or sued upon as are any other undertakings payable to the State.

(v) None of the provisions or sections herein set forth in subsections (q)-(u) shall have the force and effect nor shall the same be construed or interpreted as repealing any of the provisions of G.S. 96-15 which provide for the procedure and determination of all claims for benefits and such claims for benefits shall be prosecuted and determined as provided by said G.S. 96-15.

(w) Upon a finding of good cause, the Division shall have the power in its sole discretion to forgive, in whole or in part, any overpayment arising under G.S. 96-18(g)(2).

(x) Confidentiality of Records, Reports, and Information Obtained from Claimants, Employers, and Units of Government. - Disclosure and redisclosure of confidential information shall be consistent with 20 C.F.R. Part 603 and any written guidance promulgated and issued by the U.S. Department of Labor consistent with this regulation and any successor regulation. To the extent a disclosure or redisclosure of confidential information is permitted or required by this federal regulation, the Department's authority to disclose or redisclose the information includes the following:

(1) Confidentiality of Information Contained in Records and Reports. - (i) Except as hereinafter otherwise provided, it shall be unlawful for any person to obtain, disclose, or use, or to authorize or permit the use of any information which is obtained from an employer, individual, or unit of government pursuant to the administration of this Chapter or G.S. 108A-29. (ii) Any claimant or employer or their legal representatives shall be supplied with information from the records of the Division to the extent necessary for the proper presentation of claims or defenses in any proceeding under this Chapter. Notwithstanding any other provision of law, any claimant may be supplied, subject to restrictions as the Division may by regulation prescribe, with any information contained in his payment record or on his most recent monetary determination, and any individual, as well as any interested employer, may be supplied with information as to the individual's potential benefit rights from claim records. (iii) Subject to restrictions as the Secretary may by regulation provide, information from the

records of the Division may be made available to any agency or public official for any purpose for which disclosure is required by statute or regulation. (iv) The Division may, in its sole discretion, permit the use of information in its possession by public officials in the performance of their public duties. (v) The Division shall release the payment and the amount of unemployment compensation benefits upon receipt of a subpoena in a proceeding involving child support. (vi) The Division shall furnish to the State Controller any information the State Controller needs to prepare and publish a comprehensive annual financial report of the State or to track debtors of the State. (vii) The Secretary may disclose or authorize redisclosure of any confidential information to an individual, agency, or entity, public or private, consistent with the requirements enumerated in 20 C.F.R. Part 603 or any successor regulation and any written guidance promulgated and issued by the U.S. Department of Labor consistent with 20 C.F.R. Part 603.

(2) Job Service Information. - (i) Except as hereinafter otherwise provided it is unlawful for any person to disclose any information obtained by the Division from workers, employers, applicants, or other persons or groups of persons in the course of administering the State Public Employment Service Program. Provided, however, that if all interested parties waive in writing the right to hold such information confidential, the information may be disclosed and used but only for those purposes that the parties and the Division have agreed upon in writing. (ii) The Division shall make public, through the newspapers and any other suitable media, information as to job openings and available applicants for the purpose of supplying the demand for workers and employment. (iii) The Labor Market Information Unit shall collect, collate, and publish statistical and other information relating to the work under the Division's jurisdiction; investigate economic developments, and the extent and causes of unemployment and its remedies with the view of preparing for the information of the General Assembly such facts as in the Division's opinion may make further legislation desirable. (iv) Except as provided by rules adopted by the Division, any information published pursuant to this subdivision shall not be published in any manner revealing the identity of the applicant or the employer.

(3) Penalties for Disclosure or Improper Use. - Any person violating any provision of this section may be fined not less than twenty dollars ($20.00) nor more than two hundred dollars ($200.00).

(4) Regulations. - The Division may provide by rule for procedures by which requests for information will be considered and the methods by which such information may be disclosed. The Division is authorized to provide by

regulation for the assessment of fees for securing and copying information released under this section.

(5)   Privileged Status of Letters and Reports and Other Information Relating to Administration of this Chapter. - All letters, reports, communication, or any other matters, either oral or written, including any testimony at any hearing, from the employer or employee to each other or to the Division or any of its agents, representatives, or employees, which letters, reports, or other communication shall have been written, sent, delivered, or made in connection with the requirements of the administration of this Chapter, shall be absolutely privileged communication in any civil or criminal proceedings except proceedings pursuant to or involving the administration of this Chapter and except proceedings involving child support and only for the purpose of establishing the payment and amount of unemployment compensation benefits. Nothing in this subdivision shall be construed to prohibit the Division, upon written request and on a reimbursable basis only, from disclosing information from the records of a proceeding compiled for the purpose of resolving issues raised pursuant to the Employment Security Law.

(6)   Nothing in this subsection (x) shall operate to relieve any claimant or employer from disclosing any information required by this Chapter or by regulations promulgated thereunder.

(7)   Nothing in this subsection (x) shall be construed to prevent the Division from allowing any individual or entity to examine and copy any report, return, or any other written communication made by that individual or entity to the Division, its agents, or its employees.

(7a)   Nothing in this subsection shall be construed to prevent the Division from disclosing, upon request and on a reimbursable basis only, to officers and employees of the Department of Housing and Urban Development and to representatives of a public housing agency as defined in Section 303(i)(4) of the Social Security Act, any information from the records of the Division with respect to individuals applying for or participating in any housing assistance program administered by the Department of Housing and Urban Development who have signed an appropriate consent form approved by the Secretary of Housing and Urban Development. It is the purpose of this paragraph to assure the compliance with Section 303(i)(1) of the Social Security Act and it shall be construed accordingly.

(7b) Nothing in this subsection shall be construed to prevent the Division from disclosing, upon request and on a reimbursable basis, to the Secretary of Health and Human Services, any information from the records of the Division as may be required by Section 303(h)(1) of the Social Security Act. It is the purpose of this paragraph to assure compliance with Section 303(h)(1) of the Social Security Act and it shall be construed accordingly.

(8) Any finding of fact or law, judgment, determination, conclusion or final order made by the Assistant Secretary, the Board of Review, a hearing officer, appeals referee, or any other person acting under authority of the Division pursuant to the Employment Security Law is not admissible or binding in any separate or subsequent action or proceeding, between a person and his present or previous employer brought before an arbitrator, court or judge of this State or the United States, regardless of whether the prior action was between the same or related parties or involved the same facts.

Provided, however, any finding of fact or law, judgment, determination, conclusion, or final order made by the Assistant Secretary, the Board of Review, a hearing officer, appeals referee, or any other person acting under the authority of the Division pursuant to the Employment Security Law shall be admissible in proceedings before the North Carolina Industrial Commission.

(y) Service of process upon the Division in any proceeding instituted before an administrative agency or court of this State shall be pursuant to G.S. 1A-1, Rule 4(j)(4); however, notice of the requirement to withhold unemployment compensation benefits pursuant to G.S. 110-136.2(f) shall be served upon the process agent for the Division by regular or courier mail.

(z) Advisory rulings may be made by the Division with respect to the applicability of any statute or rule administered by the Division, as follows:

(1) All requests for advisory rulings shall be made in writing and submitted to the Division. Such requests shall state the facts and statutes or rules on which the ruling is requested.

(2) The Division may request from any person securing an advisory ruling any additional information that is necessary. Failure to supply such additional information shall be cause for the Division to decline to issue an advisory ruling.

(3) The Division may decline to issue an advisory ruling if any administrative or judicial proceeding is pending with the person requesting the ruling on the

same factual grounds. The Division may decline to issue an advisory ruling if such a ruling may harm the Division's interest in any litigation in which it is or may be a party.

(4)   All advisory rulings shall be issued no later than 30 days from the date all information necessary to make a ruling has been received by the Division.

(5)   No advisory ruling shall be binding upon the Division provided that in any subsequent enforcement action initiated by the Division, any person's reliance on such ruling shall be considered in mitigation of any penalty sought to be assessed. (Ex. Sess. 1936, c. 1, s. 11; 1939, c. 2; c. 27, s. 8; c. 52, s. 5; cc. 207, 209; 1941, c. 279, ss. 4, 5; 1943, c. 377, ss. 16-23; 1945, c. 522, ss. 1-3; 1947, c. 326, ss. 1, 3, 4, 26; c. 598, ss. 1, 6, 7; 1949, c. 424, s. 1; 1951, c. 332, ss. 1, 18; 1953, c. 401, ss. 1-4; 1955, c. 385, ss. 1, 2; c. 479; 1957, c. 1059, s. 1; 1969, c. 44, s. 63; c. 575, ss. 1, 2; 1971, c. 673, ss. 1, 2; 1977, c. 727, ss. 8-10; 1979, c. 660, s. 2; 1979, 2nd Sess., c. 1212, s. 2; 1981, c. 160, s. 1; 1983, c. 625, s. 16; 1983 (Reg. Sess., 1984), c. 995, s. 6; 1985, c. 197, ss. 1, 6, 7; c. 552, s. 23; 1987, c. 273; c. 764, ss. 4, 4.1, 5; 1989, c. 583, ss. 1, 2; c. 707, ss. 1, 2; 1991, c. 603, s. 1; c. 723, s. 3; 1993, c. 343, s. 1; c. 512, s. 3; 1995, c. 507, s. 27.8(n); 1999-340, s. 10; 2000-140, s. 93.1(a); 2001-424, s. 12.2(b); 2004-203, s. 8; 2007-251, ss. 1, 2; 2011-401, s. 2.3; 2012-134, s. 6(a); 2013-2, s. 9(b); 2013-224, ss. 1, 2, 19, 20(a), (b).)

§ 96-4.1. Funds used in administering the unemployment compensation laws.

Four funds are established to administer this Chapter. The State Treasurer is responsible for investing all revenue received by the funds as provided in G.S. 147-69.2 and G.S. 147-69.3. Interest and other investment income earned by a fund accrues to it. Payments from a fund may be made only upon the warrant of the Secretary of Commerce.

The four funds are:

(1)   The Employment Security Administration Fund established under G.S. 96-5.

(2)   The Supplemental Employment Security Administration Fund established under G.S. 96-5.1.

(3) The Unemployment Insurance Fund established under G.S. 96-6.

(4) The Unemployment Insurance Reserve Fund established under G.S. 96-6.2. (2013-2, s. 1(b); 2013-224, s. 19.)

§ 96-5. Employment Security Administration Fund.

(a) Fund Established. - The Employment Security Administration Fund is created as a special revenue fund. The fund consists of the following:

(1) Monies appropriated by this State.

(2) Monies received from the United States or another source for the administration of this Chapter.

(3) Monies received from any agency of the United States or any other state as compensation for services or facilities supplied to the agency or state.

(4) Monies received pursuant to any surety bond or insurance policy or from other sources for losses sustained by the Employment Security Administration Fund or by reason of damage to equipment or supplies purchased from monies in the fund.

(5) Proceeds realized from the sale or disposition of equipment or supplies purchased from monies in the fund.

(b) Use of Fund. - Monies in the Employment Security Administration Fund may be used by the Division only to administer this Chapter. Monies received in the fund from a source other than an appropriation by the General Assembly are appropriated for the purpose of administering this Chapter. The Secretary is authorized to requisition and receive from the State's account in the Unemployment Trust Fund any monies standing to the State's credit that are permitted by federal law to be used for administering this Chapter and to expend the monies for this purpose, without regard to a determination of necessity by a federal agency.

(c) Repealed by Session Laws 2013-2, s. 1(a), effective July 1, 2013.

(c1)   Repealed by Session Laws 2004-124, s. 13.7B(b), effective July 20, 2004.

(d)   through (g) Repealed by Session Laws 2013-2, s. 1(a), effective July 1, 2013. (Ex. Sess. 1936, c. 1, s. 13; 1941, c. 108, ss. 12, 13; 1947, c. 326, s. 5; c. 598, s. 1; 1949, c. 424, s. 2; 1951, c. 332, s. 18; 1953, c. 401, ss. 1, 5; 1977, c. 727, ss. 11-13; 1981, c. 160, s. 2; 1987, c. 17, ss. 1, 2; 1991, c. 689, s. 142; 1991, Ex. Sess., c. 6, s. 1; 1995 (Reg. Sess., 1996), c. 608, s. 2; 1996, 2nd Ex. Sess., c. 18, s. 26.6; 2004-124, s. 13.7B(b); 2005-276, s. 6.37(h); 2006-203, s. 22; 2011-401, s. 2.4; 2013-2, s. 1(a), (b); 2013-224, s. 19.)

§ 96-5.1. Supplemental Employment Security Administration Fund.

(a)   Fund Established. - The Supplemental Employment Security Administration Fund is created as a special revenue fund. The fund consists of all interest and penalties paid under this Chapter by employers on overdue contributions and any appropriations made to the fund by the General Assembly. Penalties collected on unpaid taxes imposed by this section must be transferred to the Civil Penalty and Forfeiture Fund established in G.S. 115C-457.1.

(b)   Use of Funds. - Monies in the Supplemental Employment Security Administration Fund may be used by the Division only for one or more of the purposes listed below and may not be used in lieu of federal funds made available to the Division for the administration of this Chapter:

(1)   The payment of costs and charges of administration that the Secretary of Labor determines are not eligible for payment from or were improperly paid from the Employment Security Administration Fund. The Supplemental Employment Security Administration Fund must reimburse the Employment Security Administration Fund for the amount of any improper payment. If the balance in the Supplemental Fund is insufficient, the Secretary must notify the Governor, who must request an appropriation for that purpose.

(2)   The temporary stabilization of federal funds cash flow.

(3)   Security for loans from the Unemployment Trust Fund.

(4) The refund of an overpayment of interest previously credited to the fund. If an employer takes credit for a previous overpayment of interest when remitting contributions, the amount of credit taken for the overpayment of interest must be reimbursed to the Unemployment Insurance Fund. (2013-2, s. 1(b); 2013-224, ss. 3, 19.)

§ 96-6. Unemployment Insurance Fund.

(a) Establishment and Use. - The Unemployment Insurance Fund is established as an enterprise fund. The Division must administer the fund solely for the payment of unemployment compensation as that term is defined by section 3306(h) of the Code, exclusive of expenses of administration, and for refunds of sums erroneously paid into the fund. No money in the fund may be used, directly or indirectly, to pay interest on an advance received from the Unemployment Trust Fund.

This fund consists of the following sources of revenue:

(1) Contributions collected under this Chapter.

(2) Property or securities acquired through the use of monies belonging to the fund.

(3) Interest and investment earnings of the fund.

(4) Monies received from this State's account in the Unemployment Trust Fund in accordance with Title XII of the Social Security Act, as amended.

(5) Monies credited to this State's account in the Unemployment Trust Fund pursuant to section 903 of Title IX of the Social Security Act, as amended.

(6) Monies paid to this State pursuant to section 204 of the Federal-State Extended Unemployment Compensation Act of 1970.

(7) Reimbursement payments in lieu of contributions.

(8) Any federally mandated penalty amount assessed under G.S. 96-18(h).

(9) Amounts transferred from the Unemployment Insurance Reserve Fund.

(b) Accounts. - The State Treasurer must maintain within the fund three separate accounts:

(1) A clearing account.

(2) An unemployment trust fund account.

(3) A benefit account.

(b1) Clearing Account. - The Division must credit monies payable to the Unemployment Insurance Fund to the clearing account. The Controller must immediately deposit amounts in the clearing account with the secretary of the treasury of the United States to the credit of the account of this State in the Unemployment Trust Fund.

(b2) Unemployment Trust Fund Account. - The unemployment trust fund account consists of monies requisitioned from the State's account in the Unemployment Trust Fund to make refunds of overpayments of contributions. To obtain funds needed to make refunds, the Controller must requisition the amount needed from the Unemployment Trust Fund and credit the amount received to this account.

(c) Benefit Account. - The benefit account consists of monies requisitioned from the State's account in the Unemployment Trust Fund to pay benefits. To obtain funds to pay benefits under this Chapter, the Controller must requisition the amount needed from the State's account in the Unemployment Trust Fund and credit the amount received to this account. Warrants for the payment of benefits are payable from this account. Amounts in the benefit account that are not needed to pay the benefits for which they were requisitioned may be applied to the payment of benefits for succeeding periods or, in the discretion of the Controller, deposited to the credit of the State's account in the Unemployment Trust Fund.

(d) Discontinuance of Unemployment Trust Fund. - If the Unemployment Trust Fund or the State's account within the federal Fund ceases to exist, the credit balance of the State's account in that Fund must be transferred to the Unemployment Insurance Fund and credited to the benefit account.

(e), (f) Repealed by Session Laws 2013-2, s. 1(b), effective July 1, 2013. (Ex. Sess. 1936, c. 1, ss. 9, 18; 1939, c. 27, s. 7; c. 52, s. 4; c. 208; 1941, c.

108; 1945, c. 522, s. 4; 1947, c. 326, s. 6; 1953, c. 401, ss. 1, 6; 1959, c. 362, s. 1; 1961, c. 454, ss. 1-3; 1969, c. 575, s. 3; 1971, c. 673, ss. 3, 4; 1985, c. 197, s. 2; 2006-66, s. 6.19(a); 2006-203, s. 23; 2006-221, s. 3A; 2006-259, s. 40(a); 2011-401, s. 2.5; 2012-134, s. 3(e); 2013-2, s. 1(b); 2013-224, s. 19; 2013-391, s. 1.)

§ 96-6.1: Repealed pursuant to the terms of G.S. 96-6.1(c), effective with respect to calendar quarters beginning on or after January 1, 2011.

§ 96-6.2. Unemployment Insurance Reserve Fund.

(a) Establishment and Use. - The Unemployment Insurance Reserve Fund is established as an enterprise fund. The Fund consists of the revenues derived from the surtax imposed under G.S. 96-9.7. Monies in the Fund may be used only for the following purposes:

(1) Interest payments required on advances under Title XII of the Social Security Act.

(2) Principal payments on advances under Title XII of the Social Security Act.

(3) Transfers to the Unemployment Insurance Fund for payment of benefits.

(4) Administrative costs for the collection of the surtax.

(5) Refunds of the surtax.

(b) Fund Capped. - The balance in the Unemployment Insurance Reserve Fund on January 1 of any year may not exceed the greater of fifty million dollars ($50,000,000) or the amount of interest paid the previous September on advances under Title XII of the Social Security Act. Any amount in the fund that exceeds the cap must be transferred to the Unemployment Insurance Fund. (2013-2, s. 1(b); 2013-224, ss. 4, 19.)

§ 96-7. Representation in court.

(a)   In any civil action to enforce the provisions of this Chapter, the Secretary, the Department, and the State may be represented by any qualified attorney who is designated by it for this purpose.

(b)   All criminal actions for violation of any provision of this Chapter, or of any rules or regulations issued pursuant thereto, shall be prosecuted as now provided by law by the district attorney or by the prosecuting attorney of any county or city in which the violation occurs. (Ex. Sess. 1936, c. 1, s. 17; 1937, c. 150; 1973, c. 47, s. 2; 2011-401, s. 2.6.)

Article 2.

Contributions and Payments by Employers.

§§ 96-8, 96-9: Repealed by Session Laws 2013-2, s. 2(a), effective July 1, 2013.

§ 96-9.1. Purpose.

The purpose of this Article is to provide revenue to finance the unemployment benefits allowed under this Chapter and to do so in as simple a manner as possible by imposing a State unemployment tax that is similar to the federal unemployment tax imposed under FUTA. All employers that are liable for the federal unemployment tax on wages paid for services performed in this State and all employers that are required by FUTA to be given a state reimbursement option are liable for a State unemployment tax on wages. Revenue from this tax, referred to as a contribution, is credited to the Unemployment Insurance Fund established in G.S. 96-6. (2013-2, s. 2(b); 2013-224, s. 19.)

§ 96-9.2. Required contributions to the Unemployment Insurance Fund.

(a) Required Contribution. - An employer is required to make a contribution in each calendar year to the Unemployment Insurance Fund in an amount equal to the applicable percentage of the taxable wages the employer pays its employees during the year for services performed in this State. An employer may not deduct the contributions due in whole or in part from the remuneration of the individuals employed. Taxable wages are determined in accordance with G.S. 96-9.3. The applicable percentage for an employer is considered the employer's contribution rate and determined in accordance with this section.

(b) Contribution Rate for Beginning Employer. - The contribution rate for a beginning employer until the employer's account has been chargeable with benefits for at least 12 calendar months ending July 31 immediately preceding the computation date is one percent (1%). An employer's account has been chargeable with benefits for at least 12 calendar months if the employer has reported wages paid in four completed calendar quarters and its liability extends over all or part of two consecutive calendar years.

(c) Contribution Rate for Experience-Rated Employer. - The contribution rate for an experience-rated employer who does not qualify as a beginning employer under subsection (b) of this section is determined in accordance with the table set out below and then rounded to the nearest one-hundredth percent (0.01%), subject to the minimum and maximum contribution rates. The minimum contribution rate is six-hundredths of one percent (0.06%). The maximum contribution rate is five and seventy-six hundredths percent (5.76%). "Total insured wages" are the total wages reported by all insured employers for the 12-month period ending on July 31 preceding the computation date. An employer's experience rating is computed as a reserve ratio in accordance with G.S. 96-9.4. An employer's reserve ratio percentage (ERRP) is the employer's reserve ratio multiplied by sixty-eight hundredths. A positive ERRP produces a lower contribution rate, and a negative ERRP produces a higher contribution rate.

UI Trust Fund Balance as Percentage of Total Insured Wages	Contribution Rate
Less than or equal to 1%	2.9% minus ERRP
Greater than 1% but less	

than or equal to 1.25%	2.4% minus ERRP
Greater than 1.25%	1.9% minus ERRP

(d) Notification of Contribution Rate. - The Division must notify an employer of the employer's contribution rate for a calendar year by January 1 of that year. The contribution rate becomes final unless the employer files an application for review and redetermination prior to May 1 following the effective date of the contribution rate. The Division may redetermine the contribution rate on its own motion within the same time period.

(e) Voluntary Contribution. - An employer that is subject to this section may make a voluntary contribution to the Unemployment Insurance Fund in addition to its required contribution. A voluntary contribution is credited to the employer's account. A voluntary contribution made by an employer within 30 days after the date on an annual notice of its contribution rate is considered to have been made as of the previous July 31. (2013-2, s. 2(b); 2013-224, ss. 5, 19; 2013-391, s. 2.)

§ 96-9.3. Determination of taxable wages.

(a) Determination. - The Division must determine the taxable wages for each calendar year. An employer is not liable for contributions on wages paid to an employee in excess of taxable wages. The taxable wages of an employee is an amount equal to the greater of the following:

(1) The federal taxable wages set in section 3306 of the Code.

(2) Fifty percent (50%) of the average yearly insured wage, rounded to the nearest multiple of one hundred dollars ($100.00). The average yearly insured wage is the average weekly wage on the computation date multiplied by 52.

(b) Wages Included. - The following wages are included in determining whether the amount of wages paid to an individual in a single calendar year exceeds taxable wages:

(1) Wages paid to an individual in this State by an employer that made contributions in another state upon the wages paid to the individual because the work was performed in the other state.

(2) Wages paid by a successor employer to an individual when all of the following apply:

a. The individual was an employee of the predecessor and was taken over as an employee by the successor as a part of the organization acquired.

b. The predecessor employer paid contributions on the wages paid to the individual while in the predecessor's employ during the year of acquisition.

c. The account of the predecessor is transferred to the successor. (2013-2, s. 2(b); 2013-224, s. 19.)

§ 96-9.4. Determination of employer's reserve ratio.

(a) Account Balance. - The Division must determine the balance of an employer's account on the computation date by subtracting the total amount of all benefits charged to the employer's account for all past periods from the total of all contributions and other amounts credited to the employer for those periods. If the Division finds that an employer failed to file a report or finds that a report filed by an employer is incorrect or insufficient, the Division must determine the employer's account balance based upon the best information available to it and must notify the employer that it will use this balance to determine the employer's reserve ratio unless the employer provides additional information within 15 days of the date of the notice.

(b) Reserve Ratio. - The Division must determine an employer's reserve ratio, which is used to determine the employer's contribution rate. The employer's reserve ratio is the quotient obtained by dividing the employer's account balance on the computation date by the total taxable payroll of the employer for the 36 calendar month period ending June 30 preceding the computation date, expressed as a percentage. (2013-2, s. 2(b); 2013-224, s. 19.)

§ 96-9.5. Performance of services in this State.

A service is performed in this State if it meets one or more of the following descriptions:

(1) The service is localized in this State. Service is localized in this State if it meets one of the following conditions:

a. It is performed entirely within the State.

b. It is performed both within and without the State, but the service performed without the State is incidental to the individual's service within the State. For example, the individual's service without the State is temporary or transitory in nature or consists of isolated transactions.

(2) The service is not localized in any state but some of the service is performed in this State, and one or more of the following applies:

a. The base of operations is in this State.

b. There is no base of operations and the place from which the service is directed or controlled is in this State.

c. The service is not performed in any state that has a base of operations or a place from which the service is directed or controlled and the individual who performs the service is a resident of this State.

(3) The service, wherever performed, is within the United States or Canada and both of the following apply:

a. The service is not covered under the employment security law of any other state or Canada.

b. The place from which the service is directed or controlled is in this State.

(4) The service is performed outside the United States or Canada by a citizen of the United States in the employ of an American employer and at least one of the following applies. For purposes of this subdivision, the term "American employer" has the same meaning as defined in section 3306 of the Code:

a. The employer's principal place of business in the United States is located in this State.

b. The employer has no place of business in the United States, but the employer is one of the following:

1. An individual who is a resident of this State.

2. A corporation that is organized under the laws of this State.

3. A partnership or a trust and more of its partners or trustees are residents of this State than of any other state.

4. A limited liability company and more of its members are residents of this State than of any other state.

c. The employer has elected coverage in this State in accordance with G.S. 96-9.8.

d. The employer has not elected coverage in any state and the employee has filed a claim for benefits under the law of this State based on the service provided to the employer. (2013-2, s. 2(b); 2013-224, ss. 19, 20(c).)

§ 96-9.6. Election to reimburse Unemployment Insurance Fund in lieu of contributions.

(a) Applicability. - This section applies to a governmental entity, a nonprofit organization, and an Indian tribe that is required by section 3309 of the Code to have a reimbursement option. Each of these employers must finance benefits under the contributions method imposed under G.S. 96-9.2 unless the employer elects to finance benefits by making reimbursable payments to the Division for the Unemployment Insurance Fund.

(b) Election. - An employer may make an election under this section by filing a written notice of its election with the Division at least 30 days before the January 1 effective date of the election. An Indian tribe may make separate elections for itself and each subdivision, subsidiary, or business enterprise wholly owned by the tribe. A new employer may make an election under this section by filing a written notice of its election within 30 days after the employer receives notification from the Division that it is eligible to make an election under this section.

An election is valid for a minimum of four years and is binding until the employer files a notice terminating its election. An employer must file a written notice of termination with the Division at least 30 days before the January 1 effective date of the termination. The Division must notify an employer of a determination of the effective date of an election the employer makes and of any termination of the election. These determinations are subject to reconsideration, appeal, and review. An employer that makes the election allowed by this section may not deduct any amount due under this section from the remuneration of the individuals it employs.

(c) Reimbursable Amount. - An employer must reimburse the Unemployment Insurance Fund for the amount of benefits that are paid to an individual for weeks of unemployment that begin within a benefit year established during the effective period of the employer's election and are attributable to service that is covered by section 3309 of the Code and was performed in the employ of the employer. For regular benefits, the reimbursable amount is the amount of regular benefits paid. For extended benefits, the reimbursable amount is the amount not reimbursed by the federal government.

(d) Account. - The Division must establish a separate account for each reimbursing employer. The Division must credit payments made by the employer to the account. The Division must charge to the account benefits that are paid by the Unemployment Insurance Fund to individuals for weeks of unemployment that begin within a benefit year established during the effective period of the election and are attributable to service in the employ of the employer. All benefits paid must be charged to the employer's account except benefits paid through error.

The Division must furnish an employer with a statement of all credits and charges made to its account as of the computation date prior to January 1 of the succeeding year. The Division may, in its sole discretion, provide a reimbursing employer with informational bills or lists of charges on a basis more frequent than yearly if the Division finds it is in the best interest of the Division and the affected employer to do so.

(e) Annual Reconciliation. - A reimbursing employer must maintain an account balance equal to one percent (1%) of its taxable wages. The Division must determine the balance of each employer's account on the computation date. If there is a deficit in the account, the Division must bill the employer for the amount necessary to bring its account to one percent (1%) of its taxable wages for the immediate four quarters preceding July 1. Any amount in the account in excess of the one percent (1%) of taxable wages will be retained in the employer's account as a credit and will not be refunded to the employer. The Division must send a bill as soon as practical. Payment is due within 30 days from the date a bill is mailed. Amounts unpaid by the due date accrue interest and penalties in the same manner as past-due contributions and are subject to the same collection remedies provided under G.S. 96-10 for past-due contributions.

(f)   Quarterly Wage Reports. - A reimbursing employer must submit quarterly wage reports to the Division on or before the last day of the month following the close of the calendar quarter in which the wages are paid. During the first four quarters following an election to be a reimbursing employer, the employer must submit an advance payment with its quarterly report. The amount of the advance payment is equal to one percent (1%) of the taxable wages reported on the quarterly wage report. The Division must remit the payments to the Unemployment Insurance Fund and credit the payments to the employer's account.

(g)   Change in Election. - The Division must close the account of an employer that has been paying contributions under G.S. 96-9.2 and that elects to change to a reimbursement basis under this section. A closed account may not be used in any future computation of a contribution rate. The Division must close the account of an employer that terminates its election to reimburse the Unemployment Insurance Fund in lieu of making contributions. An employer that terminates its election under this section is subject to the standard beginning rate.

(h)   Noncompliance by Indian Tribes. - An Indian tribe that makes an election under this section and then fails to comply with this section is subject to the following consequences:

(1)   An employer that fails to pay an amount due within 90 days after receiving a bill and has not paid this liability as of the computation date loses the option to make reimbursable payments in lieu of contributions for the following calendar year. An employer that loses the option to make reimbursable payments in lieu of contributions for a calendar year regains that option for the following calendar year if it pays its outstanding liability and makes all contributions during the year for which the option was lost.

(2)   Services performed for an employer that fails to make payments, including interest and penalties, required under this section after all collection activities considered necessary by the Division have been exhausted, are no longer treated as "employment" for the purpose of coverage under this Chapter. An employer that has lost coverage regains coverage under this Chapter for

services performed if the Division determines that all contributions, payments in lieu of contributions, penalties, and interest have been paid. The Division must notify the Internal Revenue Service and the United States Department of Labor of any termination or reinstatement of coverage pursuant to this subsection.

(i) (Expires January 1, 2016) Transition. - This subsection provides a transitional adjustment period for an employer that elected to be a reimbursing employer prior to January 1, 2013, and was not required to submit an advance payment with its first four quarterly reports equal to one percent (1%) of its reported taxable wages. This subsection expires January 1, 2016:

(1) Governmental entities. - An employer that is a State or local governmental unit must reimburse the Division in the amount required by subsection (c) of this section for benefits paid on its behalf, as determined on the computation date in 2013, but it does not have to reconcile its account balance, as required under subsection (e) of this section, until 2014. If the employer's account balance on the computation date in 2014 does not equal one percent (1%) of its taxable wages reported for the preceding fiscal year, the Division will bill the employer for the deficiency.

(2) Nonprofit organization. - An employer that is a nonprofit organization may not secure its election to reimburse in lieu of paying contributions by posting a surety bond or a line of credit after July 1, 2013. An employer whose election is secured by a surety bond or line of credit is not required to begin making quarterly advance payments until the quarter following the quarter that its surety bond or line of credit expires and is not required to meet the annual reconciliation requirement until the employer has made at least four quarterly payments. (2013-2, s. 2(b); 2013-224, ss. 6, 7, 19.)

§ 96-9.7. Surtax for the Unemployment Insurance Reserve Fund.

(a) Surtax Imposed. - A surtax is imposed on an employer who is required to make a contribution to the Unemployment Insurance Fund equal to twenty percent (20%) of the contribution due under G.S. 96-9.2. Except as provided in this section, the surtax is collected and administered in the same manner as contributions. Surtaxes collected under this section must be credited to the Unemployment Insurance Reserve Fund established under G.S. 96-6.2. Interest and penalties collected on unpaid surtaxes imposed by this section must be credited to the Supplemental Employment Security Administration Fund.

Penalties collected on unpaid surtaxes imposed by this section must be transferred to the Civil Penalty and Forfeiture Fund established in G.S. 115C-457.1.

(b) Suspension of Tax. - The tax does not apply in a calendar year if, as of the preceding August 1 computation date, the amount in the State's account in the Unemployment Trust Fund equals or exceeds one billion dollars ($1,000,000,000). (2013-2, s. 2(b); 2013-224, ss. 8, 19.)

§ 96-9.8. Voluntary election to pay contributions.

(a) When Allowed. - An employer may elect to be subject to the contribution requirement imposed by G.S. 96-9.2 and thereby provide benefit coverage for its employees as follows:

(1) An employer that is not otherwise liable for contributions under G.S. 96-9.2 may elect to pay contributions to the same extent as an employer that is liable for those contributions.

(2) An employer that pays for services that are not otherwise subject to the contribution requirement may elect to pay contributions on those services performed by individuals in its employ in one or more distinct establishments or places of business.

(3) An employer that employs the services of an individual who resides within this State but performs the services entirely without the State may elect to have the individual's service constitute employment subject to contributions if no contributions are required or paid with respect to the services under an employment security law of any other state or of the federal government.

(b) Election. - To make an election under this section, an employer must file an application with the Division. An election is effective on the date stated by the Division in a letter approving the election. An election is irrevocable for the two-year period beginning on the effective date.

(c) Termination. - The Division may, on its own motion, terminate coverage of an employer who has become subject to this Chapter solely by electing coverage under this section. This termination may occur within the two-year minimum election period. The Division must give the employer 30 days written notice of a decision to terminate an election. The notice must be mailed to the employer's last known address. An employer that elects coverage under this section may, subsequent to the two-year minimum election period, terminate the election by filing a notice of termination with the Division. The notice must be given prior to the first day of March following the first day of January of the calendar year for which the employer wishes to cease coverage under this section. (2013-2, s. 2(b); 2013-224, s. 19.)

§ 96-9.9: Reserved for future codification purposes.

§ 96-9.10: Reserved for future codification purposes.

§ 96-9.11: Reserved for future codification purposes.

§ 96-9.12: Reserved for future codification purposes.

§ 96-9.13: Reserved for future codification purposes.

§ 96-9.14: Reserved for future codification purposes.

Article 2A.

Administration and Collection of Contributions.

§ 96-9.15. Report and payment.

(a) Report and Payment. - Contributions are payable to the Division when a report is due. A report is due on or before the last day of the month following the close of the calendar quarter in which the wages are paid. The Division must remit the contributions to the Unemployment Insurance Fund. If the amount of the contributions shown to be due after all credits is less than five dollars ($5.00), no payment need be made.

(b) Overpayment. - If an employer remits an amount in excess of the amount of contributions due, including any applicable penalty and interest, the excess amount remitted is considered an overpayment. The Division must refund an overpayment unless the amount of the overpayment is less than five dollars ($5.00). Overpayments of less than five dollars ($5.00) may be refunded only upon receipt of a written demand for the refund from the employer within the time allowed under G.S. 96-10(e).

(c)   Method of Payment. - An employer may pay contributions by electronic funds transfer. When an electronic funds transfer cannot be completed due to insufficient funds or the nonexistence of an account of the transferor, the Division may assess a penalty equal to ten percent (10%) of the amount of the transfer, subject to a minimum of one dollar ($1.00) and a maximum of one thousand dollars ($1,000). The Division may waive this penalty for good cause shown.

The Division may allow an employer to pay contributions by credit card. An employer that pays by credit card must include an amount equal to any fee charged by the Division for the use of the card. A payment of taxes that is made by credit card and is not honored by the card issuer does not relieve the employer of the obligation to pay the taxes.

An employer that does not pay by electronic funds transfer or by credit card must pay by check or cash. A check must be drawn on a United States bank and cash must be in currency of the United States.

(d)   Form of Report. - An employer must complete the tax form prescribed by the Division. An employer or an agent of an employer that reports wages for at least 25 employees must file the portion of the "Employer's Quarterly Tax and Wage Report" that contains the name, social security number, and gross wages of each employee in an electronic format prescribed by the Division. For failure of an employer to comply with this subsection, the Division must assess a penalty of twenty-five dollars ($25.00). For failure of an agent of an employer to comply with this subsection, the Division may deny the agent the right to report wages and file reports for that employer for a period of one year following the calendar quarter in which the agent filed the improper report. The Division may reduce or waive a penalty for good cause shown.

(e)   Jeopardy Assessment. - The Secretary may immediately assess and collect a contribution the Secretary finds is due from an employer if the Secretary determines that collection of the tax is in jeopardy and immediate assessment and collection are necessary in order to protect the interest of the State and the Unemployment Insurance Fund.

(f)   Domestic Employer Exception. - The Division may authorize an employer of domestic service employees to file an annual report and to file that report by telephone. An annual report allowed under this subsection is due on or before the last day of the month following the close of the calendar year in which the wages are paid. A domestic service employer that files a report by telephone must contact either the tax auditor assigned to the employer's account or the Employment Insurance Section in Raleigh and report the required information to that auditor or to that section by the date the report is due. (2013-2, s. 3(b); 2013-224, ss. 18, 19.)

§ 96-10. Collection of contributions.

(a) Interest on Past-Due Contributions. - Contributions unpaid on the date on which they are due and payable, as prescribed by the Division, shall bear interest at the rate set under G.S. 105-241.21 per month from and after that date until payment plus accrued interest is received by the Division. An additional penalty in the amount of ten percent (10%) of the taxes due shall be added. The clear proceeds of any civil penalties levied pursuant to this section shall be remitted to the Civil Penalty and Forfeiture Fund in accordance with G.S. 115C-457.2. Interest collected pursuant to this subsection shall be paid into the Special Employment Security Administration Fund. If any employer, in good faith, pays contributions to another state or to the United States under the Federal Unemployment Tax Act, prior to a determination of liability by this Division, and the contributions were legally payable to this State, the contributions, when paid to this State, shall be deemed to have been paid by the due date under the law of this State if they were paid by the due date of the other state or the United States.

(b) Collection. -

(1) If, after due notice, any employer defaults in any payment of contributions or interest thereon, the amount due shall be collected by civil action in the name of the Division, and the employer adjudged in default shall pay the costs of such action. Civil actions brought under this section to collect contributions or interest thereon from an employer shall be heard by the court at the earliest possible date, and shall be entitled to preference upon the calendar of the court over all other civil actions, except petitions for judicial review under this Chapter and cases arising under the Workers' Compensation Law of this State; or, if any contribution imposed by this Chapter, or any portion thereof, and/or penalties duly provided for the nonpayment thereof shall not be paid within 30 days after the same become due and payable, and after due notice

and reasonable opportunity for hearing, the Division, under the hand of the Assistant Secretary, may certify the same to the clerk of the superior court of the county in which the delinquent resides or has property, and additional copies of said certificate for each county in which the Division has reason to believe the delinquent has property located. If the amount of a delinquency is less than fifty dollars ($50.00), the Division may not certify the amount to the clerk of court until a field tax auditor or another representative of the Division personally contacts, or unsuccessfully attempts to personally contact, the delinquent and collect the amount due. A certificate or a copy of a certificate forwarded to the clerk of the superior court shall immediately be docketed and indexed on the cross index of judgments, and from the date of such docketing shall constitute a preferred lien upon any property which said delinquent may own in said county, with the same force and effect as a judgment rendered by the superior court. The Division shall forward a copy of said certificate to the sheriff or sheriffs of such county or counties, or to a duly authorized agent of the Division, and when so forwarded and in the hands of such sheriff or agent of the Division, shall have all the force and effect of an execution issued to such sheriff or agent of the Division by the clerk of the superior court upon a judgment of the superior court duly docketed in said county. Provided, however, the Division may in its discretion withhold the issuance of said certificate or execution to the sheriff or agent of the Division for a period not exceeding 180 days from the date upon which the original certificate is certified to the clerk of superior court. The Division is further authorized and empowered to issue alias copies of said certificate or execution to the sheriff or sheriffs of such county or counties, or to a duly authorized agent of the Division in all cases in which the sheriff or duly authorized agent has returned an execution or certificate unsatisfied; when so issued and in the hands of the sheriff or duly authorized agent of the Division, such alias shall have all the force and effect of an alias execution issued to such sheriff or duly authorized agent of the Division by the clerk of the superior court upon a judgment of the superior court duly docketed in said county. Provided, however, that notwithstanding any provision of this subsection, upon filing one written notice with the Division, the sheriff of any county shall have the sole and exclusive right to serve all executions and make all collections mentioned in this subsection and in such case no agent of the Division shall have the authority to serve any executions or make any collections therein in such county. A return of such execution, or alias execution, shall be made to the Division, together with all moneys collected thereunder, and when such order, execution, or alias is referred to the agent of the Division for service the said agent of the Division shall be vested with all the powers of the sheriff to the extent of serving such order, execution or alias and levying or collecting thereunder. The agent of the Division to whom such order or execution is referred shall give a bond not to exceed three thousand dollars ($3,000) approved by the Division for the faithful performance of such duties. The liability of said agent shall be in the same manner and to the same extent as is now imposed on sheriffs in the service of executions. If any sheriff of this State or any agent of the Division who is charged with the duty of serving executions shall willfully fail, refuse, or neglect to execute any order directed to him by the said Division and within the time provided by law, the official bond of such sheriff or of such agent of the Division shall be liable for the contributions, penalty, interest, and costs due by the employer.

(2) Any representative of the Division may examine and copy the county tax listings, detailed inventories, statements of assets or similar information required under General Statutes, Chapter 105, to be filed with the tax supervisor of any county in this State by any person, firm, partnership, or corporation, domestic or foreign, engaged in operating any business enterprise in such county. Any such information obtained by an agent or employee of the Division shall not be divulged, published, or open to public inspection other than to the Division's employees in the performance of their public duties. Any employee of the Division who violates any provision of this section shall be fined not less than twenty dollars ($20.00), nor more than two hundred dollars ($200.00), or imprisoned for not longer than 90 days, or both.

(3) When the Division furnishes the clerk of superior court of any county in this State a written statement or certificate to the effect that any judgment docketed by the Division against any firm or individual has been satisfied and paid in full, and said statement or certificate is signed by the Secretary of Commerce and attested by the Assistant Secretary, with the seal of the Division affixed, it shall be the duty of the clerk of superior court to file said certificate and enter a notation thereof on the margin of the judgment docket to the effect that said judgment has been paid and satisfied in full, and is in consequence canceled of record. The cancellation shall have the full force and effect of a cancellation entered by an attorney of record for the Division. It shall also be the duty of such clerk, when any such certificate is furnished him by the Division showing that a judgment has been paid in part, to make a notation on the margin of the judgment docket showing the amount of such payment so certified and to file said certificate. This paragraph shall apply to judgments already docketed, as well as to the future judgments docketed by the Division. For the filing of said statement or certificate and making new notations on the record, the clerk of superior court shall be paid a fee of fifty cents (50¢) by the Division.

(c) Priorities under Legal Dissolution or Distributions. - In the event of any distribution of an employer's assets pursuant to an order of any court under the laws of this State, including any receivership, assignment for benefit of creditors, adjudicated insolvency, composition, or similar proceeding, contributions then or thereafter due shall be paid in full prior to all other claims except taxes, and claims for remuneration of not more than two hundred and fifty dollars ($250.00) to each claimant, earned within six months of the commencement of the proceeding. In the event of an employer's adjudication in bankruptcy, judicially confirmed extension proposal, or composition, under the Federal Bankruptcy Act of 1898, as amended, contributions then or thereafter due shall be entitled to such priority as is provided in section 64(a) of that act (U.S.C., Title 11, section 104(a)), as amended.

A receiver of any covered employer placed into an operating receivership pursuant to an order of any court of this State shall pay to the Division any contributions, penalties or interest then due out of moneys or assets on hand or coming into his possession before any such moneys or assets may be used in any manner to continue the operation of the business of the employer while it is in receivership.

(d) Collections of Contributions upon Transfer or Cessation of Business. - The contribution or tax imposed by G.S. 96-9.2, and subsections thereunder, of this Chapter shall be a lien upon the assets of the business of any employer subject to the provisions hereof who shall lease, transfer or sell out his business, or shall cease to do business and such employer shall be required, by the next reporting date as prescribed by the Division, to file with the Division all reports and pay all contributions due with respect to wages payable for employment up to the date of such lease, transfer, sale or cessation of the business and such employer's successor in business shall be required to withhold sufficient of the purchase money to cover the amount of said contributions due and unpaid until such time as the former owner or employer shall produce a receipt from the Division showing that the contributions have been paid, or a certificate that no contributions are due. If the purchaser of a business or a successor of such employer shall fail to withhold purchase money or any money due to such employer in consideration of a lease or other transfer and the contributions shall be due and unpaid after the next reporting date, as above set forth, such successor shall be personally liable to the extent of the assets of the business so acquired for the payment of the contributions accrued and unpaid on account of the operation of the business by the former owner or employer.

(e) Refunds. - If not later than five years from the last day of the calendar year with respect to which a payment of any contributions or interest thereon was made, or one year from the date on which such payment was made, whichever shall be the later, an employer or employing unit who has paid such contributions or interest thereon shall make application for an adjustment thereof in connection with subsequent contribution payments, or for a refund, and the Division shall determine that such contributions or any portion thereof was erroneously collected, the Division shall allow such employer or employing unit to make an adjustment thereof, without interest, in connection with subsequent contribution payments by him, or if such an adjustment cannot be made in the next succeeding calendar quarter after such application for such refund is received, a cash refund may be made, without interest, from the fund: Provided, that any interest refunded under this subsection, which has been paid into the Special Employment Security Administration Fund established pursuant to G.S. 96-5(c), shall be paid out of such fund. For like cause and within the same period, adjustment or refund may be so made on the Division's own initiative. Provided further, that nothing in this section or in any other section of this Chapter shall be construed as permitting the refund of moneys due and payable under the law and regulations in effect at the time such moneys were paid. In any case, where the Division finds that any employing unit has erroneously paid to this State contributions or interest upon wages earned by individuals in employment in another state, refund or adjustment thereof shall be made, without interest, irrespective of any other provisions of this subsection, upon satisfactory proof to the Division that such other state has determined the employing unit liable under its law for such contributions or interest.

(f) No injunction shall be granted by any court or judge to restrain the collection of any tax or contribution or any part thereof levied under the provisions of this Chapter nor to restrain the sale of any property under writ of execution, judgment, decree or order of court for the nonpayment thereof. Whenever any employer, person, firm or corporation against whom taxes or contributions provided for in this Chapter have been assessed, shall claim to have a valid defense to the enforcement of the tax or contribution so assessed or charged, such employer, person, firm or corporation shall pay the tax or contribution so assessed to the Division; but if at the time of such payment he shall notify the Division in writing that the same is paid under protest, such payment shall be without prejudice to any defenses or rights he may have in the premises, and he may, at any time within 30 days after such payment, demand the same in writing from the Division; and if the same shall not be refunded within 90 days thereafter, he may sue the Division for the amount so demanded; such suit against the Division must be brought in the Superior Court of Wake

County, or in the county in which the taxpayer resides, or in the county where the taxpayer conducts his principal place of business; and if, upon the trial it shall be determined that such tax or contribution or any part thereof was for any reason invalid, excessive or contrary to the provisions of this Chapter, the amount paid shall be refunded by the Division accordingly. The remedy provided by this subsection shall be deemed to be cumulative and in addition to such other remedies as are provided by other subsections of this Chapter. No suit, action or proceeding for refund or to recover contributions or payroll taxes paid under protest according to the provisions of this subsection shall be maintained unless such suit, action or proceeding is commenced within one year after the expiration of the 90 days mentioned in this subsection, or within one year from the date of the refusal of the Division to make refund should such refusal be made before the expiration of said 90 days above mentioned. The one-year limitation here imposed shall not be retroactive in its effect, shall not apply to pending litigation nor shall the same be construed as repealing, abridging or extending any other limitation or condition imposed by this Chapter.

(g) Upon the motion of the Division, any employer refusing to submit any report required under this Chapter, after 10 days' written notice sent by the Division by registered or certified mail to the employer's last known address, may be enjoined by any court of competent jurisdiction from hiring and continuing in employment any employees until such report is properly submitted. When an execution has been returned to the Division unsatisfied, and the employer, after 10 days' written notice sent by the Division by registered or certified mail to the employer's last known address, refuses to pay the contributions covered by the execution, such employer shall upon the motion of the Division be enjoined by any court of competent jurisdiction from hiring and continuing in employment any employees until such contributions have been paid.

An employer who fails to file a report within the required time shall be assessed a late filing penalty of five percent (5%) of the amount of contributions due with the report for each month or fraction of a month the failure continues. The penalty may not exceed twenty-five percent (25%) of the amount of contributions due. An employer who fails to file a report within the required time but owes no contributions shall not be assessed a penalty unless the employer's failure to file continues for more than 30 days.

(h) When any uncertified check is tendered in payment of any contributions to the Division and such check shall have been returned unpaid on account of insufficient funds of the drawer of said check in the bank upon which same is drawn, a penalty shall be payable to the Division, equal to ten percent (10%) of the amount of said check, and in no case shall such penalty be less than one dollar ($1.00) nor more than two hundred dollars ($200.00).

(i) Except as otherwise provided in this subsection, no suit or proceedings for the collection of unpaid contributions may be begun under this Chapter after five years from the date on which the contributions become due, and no suit or proceeding for the purpose of establishing liability and/or status may be begun with respect to any period occurring more than five years prior to the first day of January of the year within which the suit or proceeding is instituted. This subsection shall not apply in any case of willful attempt in any manner to defeat or evade the payment of any contributions becoming due under this Chapter. A proceeding shall be deemed to have been instituted or begun upon the date of issuance of an order by the Assistant Secretary of the Division directing a hearing to be held to determine liability or nonliability, and/or status under this Chapter of an employing unit, or upon the date notice and demand for payment is mailed by certified mail to the last known address of the employing unit. The order shall be deemed to have been issued on the date the order is mailed by certified mail to the last known address of the employing unit. The running of the period of limitations provided in this subsection for the making of assessments or collection shall, in a case under Title II of the United States Code, be suspended for the period during which the Division is prohibited by reason of the case from making the assessment or collection and for a period of one year after the prohibition is removed.

(j) Waiver of Interest and Penalties. - The Division may, for good cause shown, reduce or waive any interest assessed on unpaid contributions under this section. The Division may reduce or waive any penalty provided in G.S. 96-10(a) or G.S. 96-10(g). The late filing penalty under G.S. 96-10(g) shall be waived when the mailed report bears a postmark that discloses that it was mailed by midnight of the due date but was addressed or delivered to the wrong State or federal agency. The late payment penalty and the late filing penalty imposed by G.S. 96-10(a) and G.S. 96-10(g) shall be waived where the delay was caused by any of the following:

(1) The death or serious illness of the employer or a member of his immediate family, or by the death or serious illness of the person in the employer's organization responsible for the preparation and filing of the report;

(2) Destruction of the employer's place of business or business records by fire or other casualty;

(3) Failure of the Division to furnish proper forms upon timely application by the employer, by reason of which failure the employer was unable to execute and file the report on or before the due date;

(4) The inability of the employer or the person in the employer's organization responsible for the preparation and filing of reports to obtain an interview with a representative of the Division upon a personal visit to the central office or any local office for the purpose of securing information or aid in the proper preparation of the report, which personal interview was attempted to be had within the time during which the report could have been executed and filed as required by law had the information at the time been obtained;

(5) The entrance of one or more of the owners, officers, partners, or the majority stockholder into the Armed Forces of the United States, or any of its allies, or the United Nations, provided that the entrance was unexpected and is not the annual two weeks training for reserves; and

(6) Other circumstances where, in the opinion of the Secretary, Assistant Secretary, or their designees, the imposition of penalties would be inequitable.

In the waiver of any penalty, the burden shall be upon the employer to establish to the satisfaction of the Secretary, Assistant Secretary, or their designees, that the delinquency for which the penalty was imposed was due to any of the foregoing facts or circumstances.

The waiver or reduction of interest or a penalty under this subsection shall be valid and binding upon the Division. The reason for any reduction or waiver shall be made a part of the permanent records of the employing unit to which it applies. (Ex. Sess. 1936, c. 1, s. 14; 1939, c. 27, ss. 9, 10; 1941, c. 108, ss. 14-16; 1943, c. 377, ss. 24-28; 1945, c. 221, s. 1; c. 288, s. 1; c. 522, ss. 17-20; 1947, c. 326, ss. 18-20; c. 598, s. 9; 1949, c. 424, ss. 14-16; 1951, c. 332, ss. 8, 20; 1953, c. 401, s. 15; 1959, c. 362, s. 9; 1965, c. 795, s. 11; 1971, c. 673, s. 21; 1973, c. 108, s. 43; c. 172, s. 4; 1977, c. 727, s. 50; 1979, c. 660, s. 16; 1981, c. 160, s. 16; 1989, c. 770, s. 21; 1991, c. 422, s. 1; 1995, c. 463, ss. 4-6; 1997-398, ss. 1-3; 2001-207, ss. 2, 3; 2005-276, s. 6.37(k); 2007-491, s. 44(1)a; 2011-401, s. 2.9; 2013-224, ss. 9, 20(d).)

§ 96-10.1. Compromise of liability.

(a) Authority. - The Secretary may compromise an employer's liability under this Article when the Secretary determines that the compromise is in the best interest of the State and makes one or more of the following findings:

(1) There is a reasonable doubt as to the amount of the liability of the employer under the law and the facts.

(2) The employer is insolvent and the Secretary probably could not otherwise collect an amount equal to, or in excess of, the amount offered in compromise. An employer is considered insolvent only in one of the following circumstances:

a. It is plain and indisputable that the employer is clearly insolvent and will remain so in the reasonable future.

b. The employer has been determined to be insolvent in a judicial proceeding.

(3) Collection of a greater amount than that offered in compromise is improbable, and the funds or a substantial portion of the funds offered in the settlement come from sources from which the Secretary could not otherwise collect.

(b) Written Statement. - When the Secretary compromises an employer's liability under this section and the amount of the liability is at least one thousand dollars ($1,000), the Secretary must make a written statement that sets out the amount of the liability, the amount accepted under the compromise, a summary of the facts concerning the liability, and the findings on which the compromise is based. The Secretary must sign the statement and keep a record of the statement. (2013-2, s. 3(b); 2013-224, s. 19.)

Article 2B.

Administration of Employer Accounts.

§ 96-11: Repealed by Session Laws 2013-2, s. 2(a), effective July 1, 2013.

§ 96-11.1. Employer accounts.

The Division must maintain a separate account for each employer. The Division must credit the employer's account with all contributions paid by the employer or on the employer's behalf and must charge the employer's account for benefits as provided in this Chapter. The Division must prepare an annual statement of all charges and credits made to the employer's account during the 12 months preceding the computation date. The Division must send the statement to the employer when the Division notifies the employer of the employer's contribution rate for the succeeding calendar year. The Division may provide a statement of charges and credits more frequently upon a request by the employer. (2013-2, s. 4; 2013-224, s. 19.)

§ 96-11.2. Allocation of charges to base period employers.

Benefits paid to an individual are charged to an employer's account when the individual's benefit year has expired. Benefits paid to an individual must be allocated to the account of each base period employer in the proportion that the base period wages paid to the individual in a calendar quarter by each base period employer bears to the total wages paid to the individual in the base period by all base period employers. The amount allocated to an employer that pays contributions is multiplied by one hundred twenty percent (120%) and charged to that employer's account. The amount allocated to an employer that elects to reimburse the Unemployment Insurance Fund in lieu of paying contributions is the amount of benefits charged to that employer's account. (2013-2, s. 4; 2013-224, ss. 10, 19.)

§ 96-11.3. Noncharging of benefits.

(a)   To Specific Employer. - Benefits paid to an individual under a claim filed for a period occurring after the date of the individual's separation from employment may not be charged to the account of the employer by whom the individual was employed at the time of the separation if the separation is due to one of the reasons listed below and the employer promptly notifies the Division, in accordance with rules adopted by the Division, of the reason:

(1)   The individual left work without good cause attributable to the employer.

(2)   The employer discharged the individual for misconduct in connection with the work.

(3)   The employer discharged the individual solely for a bona fide inability to do the work for which the individual was hired and the individual's period of employment was 100 days or less.

(4)   The separation is a disqualifying separation under G.S. 96-14.7.

(b)   To Any Base Period Employer. - Benefits paid to an individual may not be charged to the account of an employer of the individual if the benefits paid meet any of the following descriptions:

(1)   They were paid to an individual who is attending a vocational school or training program approved by the Division.

(2)   They were paid to an individual for unemployment due directly to a major natural disaster declared by the President pursuant to the Disaster Relief Act of 1970, and the individual receiving the benefits would have been eligible for disaster unemployment assistance under this federal act if the individual had not received benefits under this Chapter.

(3)   They were paid to an individual who left work for good cause under G.S. 96-14.8.

(4)   They were paid as a result of a decision by the Division and the decision is ultimately reversed upon final adjudication.

(c)   Current Employer. - At the request of the employer, no benefit charges may be made to the account of an employer that has furnished work to an individual who, because of the loss of employment with one or more other employers, is eligible for partial benefits while still being furnished work by the employer on substantially the same basis and substantially the same wages as had been made available to the individual during the individual's base period. This prohibition applies regardless of whether the employments were simultaneous or successive. A request made under this subsection must be filed in accordance with rules adopted by the Division. (2013-2, s. 4; 2013-224, s. 19.)

§ 96-11.4. No relief for errors resulting from noncompliance.

(a) Charges for Errors. - An employer's account may not be relieved of charges relating to benefits paid erroneously from the Unemployment Insurance Fund if the Division determines that both of the following apply:

(1) The erroneous payment was made because the employer, or the agent of the employer, was at fault for failing to respond timely or adequately to a written request from the Division for information relating to the claim for unemployment compensation. An erroneous payment is one that would not have been made but for the failure of the employer or the employer's agent to respond to the Division's request for information related to that claim.

(2) The employer or agent has a pattern of failing to respond timely or adequately to requests from the Division for information relating to claims for unemployment compensation. In determining whether the employer or agent has a pattern of failing to respond timely or adequately, the Division must consider the number of documented instances of that employer's or agent's failures to respond in relation to the total requests made to that employer or agent. An employer or agent may not be determined to have a pattern of failing to respond if the number of failures during the year prior to the request is fewer than two or less than two percent (2%) of the total requests made to that employer or agent, whichever is greater.

(b) Appeals. - An employer may appeal a determination by the Division prohibiting the relief of charges under this section in the same manner as other determinations by the Division with respect to the charging of employer accounts.

(c) Applicability. - This section applies to erroneous payments established on or after October 21, 2013. (2013-2, s. 4; 2013-224, ss. 11, 19.)

§ 96-11.5. Contributions credited to wrong account.

(a) Refund of Contributions Credited to Wrong Account. - When contributions are credited to the wrong account, the erroneous credit may be adjusted only by refunding the employer who made the payment that was credited in error. This applies regardless of whether the employer to whom the payment was credited in error is a related entity of the employer to whom the payment should have been credited. An employer whose payment is credited to the wrong account may request a refund of the amount erroneously credited by filing a request for refund within five years of the last day of the calendar year in which the erroneous credit occurred.

(b) Effect on Contribution Rate. - Failure of the Division to credit the correct account for contributions does not affect the contribution rate determined under G.S. 96-9.2 for either the employer whose account should have been credited for the contributions or the employer whose account was credited, and it does not affect the liability of an employer for contributions determined under those rates. No prior contribution rate for either of the employers may be adjusted even though the contribution rates were based on incorrect amounts in their account. An employer is liable for contributions determined under those rates for the five calendar years preceding the year in which the error is determined. This applies regardless of whether the employer acted in good faith. (2013-2, s. 4; 2013-224, s. 19.)

§ 96-11.6. Interest on Unemployment Insurance Fund allocated among employers' accounts.

The Division must determine the ratio of the credit balance in each employer's account to the total of the credit balances in all employers' accounts as of the computation date. The Division must allocate an amount equal to the interest credited to this State's account in the Unemployment Trust Fund for the four completed calendar quarters preceding the computation date on a pro rata basis to these accounts. The amount must be prorated to an employer's account in the same ratio that the credit balance in the employer's account bears to the total of the credit balances in all the accounts. Voluntary contributions made by an employer after July 31 of a year are not considered a part of the employer's account balance used in determining the allocation under this section until the computation date in the following year. (2013-2, s. 4; 2013-224, s. 19.)

§ 96-11.7. Acquisition of employer and transfer of account to another employer.

(a) Mandatory Transfer. - When an employer acquires all of the organization, trade, or business of another employer, the account of the predecessor must be transferred as of the date of the acquisition to the successor employer for use in the determination of the successor's contribution rate. This mandatory transfer does not apply when there is no common ownership between the predecessor and the successor and the successor acquired the assets of the predecessor in a sale in bankruptcy. In this circumstance, the successor's contribution rate is determined without regard to the predecessor's contribution rate.

(b) Consent. - When a distinct and severable portion of an employer's organization, trade, or business is transferred to a successor employer and the successor employer continues to operate the acquired organization, trade, or business, the portion of the account of the transferring employer that related to the transferred business may, with the approval of the Division, be transferred by mutual consent from the transferring employer to the successor employer. A successor employer that is a related entity of the transferring employer is eligible for a transfer from the transferring employer's account only to the extent permitted by rules adopted by the Division. No transfer may be made to the account of an employer that has ceased to be an employer under G.S. 96-11.9.

If a transfer of part or all of an account is allowed but is not mandatory, the successor employer requesting the transfer may make a request for transfer by filing an application for transfer with the Division within two years after the date the business was transferred or the date of notification by the Division of the right to request an account transfer, whichever is later. If the application is approved and the application was filed within 60 days after notification from the Division of the right to request a transfer, the transfer is effective as of the date the business was transferred. If the application is approved and the application was filed later than 60 days after notification from the Division, the effective date of the transfer is the first day of the calendar quarter in which the application was filed.

If the effective date of a transfer of an account under this subsection is after the computation date in a calendar year, the Division must recalculate the contribution rate for the transferring employer and the successor employer based on their account balances on the effective date of the account transfer. The recalculated contribution rate applies for the calendar year beginning after the computation date.

(c) Employer Number. - A new employer shall not be assigned a discrete employer number when there is an acquisition or change in the form or organization of an existing business enterprise, or severable portion thereof, and there is a continuity of control of the business enterprise. That new employer shall continue to be the same employer for the purposes of this Chapter as before the acquisition or change in form. The following assumptions apply in this subsection:

(1) "Control of the business enterprise" may occur by means of ownership of the organization conducting the business enterprise, ownership of assets necessary to conduct the business enterprise, security arrangements or lease arrangements covering assets necessary to conduct the business enterprise, or a contract when the ownership, stated arrangements, or contract provide for or allow direction of the internal affairs or conduct of the business enterprise.

(2) A "continuity of control" will exist if one or more persons, entities, or other organizations controlling the business enterprise remain in control of the business enterprise after an acquisition or change in form. Evidence of continuity of control includes changes of an individual proprietorship to a corporation, partnership, limited liability company, association, or estate; a partnership to an individual proprietorship, corporation, limited liability company, association, estate, or the addition, deletion, or change of partners; a limited liability company to an individual proprietorship, partnership, corporation, association, estate, or to another limited liability company; a corporation to an individual proprietorship partnership, limited liability company, association, estate, or to another corporation or from any form to another form.

(d) Contribution Rate. - Notwithstanding the other provisions in this section, when an account is transferred in its entirety to a successor employer, the transferring employer's contribution rate is the standard beginning rate.

Notwithstanding the other provisions in this section, if a successor employer to whom an account is transferred was an employer as of the date of the business transfer, the account transfer does not affect the successor employer's contribution rate for the calendar year in which the business was transferred. If the successor employer was not an employer as of the date of the business transfer, the successor employer's contribution rate for the year in which the business transfer occurs is the standard beginning rate unless one of the following applies:

(1) The account transfer is a mandatory transfer, in which case the contribution rate of the successor employer is the contribution rate of the transferring employer.

(2) The account transfer is by consent and the successor employer filed an application within 60 days of the business transfer, in which case the contribution rate of the successor employer is the contribution rate of the transferring employer. If the business was transferred from more than one employer and the transferring employers had different contribution rates, the contribution rate of the successor employer is the rate calculated as of the effective date of the account transfers.

(e) Liability for Contributions. - An employer that, by operation of law, purchase, or otherwise is the successor to an employer liable for contributions becomes liable for contributions on the day of the succession. This provision does not affect the successor's liability as otherwise prescribed by law for unpaid contributions due from the predecessor.

(f) Deceased or Insolvent Employer. - When the organization, trade, or business of a deceased person or of an insolvent debtor is taken over and operated by an administrator, executor, receiver, or trustee in bankruptcy, the new employer automatically succeeds to the account and contribution rate of the deceased person or insolvent debtor without the necessity of filing an application for the transfer of the account. (2013-2, s. 4; 2013-224, s. 19.)

§ 96-11.8. Closure of account.

(a) Account Closed. - When an employer ceases to be an employer under G.S. 96-11.9, the employer's account must be closed and may not be used in any future computation of the employer's contribution rate. An employer has no right or claim to any amounts paid by the employer into the Unemployment Insurance Fund.

(b) Exception for Active Duty. - If the Division finds that an employer's business is closed solely because one or more of its owners, officers, or partners or its majority stockholder enters into the Armed Forces of the United States, an ally, or the United Nations, the employer's account may not be terminated. If the business resumes within two years after the discharge or release of the affected individual from active duty in the Armed Forces of the United States, the employer's account is considered to have been chargeable with benefits throughout more than 13 consecutive calendar months ending July 31 immediately preceding the computation date. This subsection applies only to an employer that makes contributions under G.S. 96-9.2. This subsection does not apply to an employer that makes payments in lieu of contributions under G.S. 96-9.6. (2013-2, s. 4; 2013-224, s. 19.)

§ 96-11.9. Termination of coverage.

(a) By Law. - An employer that has not paid wages for two consecutive calendar years ceases to be an employer liable for contributions under this Chapter.

(b) By Application. - An employer may file an application with the Division to terminate coverage. An application for termination must be filed prior to March 1 of the calendar year for which the employer wishes to cease coverage. The Division may terminate coverage if it finds that the employer was not liable for contributions during the preceding calendar year. Termination of coverage under this subsection is effective as of January 1 of the calendar year in which the application is granted.

(c) After Reactivation. - If the Division reactivates the account of an employer that has been closed, the employer may file an application with the Division to terminate coverage. The application must be filed within 120 days after the Division notifies the employer of the reactivation of the employer's account. The Division may terminate coverage if it finds that the employer was not liable for contributions during the preceding calendar year. Termination of coverage under this subsection is effective as of January 1 of the calendar year in which the application is granted. An employer's protest of liability upon reactivation is considered an application for termination.

(d) After Discovery. - When the Division discovers that an employer is liable for contributions for a period of more than two years, the employer may file an application with the Division to terminate coverage. The application must be filed within 90 days after the Division notifies the employer of the discovered liability. The Division may terminate coverage if it finds that the employer was not liable for contributions during the preceding calendar year. An employer's protest of liability upon discovery is considered an application for termination. An employer is not eligible for termination of liability under this subsection if the employer willfully attempted to defeat or evade the payment of contributions. (2013-2, s. 4; 2013-224, s. 19.)

Article 2C.

Benefits Payable for Unemployment Compensation.

§ 96-12: Repealed by Session Laws 2013-2, s. 2(a), effective July 1, 2013.

§ 96-12.01: Recodified as G.S. 96-14.14 by Session Laws 2013-2, s. 6, effective July 1, 2013.

§§ 96-12.1 through 96-14: Repealed by Session Laws 2013-2, s. 2(a), effective July 1, 2013.

§ 96-14.1. Unemployment benefits.

(a)   Purpose. - The purpose of this Article is to provide temporary unemployment benefits as required by federal law to an individual who is unemployed through no fault on the part of the individual and who is able, available, and actively seeking work. Benefits are payable on the basis of service, to which section 3309(a)(1) of the Code applies, performed for a governmental entity, a nonprofit organization, and an Indian tribe in the same amount, on the same terms, and subject to the same conditions as compensation payable on the basis of other service.

(b)   Valid Claim. - To obtain benefits, an individual must file a valid claim for unemployment benefits and register for work. An individual must serve a one-week waiting period for each claim filed. A valid claim is one that meets the employment and wage standards in this subsection for the individual's base period. A valid claim for a second benefit year is one that meets the employment and wage standards in this subsection since the beginning date of the prior benefit year and before the date the new benefit claim is filed:

(1)   Employment. - The individual has been paid wages in at least two quarters of the individual's base period.

(2) Wages. - The individual has been paid wages totaling at least six times the average weekly insured wage during the individual's base period. If an individual lacks sufficient base period wages, then the wage standard for that individual is determined using the last four completed calendar quarters immediately preceding the first day of the individual's benefit year. This alternative base period may not be used by an individual in making a claim for benefits in the next benefit year.

(c) Qualification Determination. - An individual's qualification for benefits is determined based on the reason for separation from employment from the individual's bona fide employer. The individual's bona fide employer is the most recent employer for whom the individual began employment for an indefinite duration or a duration of more than 30 consecutive calendar days, regardless of whether work was performed on all of those days. An individual who is disqualified has no right to benefits. An individual who is disqualified may have the disqualification removed if the individual files a valid claim based on employment with a bona fide employer that employed the individual subsequent to the employment that resulted in disqualification. An individual who had a prior disqualification removed may be determined to be disqualified based on the reason for separation from employment from the individual's most recent bona fide employer, and the individual must be otherwise eligible for benefits.

(d) Eligibility for Benefits. - The Division must calculate a weekly benefit amount and determine the duration of benefits for an individual who files a valid claim and qualifies for benefits. To receive the weekly benefit amount, the Division must find that the individual meets the work search eligibility requirements for each week of the benefit period. An individual who fails to meet the work search requirements for a given week is ineligible to receive a benefit until the condition causing the ineligibility ceases to exist.

(e) Federal Restrictions. - Benefits are not payable for services performed by the following individuals, to the maximum extent allowed by section 3304 of the Code:

(1) Instructional, research, or principal administrative employees of educational institutions.

(2) Employees who provide services in any other capacity for an educational institution.

(3) Individuals who performed services described in either subdivision (1) or (2) of this subsection in an educational institution while in the employ of an educational service agency. The term "educational service agency" has the same meaning as defined in section 3304 of the Code.

(4) Professional athletes.

(5) Aliens. (2013-2, s. 5; 2013-224, ss. 12, 19; 2013-391, s. 3.)

§ 96-14.2. Weekly benefit amount.

(a) Weekly Benefit Amount. - The weekly benefit amount for an individual who is totally unemployed is an amount equal to the wages paid to the individual in the last two completed quarters of the individual's base period divided by 52 and rounded to the next lower whole dollar. If this amount is less than fifteen dollars ($15.00), the individual is not eligible for benefits. The weekly benefit amount may not exceed three hundred fifty dollars ($350.00).

(b) Partial Weekly Benefit Amount. - The weekly benefit amount for an individual who is partially unemployed or part-totally employed is the amount the individual would receive under subsection (a) of this section if the individual were totally unemployed, reduced by the amount of any wages the individual receives in the benefit week in excess of twenty percent (20%) of the benefit amount applicable to total unemployment. If the amount so calculated is not a whole dollar, the amount must be rounded to the next lower whole dollar. Payments received by an individual under a supplemental benefit plan do not affect the computation of the individual's partial weekly benefit.

(c) Retirement Reduction. - The amount of benefits payable to an individual must be reduced as provided in section 3304(a)(15) of the Code. This subsection does not apply to social security retirement benefits.

(d) Income Tax Withholding. - An individual may elect to have federal income tax deducted and withheld from the individual's unemployment benefits in the amount specified in section 3402 of the Code. An individual may elect to have State income tax deducted and withheld from the individual's unemployment benefits in an amount determined by the individual. The individual may change a previously elected withholding status. The amounts deducted and withheld from unemployment benefits remain in the

Unemployment Insurance Fund until transferred to the appropriate taxing authority as a payment of income tax. The Division must advise an individual in writing at the time the individual files a claim for unemployment benefits that the benefits paid are subject to federal and State income tax, that requirements exist pertaining to estimated tax payments, and that the individual may elect to have the amounts withheld. (2013-2, s. 5; 2013-224, s. 19; 2013-391, s. 4.)

§ 96-14.3. Minimum and maximum duration of benefits.

The minimum and maximum number of weeks an individual is allowed to receive unemployment benefits depends on the seasonal adjusted statewide unemployment rate that applies to the six-month base period in which the claim is filed. One six-month base period begins on January 1 and one six-month base period begins on July 1. For the base period that begins January 1, the average of the seasonal adjusted unemployment rates for the State for the preceding months of July, August, and September applies. For the base period that begins July 1, the average of the seasonal adjusted unemployment rates for the State for the preceding months of January, February, and March applies. The Division must use the most recent seasonal adjusted unemployment rate determined by the U.S. Department of Labor, Bureau of Labor Statistics, and not the rate as revised in the annual benchmark. The number of weeks allowed for an individual is determined in accordance with G.S. 96-14.4.

Seasonal Adjusted Unemployment Rate	Minimum Number of Weeks	Maximum Number of Weeks
Less than or equal to 5.5%	5	12
Greater than 5.5% up to 6%	6	13
Greater than 6% up to 6.5%	7	14
Greater than 6.5% up to 7%	8	15
Greater than 7% up to 7.5%	9	16
Greater than 7.5% up to 8%	10	17

Greater than 8% up to 8.5%	11	18
Greater than 8.5% up to 9%	12	19
Greater than 9%	13	20

(2013-2, s. 5; 2013-224, ss. 13, 19.)

§ 96-14.4. Duration of benefits for individual claimant.

(a) Total Benefit Amount. - The total amount of benefits paid to an individual may not exceed the individual's total benefit amount. The total benefit amount for an individual is determined as follows:

(1) Divide the individual's base-period wages by the average of the wages paid to the individual in the last two completed quarters of the base period.

(2) Multiply the quotient by eight and two-thirds.

(3) Round the product to the nearest whole number.

(4) Multiply the resulting amount by the individual's weekly benefit amount as determined under G.S. 96-14.2.

(b) Duration. - The number of weeks an individual may receive benefits varies depending on the seasonal adjusted statewide unemployment rate that applies at the time the regular unemployment claim is filed. The total benefits paid to an individual may not be less than the individual's average weekly benefit amount multiplied by the minimum number of weeks allowed in accordance with G.S. 96-14.3. The total benefits paid to an individual may not exceed the lesser of the following:

(1) The individual's average weekly benefit amount multiplied by the maximum number of weeks allowed in accordance with G.S. 96-14.3.

(2) The individual's total benefit amount, as calculated under subsection (a) of this section. (2013-2, s. 5; 2013-224, s. 19.)

§ 96-14.5. Disqualification for good cause not attributable to the employer.

(a) Determination. - The Division must determine the reason for an individual's separation from work. An individual does not have a right to benefits and is disqualified from receiving benefits if the Division determines that the individual left work for a reason other than good cause attributable to the employer. When an individual leaves work, the burden of showing good cause attributable to the employer rests on the individual and the burden may not be shifted to the employer.

(b) Reduced Work Hours. - When an individual leaves work due solely to a unilateral and permanent reduction in work hours of more than fifty percent (50%) of the customary scheduled full-time work hours in the establishment, plant, or industry in which the individual was employed, the leaving is presumed to be good cause attributable to the employer. The employer may rebut the presumption if the reduction is temporary or was occasioned by malfeasance, misfeasance, or nonfeasance on the part of the individual.

(c) Reduced Rate of Pay. - When an individual leaves work due solely to a unilateral and permanent reduction in the individual's rate of pay of more than fifteen percent (15%), the leaving is presumed to be good cause attributable to the employer. The employer may rebut the presumption if the reduction is temporary or was occasioned by malfeasance, misfeasance, or nonfeasance on the part of the individual. (2013-2, s. 5; 2013-224, s. 19.)

§ 96-14.6. Disqualification for misconduct.

(a) Disqualification. - An individual who the Division determines is unemployed for misconduct connected with the work is disqualified for benefits. The period of disqualification begins with the first day of the first week the individual files a claim for benefits after the misconduct occurs.

(b) Misconduct. - Misconduct connected with the work is either of the following:

(1) Conduct evincing a willful or wanton disregard of the employer's interest as is found in deliberate violation or disregard of standards of behavior that the employer has the right to expect of an employee or has explained orally or in writing to an employee.

(2) Conduct evincing carelessness or negligence of such degree or recurrence as to manifest an intentional and substantial disregard of the employer's interests or of the employee's duties and obligations to the employer.

(c) Examples. - The following examples are prima facie evidence of misconduct that may be rebutted by the individual making a claim for benefits:

(1) Violation of the employer's written alcohol or illegal drug policy.

(2) Reporting to work significantly impaired by alcohol or illegal drugs.

(3) Consumption of alcohol or illegal drugs on the employer's premises.

(4) Conviction by a court of competent jurisdiction for manufacturing, selling, or distributing a controlled substance punishable under G.S. 90-95(a)(1) or G.S. 90-95(a)(2) if the offense is related to or connected with an employee's work for the employer or is in violation of a reasonable work rule or policy.

(5) Termination or suspension from employment after arrest or conviction for an offense involving violence, sex crimes, or illegal drugs if the offense is related to or connected with the employee's work for an employer or is in violation of a reasonable work rule or policy.

(6) Any physical violence whatsoever related to the employee's work for an employer, including physical violence directed at supervisors, subordinates, coworkers, vendors, customers, or the general public.

(7) Inappropriate comments or behavior toward supervisors, subordinates, coworkers, vendors, customers, or to the general public relating to any federally protected characteristic that creates a hostile work environment.

(8) Theft in connection with the employment.

(9) Forging or falsifying any document or data related to employment, including a previously submitted application for employment.

(10) Violation of an employer's written absenteeism policy.

(11) Refusal to perform reasonably assigned work tasks or failure to adequately perform employment duties as evidenced by no fewer than three

written reprimands in the 12 months immediately preceding the employee's termination. (2013-2, s. 5; 2013-224, s. 19.)

§ 96-14.7. Other reasons to be disqualified from receiving benefits.

(a) Failure to Supply Necessary License. - An individual is disqualified for benefits if the Division determines that the individual is unemployed for failure to possess a license, certificate, permit, bond, or surety that is necessary for the performance of the individual's employment if it was the individual's responsibility to supply the necessary documents and the individual's inability to do so was within the individual's control. The period of disqualification begins with the first day of the first week the individual files a claim for benefits after the individual's failure occurs.

(b) Labor Dispute. - An individual is disqualified for benefits if the Division determines the individual's total or partial unemployment is caused by a labor dispute in active progress at the factory, establishment, or other premises at which the individual is or was last employed or by a labor dispute at another place within this State that is owned or operated by the employer that owns or operates the factory, establishment, or other premises at which the individual is or was last employed and that supplies materials or services necessary to the continued and usual operation of the premises at which the individual is or was last employed. An individual disqualified under the provisions of this subsection continues to be disqualified after the labor dispute has ceased to be in active progress for the period of time that is reasonably necessary and required to physically resume operations in the method of operating in use at the plant, factory, or establishment. (2013-2, s. 5; 2013-224, s. 19.)

§ 96-14.8. Military spouse relocation and domestic violence are good causes for leaving.

An individual is not disqualified for benefits for leaving work for one of the reasons listed in this section. Benefits paid on the basis of this section are not chargeable to the employer's account:

(1) Military spouse relocation. - Leaving work to accompany the individual's spouse to a new place of residence because the spouse has been reassigned from one military assignment to another.

(2) Domestic violence. - Leaving work for reasons of domestic violence if the individual reasonably believes that the individual's continued employment would jeopardize the safety of the individual or of any member of the individual's immediate family. For purposes of this subdivision, an individual is a victim of domestic violence if one or more of the following applies:

a. The individual has been adjudged an aggrieved party as set forth by Chapter 50B of the General Statutes.

b. There is evidence of domestic violence, sexual offense, or stalking. Evidence of domestic violence, sexual offense, or stalking may include any one or more of the following:

1. Law enforcement, court, or federal agency records or files.

2. Documentation from a domestic violence or sexual assault program if the individual is alleged to be a victim of domestic violence or sexual assault.

3. Documentation from a religious, medical, or other professional from whom the individual has sought assistance in dealing with the alleged domestic violence, sexual abuse, or stalking.

c. The individual has been granted program participant status pursuant to G.S. 15C-4 as the result of domestic violence committed upon the individual or upon a minor child with or in the custody of the individual by another individual who has or has had a familial relationship with the individual or minor child. (2013-2, s. 5; 2013-224, s. 19.)

§ 96-14.9. Weekly certification.

(a) Requirements. - An individual's eligibility for a weekly benefit amount is determined on a week-to-week basis. An individual must meet all of the requirements of this section for each weekly benefit period. An individual who fails to meet one or more of the requirements is ineligible to receive benefits until the condition causing the ineligibility ceases to exist:

(1) File a claim for benefits.

(2) Report at an employment office as requested by the Division.

(3) Meet the work search requirements of subsection (b) of this section.

(b) Work Search Requirements. - The Division must find that the individual meets all of the following work search requirements:

(1) The individual is able to work.

(2) The individual is available to work.

(3) The individual is actively seeking work.

(4) The individual accepts suitable work when offered.

(c) Able to Work. - An individual is not able to work during any week that the individual is receiving or is applying for benefits under any other state or federal law based on the individual's temporary total or permanent total disability.

(d) Available to Work. - An individual is not available to work during any week that one or more of the following applies:

(1) The individual tests positive for a controlled substance. An individual tests positive for a controlled substance if all of the conditions of this subdivision apply. An employer must report an individual's positive test for a controlled substance to the Division:

a. The test is a controlled substance examination administered under Article 20 of Chapter 95 of the General Statutes.

b. The test is required as a condition of hire for a job.

c. The job would be suitable work for the individual.

(2) The individual is incarcerated or has received notice to report to or is otherwise detained in a state or federal jail or penal institution. This subdivision does not apply to an individual who is incarcerated solely on a weekend in a county jail and who is otherwise available for work.

(3) The individual is an alien and is not in satisfactory immigration status under the laws administered by the United States Department of Justice, Immigration and Naturalization Service.

(4) The individual is on disciplinary suspension for 30 or fewer days based on acts or omissions that constitute fault on the part of the employee and are connected with the work.

(e) Actively Seeking Work. - The Division's determination of whether an individual is actively seeking work is based upon the following:

(1) The individual is registered for employment services, as required by the Division.

(2) The individual has engaged in an active search for employment that is appropriate in light of the employment available in the labor market and the individual's skills and capabilities.

(3) The individual has sought work on at least two different days during the week and made at least two job contacts with potential employers.

(4) The individual has maintained a record of the individual's work search efforts. The record must include the potential employers contacted, the method of contact, and the date contacted. The individual must provide the record to the Division upon request.

(f) Suitable Work. - The Division's determination of whether an employment offer is suitable must vary based upon the individual's length of unemployment as follows:

(1) During the first 10 weeks of a benefit period, the Division may consider all of the following:

a. The degree of risk involved to the individual's health, safety, and morals.

b. The individual's physical fitness and prior training and experience.

c. The individual's prospects for securing local work in the individual's customary occupation.

d. The distance of the available work from the individual's residence.

e. The individual's prior earnings.

(2) During the remaining weeks of a benefit period, the Division must consider any employment offer paying one hundred twenty percent (120%) of the individual's weekly benefit amount to be suitable work.

(g) Job Attachment. - An individual who is partially unemployed and for whom the employer has filed an attached claim for benefits has satisfied the work search requirements for any given week in the benefit period associated with the attached claim if the Division determines the individual is available for work with the employer that filed the attached claim.

(h) Job Training. - An individual who is otherwise eligible may not be denied benefits for any week because of the application to any such week of requirements relating to availability for work, active search for work, or refusal to accept work if the individual is attending a training program approved by the Division.

(i) Federal Labor Standards. - An otherwise eligible individual may not be denied benefits for a given week if the Division determines the individual refused to accept new work for one or more of the following reasons:

(1) The position offered is vacant due directly to a strike, lockout, or other labor dispute.

(2) The remuneration, hours, or other conditions of the work offered are substantially less favorable to the individual than those prevailing for similar work in the locality.

(3) The individual would be required to join a company union or to resign from or refrain from joining any bona fide labor organization as a condition of employment.

(j) Trade Act of 1974. - An otherwise eligible individual may not be denied benefits for any week because the individual is in training approved under section 236(a)(1) of the Trade Act of 1974, nor may the individual be denied benefits by reason of leaving work to enter such training, provided the work left is not suitable employment, or because of the application to any such week in training of provisions in this law or of any applicable federal unemployment compensation law, relating to availability for work, active search for work, or refusal to accept work. For purposes of this subsection, the term "suitable employment" means with respect to an individual, work of a substantially equal or higher skill level than the individual's past adversely affected employment, as defined for purposes of the Trade Act of 1974, and wages for such work at not less than eighty percent (80%) of the individual's average weekly wage as determined for the purposes of the Trade Act of 1974. (2013-2, s. 5; 2013-224, ss. 14, 19; 2013-391, s. 5.)

§ 96-14.10. Disciplinary suspension.

The disciplinary suspension of an employee for 30 or fewer consecutive calendar days does not constitute good cause for leaving work. An individual who is on suspension is not available for work and is not eligible for benefits for any week during any part of the disciplinary suspension. If the disciplinary suspension exceeds 30 days, the individual is considered to have been discharged from work because of the acts or omissions that caused the suspension and the issue is whether the discharge was for disqualifying reasons. During the period of suspension of 30 or fewer days, the individual is considered to be attached to the employer's payroll, and the issue of separation from work is held in abeyance until a claim is filed for a week to which this section does not apply. (2013-2, s. 5; 2013-224, ss. 15, 19.)

§ 96-14.11. Disqualification for the remaining weeks of the benefit period.

(a) Duration. - An individual may be disqualified from receiving benefits for the remaining weeks of the claim's duration if one or more subsections of this section apply. The period of disqualification under this section begins with the first day of the first week after the disqualifying act occurs.

(b) Suitable Work. - An individual is disqualified for any remaining benefits if the Division determines that the individual has failed, without good cause, to do one or more of the following:

(1) Apply for available suitable work when so directed by the employment office of the Division.

(2) Accept suitable work when offered.

(3) Return to the individual's customary self-employment when so directed by the Division.

(c) Recall After Layoff. - An individual is disqualified for any remaining benefits if it is determined by the Division that the individual is unemployed because the individual, without good cause attributable to the employer and after receiving notice from the employer, refused to return to work for an employer under one or more of the following circumstances:

(1) The individual was recalled within four weeks after a layoff. As used in this subdivision, the term "layoff" means a temporary separation from work due to no work available for the individual at the time of separation from work and the individual is retained on the employer's payroll and is a continuing employee subject to recall by the employer.

(2) The individual was recalled in a week in which the work search requirements were satisfied under G.S. 96-14.9(g) due to job attachment. (2013-2, s. 5; 2013-224, ss. 19, 20(e); 2013-391, s. 6.)

§ 96-14.12. Limitations on company officers and spouses.

(a) Disqualification for Benefits. - An individual is disqualified for benefits if the Division determines either of the following:

(1) The individual is customarily self-employed and can reasonably return to self-employment.

(2) The individual or the individual's spouse is unemployed because the individual's ownership share of the employer was voluntarily sold and, at the time of the sale, one or more of the following applied:

a. The employer was a corporation and the individual held five percent (5%) or more of the outstanding shares of the voting stock of the corporation.

b. The employer was a partnership, limited or general, and the individual was a limited or general partner.

c. The employer was a limited liability company and the individual was a member.

d.   The employer was a proprietorship, and the individual was the proprietor.

(b)   Duration of Benefits. - This subsection applies to an individual and the spouse of an individual who is unemployed based on services performed for a corporation in which the individual held five percent (5%) or more of the outstanding shares of the voting stock of the corporation. The maximum number of weeks an individual or an individual's spouse may receive benefits is limited to the lesser of six weeks or the applicable weeks determined under G.S. 96-14.4. (2013-2, s. 5; 2013-224, s. 19.)

§ 96-14.13. Limitation on benefits due to lump sum payments.

An individual is disqualified from receiving benefits for any week for which the individual receives any sum from the employer pursuant to an order of a court, the National Labor Relations Board, or another adjudicative agency or by private agreement, consent, or arbitration for loss of pay by reason of discharge. When the employer pays a lump sum that covers a period of more than one week, the amount paid is allocated to the weeks in the period on a pro rata basis as determined by the Division. If the amount prorated to a week would, if it had been earned by the individual during that week of unemployment, have resulted in a reduced benefit payment as provided in G.S. 96-14.2, the individual is entitled to receive the reduced payment if the individual is otherwise eligible for benefits.

Benefits paid for weeks of unemployment for which back pay awards or other similar compensation are made constitutes an overpayment of benefits. The employer must deduct the overpayment from the award prior to payment to the employee and must send the overpayment to the Division within five days of the payment for application against the overpayment. Overpayments not remitted to the Division are subject to the same collection procedures as contributions. The removal of charges made against the employer's account as a result of the previously paid benefits applies to the calendar year in which the Division receives the overpayment. (2013-2, s. 5; 2013-224, s. 19.)

§ 96-14.14. Extended benefits.

(a) [General Provisions. -] Extended benefits payable under sub-subdivision (b)(5)a. of this section shall be paid as required under the Federal-State Extended Unemployment Compensation Act of 1970. Extended benefits payable under sub-subdivision (b)(5)a. of this section are not required under federal law and may be paid only if the federal government funds one hundred percent (100%) of the costs of providing them. Extended benefits are payable in the manner prescribed by this section.

(b) Definitions. - As used in this section, unless the context clearly requires otherwise:

(1) "Eligibility period" of an individual means the period consisting of the weeks in his benefit year which begin in an extended benefit period and if his benefit year ends within such extended benefit period, any weeks thereafter which begin in such period.

(2) "Exhaustee" means an individual who, with respect to any week of unemployment in his eligibility period:

a. Has received, prior to such week, all of the regular benefits that were available to him under this Chapter or any other State law (including dependents' allowances and benefits payable to federal civilian employees and ex-servicemen under 5 U.S.C. Chapter 85) in his current benefit year that includes such week;

Provided, that, for the purposes of this subdivision, an individual shall be deemed to have received all of the regular benefits that were available to him although (i) as a result of a pending appeal with respect to wages that were not considered in the original monetary determination in his benefit year, he may subsequently be determined to be entitled to added regular benefits, or (ii) he may be entitled to regular benefits with respect to future weeks of unemployment, but such benefits are not payable with respect to such week of unemployment by reason of the provisions in G.S. 96-16; or

b. His benefit year having expired prior to such week, has no, or insufficient, wages on the basis of which he could establish a new benefit year that would include such week; and

c.1. Has no right to unemployment benefits or allowances, as the case may be, under the Railroad Unemployment Insurance Act, the Trade Expansion Act of 1962, the Automotive Products Trade Act of 1965 and such other federal laws as are specified in regulations issued by the United States Secretary of Labor; and

2. Has not received and is not seeking unemployment benefits under the unemployment compensation law of Canada; but if he is seeking such benefits and the appropriate agency finally determines that he is not entitled to benefits under such law, he is considered an exhaustee.

(3) "Extended benefit period" means a period which:

a. Begins the third week after a week for which there is an "on" indicator; and

b. Ends with either of the following weeks, whichever occurs later:

1. The third week after the first week for which there is an "off" indicator; or

2. The 13th consecutive week of such period.

Provided, that no extended benefit period may begin before the 14th week following the end of a prior extended benefit period which was in effect with respect to this State.

(4) "Extended benefits" means benefits (including benefits payable to federal civilian employees and to ex-servicemen pursuant to 5 U.S.C. Chapter 85) payable to an individual under the provisions of this section for weeks of unemployment in his eligibility period.

(5) There is an "on indicator" for this State for a week if the Division determines, in accordance with the regulations of the United States Secretary of Labor, that for the period consisting of such week and the immediate preceding 12 weeks, the rate of insured unemployment (not seasonally adjusted) under this Chapter:

a. Equalled or exceeded one hundred twenty percent (120%) of the average of such rates for the corresponding 13-week period ending in each of the preceding two calendar years, and equalled or exceeded five percent (5%), or

b. Equalled or exceeded six percent (6%), or

c.   With respect to benefits for weeks of unemployment in North Carolina beginning after May 1, 2002:

1.   The average rate of total unemployment (seasonally adjusted), as determined by the United States Secretary of Labor, for the period consisting of the most recent three months for which data for all states are published before the close of such week equals or exceeds a six and one-half percent (6.5%), and

2.   The average rate of total unemployment in the State (seasonally adjusted), as determined by the United States Secretary of Labor, for the three-month period referred to in [sub-]sub-subdivision c.1. of this subdivision, equals or exceeds one hundred ten percent (110%) of such average for either or both of the corresponding three-month periods ending in the two preceding calendar years.

3.   Expired effective January 1, 2013, pursuant to Session Laws 2011-145, s. 6.16(d), as amended by Session Laws 2012-134, s. 1(c).

d.   There is a State "off indicator" for a week with respect to sub-subdivision c. of this subdivision, only if, for the period consisting of such week and the immediately preceding 12 weeks, the option specified in sub-subdivision c. does not result in an "on indicator".

e.   Total extended benefit amount -

1.   The total extended benefit amount payment to any eligible individual with respect to the applicable benefit year shall be the least of the following amounts:

I.   Fifty percent (50%) of the total amount of regular benefits which were payable to the individual under this Chapter in the individual's applicable benefit year; or

II.   Thirteen times the individual's weekly benefit amount that was payable to the individual under this Chapter for a week of total unemployment in the applicable benefit year.

2.   I.   Effective with respect to weeks beginning in a high unemployment period, [sub-]sub-subdivision e.1. of this subdivision shall be applied by substituting:

A. "Eighty percent (80%)" for "fifty percent (50%)" in [sub-sub-]sub-subdivision e.1.I., and

B. "Twenty" for "thirteen" in [sub-sub-]sub-subdivision e.1.II.

II. For purposes of [sub-sub-]sub-subdivision 2.I., the term "high unemployment period" means any period during which an extended benefit period would be in effect if sub-subdivision c. of this subdivision were applied by substituting "eight percent (8%)" for "six and one-half percent (6.5%)".

3. Expired effective January 1, 2013, pursuant to Session Laws 2011-145, s. 6.16(d), as amended by Session Laws 2012-134, s. 1(c).

(6) There is an "off indicator" for this State for a week if the Division determines, in accordance with the regulations of the United States Secretary of Labor, that for the period consisting of such week and the immediately preceding 12 weeks, the rate of insured unemployment (not seasonally adjusted) under this Chapter:

a. Was less than one hundred twenty percent (120%) of the average of such rates for the corresponding 13-week period ending in each of the preceding two calendar years, and was less than six percent (6%), or

b. Was less than five percent (5%).

(7) "Rate of insured unemployment," for the purposes of subparagraphs [subdivisions] (5) and (6) of this subsection, means the percentage derived by dividing:

a. The average weekly number of individuals filing claims for regular compensation in this State for weeks of unemployment with respect to the most recent 13 consecutive-week period, as determined by the Division, on the basis of its reports to the United States Secretary of Labor, by

b. The average monthly employment covered under this Chapter for the first four of the most recent six completed calendar quarters ending before the end of such 13-week period.

(8) "Regular benefits" means benefits payable to an individual under this Chapter or any other State law (including benefits payable to federal civilian

employees and to ex-servicemen pursuant to 5 U.S.C. Chapter 85) other than extended benefits.

(9) "State law" means the unemployment insurance law of any state approved by the United States Secretary of Labor under section 3304 of the Internal Revenue Code.

(c) Effect of State Law Provisions Relating to Regular Benefits on Claims for, and for Payment of, Extended Benefits. - Except when the result would be inconsistent with the other provisions of this section and in matters of eligibility determination, as provided by rules adopted by the Division, the provisions of this Chapter which apply to claims for, or the payment of, regular benefits shall apply to claims for, and the payment of, extended benefits.

(d) Eligibility Requirements for Extended Benefits. - An individual shall be eligible to receive extended benefits with respect to any week of unemployment in his eligibility period only if the Division finds that with respect to such week:

(1) The individual is an "exhaustee" as defined in subsection [subdivision] (b)(2).

(2) The individual has satisfied the requirements of this Chapter for the receipt of regular benefits that are applicable to individuals claiming extended benefits, including not being subject to a disqualification for the receipt of benefits. Provided, however, that for purposes of disqualification for extended benefits for weeks of unemployment beginning after March 31, 1981, the term "suitable work" means any work which is within the individual's capabilities to perform if: (i) the gross average weekly remuneration payable for the work exceeds the sum of the individual's weekly extended benefit amount plus the amount, if any, of supplemental unemployment benefits (as defined in section 501(C)(17)(D) of the Internal Revenue Code of 1954) payable to such individual for such week; and (ii) the gross wages payable for the work equal the higher of the minimum wages provided by section 6(a)(1) of the Fair Labor Standards Act of 1938 as amended (without regard to any exemption), or the State minimum wage; and (iii) the work is offered to the individual in writing and is listed with the State employment service; and (iv) the considerations contained in G.S. 96-14.9(f) for determining whether or not work is suitable are applied to the extent that they are not inconsistent with the specific requirements of this subdivision; and (v) the individual cannot furnish evidence satisfactory to the Division that his prospects for obtaining work in his customary occupation within a reasonably short period of time are good, but if the individual submits evidence which the

Division deems satisfactory for this purpose, the determination of whether or not work is suitable with respect to such individual shall be made in accordance with G.S. 96-14.9(f) without regard to the definition contained in this subdivision. Provided, further, that no work shall be deemed to be suitable work for an individual which does not accord with the labor standard provisions set forth in this subdivision, but the employment service shall refer any individual claiming extended benefits to any work which is deemed suitable hereunder. Provided, further, that any individual who has been disqualified for voluntarily leaving employment, being discharged for misconduct or substantial fault, or refusing suitable work under G.S. 96-14.11 and who has had the disqualification terminated, shall have such disqualification reinstated when claiming extended benefits unless the termination of the disqualification was based upon employment subsequent to the date of the disqualification.

(3)   After March 31, 1981, he has not failed either to apply for or to accept an offer of suitable work, as defined in G.S. 96-14.14(d)(2), to which he was referred by an employment office of the Division, and he has furnished the Division with tangible evidence that he has actively engaged in a systematic and sustained effort to find work. If an individual is found to be ineligible hereunder, he shall be ineligible beginning with the week in which he either failed to apply for or to accept the offer of suitable work or failed to furnish the Division with tangible evidence that he has actively engaged in a systematic and sustained effort to find work and such individual shall continue to be ineligible for extended benefits until he has been employed in each of four subsequent weeks (whether or not consecutive) and has earned remuneration equal to not less than four times his weekly benefit amount.

(4)   Pursuant to section 202(a)(7) of the Federal-State Extended Unemployment Compensation Act of 1970 (P.L. 91-373), as amended by section 202(b)(1) of the Unemployment Compensation Amendments of 1992 (Public Law 102-318), for any week of unemployment beginning after March 6, 1993, and before January 1, 1995, the individual is an exhaustee as defined by federal law and has satisfied the requirements of this Chapter for the receipt of regular benefits that are applicable to individuals claiming extended benefits, including not being subject to a disqualification for the receipt of benefits. Provided, the terms and conditions of State law that apply to claims for regular compensation and to the payment thereof shall apply to claims for extended benefits and to the payment thereof.

(5)   An individual shall not be eligible for extended compensation unless the individual had 20 weeks of full-time insured employment, or the equivalent in

insured wages, as determined by a calculation of base period wages based upon total hours worked during each quarter of the base period and the hourly wage rate for each quarter of the base period. For the purposes of this paragraph, the equivalent in insured wages shall be earnings covered by the State law for compensation purposes which exceed 40 times the individual's most recent weekly benefit amount or one and one-half times the individual's insured wages in that calendar quarter of the base period in which the individual's insured wages were the highest.

(e) Weekly Extended Benefit Amount. - The weekly extended benefit amount payable to an individual for a week of total unemployment in his eligibility period shall be an amount equal to the weekly benefit amount payable to him during his applicable benefit year. For any individual who was paid benefits during the applicable benefit year in accordance with more than one weekly benefit amount, the weekly extended benefit amount shall be the average of such weekly benefit amounts rounded to the nearest lower full dollar amount (if not a full dollar amount). Provided, that for any week during a period in which federal payments to states under Section 204 of the Federal-State Extended Unemployment Compensation Act of 1970, P.L. 91-373, are reduced under an order issued under Section 252 of the Balanced Budget and Emergency Deficit Control Act of 1985, P.L. 99-177, the weekly extended benefit amount payable to an individual for a week of total unemployment in his eligibility period shall be reduced by a percentage equivalent to the percentage of the reduction in the federal payment. The reduced weekly extended benefit amount, if not a full dollar amount, shall be rounded to the nearest lower full dollar amount.

(f) (1) Total Extended Benefit Amount. - Except as provided in subdivision (2) hereof, the total extended benefit amount payable to any eligible individual with respect to his applicable benefit year shall be the least of the following amounts:

a. Fifty percent (50%) of the total amount of regular benefits which were payable to him under this Chapter in his applicable benefit year; or

b. Thirteen times his weekly benefit amount which was payable to him under this Chapter for a week of total unemployment in the applicable benefit year.

Provided, that during any fiscal year in which federal payments to states under Section 204 of the Federal-State Extended Unemployment Compensation

Act of 1970, P.L. 91-373, are reduced under an order issued under Section 252 of the Balanced Budget and Emergency Deficit Control Act of 1985, P.L. 99-177, the total extended benefit amount payable to an individual with respect to his applicable benefit year shall be reduced by an amount equal to the aggregate of the reductions under G.S. 96-14.14(e) and the weekly amounts paid to the individual.

(2) Notwithstanding any other provisions of this Chapter, if the benefit year of any individual ends within an extended benefit period, the remaining balance of extended benefits that such individual would, but for this subdivision, be entitled to receive in that extended benefit period, with respect to weeks of unemployment beginning after the end of the benefit year, shall be reduced (but not below zero) by the product of the number of weeks for which the individual received any amounts as trade readjustment allowances within that benefit year, multiplied by the individual's weekly benefit amount for extended benefits.

(g) Beginning and Termination of Extended Benefit Period. -

(1) Whenever an extended benefit period is to become effective in this State as a result of an "on" indicator, or an extended benefit period is to be terminated in this State as a result of an "off" indicator, the Division shall make an appropriate public announcement; and

(2) Computations required by the provisions of subsection (a)(6) [subdivision (b)(7)] shall be made by the Division, in accordance with regulations prescribed by the United States Secretary of Labor.

(h) Prior to January 1, 1978, any extended benefits paid to any claimant under G.S. 96-14.14 shall not be charged to the account of the base period employer(s) who pay taxes as required by this Chapter. However, fifty percent (50%) of any such benefits paid shall be allocated as provided in G.S. 96-11.2 (except that G.S. 96-11.3 shall not apply), and the applicable amount shall be charged to the account of the appropriate employer paying on a reimbursement basis in lieu of taxes.

On and after January 1, 1978, the federal portion of any extended benefits shall not be charged to the account of any employer who pays taxes as required by this Chapter but the State portion of such extended benefits shall be:

(1) Charged to the account of such employer; or

(2) Not charged to the account of the employer under the provisions of G.S. 96-11.3.

All state portions of the extended benefits paid shall be charged to the account of governmental entities or other employers not liable for FUTA taxes who are the base period employers.

(i) Notwithstanding the provisions of G.S. 96-9.6, G.S. 96-14.14(h), or any other provision of this Chapter, any extended benefits paid which are one hundred percent (100%) federally financed shall not be charged in any percentage to any employer's account.

(j) For weeks of unemployment beginning on or after June 1, 1981, a claimant who is filing an interstate claim under the interstate benefit payment plan shall be eligible for extended benefits for no more than two weeks when there is an "off indicator" in the state where the claimant files. (Ex. Sess. 1936, c. 1, s. 3; 1937, c. 448, s. 1; 1939, c. 27, ss. 1-3, 14; c. 141; 1941, c. 108, s. 1; c. 276; 1943, c. 377, ss. 1-4; 1945, c. 522, ss. 24-26; 1947, c. 326, s. 21; 1949, c. 424, ss. 19-21; 1951, c. 332, ss. 10-12; 1953, c. 401, ss. 17, 18; 1957, c. 1059, ss. 12, 13; c. 1339; 1959, c. 362, ss. 12-15; 1961, c. 454, ss. 17, 18; 1965, c. 795, ss. 15, 16; 1969, c. 575, s. 9; 1971, c. 673, ss. 25, 26; 1973, c. 1138, ss. 3-7; 1975, c. 2, ss. 1-5; 1977, c. 727, s. 52; 1979, c. 660, ss. 18, 19; 1981, c. 160, ss. 17-23; 1981 (Reg. Sess., 1982), c. 1178, ss. 3-14; 1983, c. 585, ss. 12-16; c. 625, ss. 1, 7; 1985, c. 552, s. 9; 1985 (Reg. Sess., 1986), c. 918; 1987, c. 17, s. 8; 1993, c. 122, s. 2; 1993 (Reg. Sess., 1994), c. 680, ss. 1-3; 1995 (Reg. Sess., 1996), c. 646, s. 25(a); 1997-456, s. 27; 1999-340, ss. 4, 5; 2001-414, ss. 42, 43, 44; 2002-143, ss. 1, 1.1; 2011-145, s. 6.16(a), (b); 2011-401, s. 2.12; 2012-134, s. 1(c)-(e); 2013-2, s. 6; 2013-224, ss. 19, 20(f)-(j).)

Article 2D.

Administration of Benefits.

§ 96-15. Claims for benefits.

(a) Generally. - Claims for benefits must be made in accordance with rules adopted by the Division. An employer must provide individuals providing services for it access to information concerning the unemployment compensation program. The Division must supply an employer with any printed statements and other materials that the Division requires an employer to provide to individuals without cost to the employer.

(a1) Attached Claims. - An employer may file claims for employees through the use of automation in the case of partial unemployment. An employer may file an attached claim for an employee only once during a benefit year, and the period of partial unemployment for which the claim is filed may not exceed six weeks. To file an attached claim, an employer must pay the Division an amount equal to the full cost of unemployment benefits payable to the employee under the attached claim at the time the attached claim is filed. The Division must credit the amounts paid to the Unemployment Insurance Fund.

An employer may file an attached claim under this subsection only if the employer has a positive credit balance in its account as determined under Article 2B of this Chapter. If an employer does not have a positive credit balance in its account, the employer must remit to the Division an amount equal to the amount necessary to bring the employer's negative credit balance to at least zero at the time the employer files the attached claim.

(b) (1) Initial Determination. - A representative designated by the Division shall promptly examine the claim and shall determine whether or not the claim is valid. If the claim is determined to be not valid for any reason other than lack of base period earnings, the claim shall be referred to an Adjudicator for a decision as to the issues presented. If the claim is determined to be valid, a monetary determination shall be issued showing the week with respect to when benefits shall commence, the weekly benefit amount payable, and the potential maximum duration thereof. The claimant shall be furnished a copy of such monetary determination showing the amount of wages paid him by each employer during his base period and the employers by whom such wages were paid, his benefit year, weekly benefit amount, and the maximum amount of benefits that may be paid to him for unemployment during the benefit year. When a claim is not valid due to lack of earnings in his base period, the determination shall so designate. The claimant shall be allowed 10 days from the earlier of mailing or delivery of his monetary determination to him within which to protest his monetary determination and upon the filing of such protest, unless said protest be satisfactorily resolved, the claim shall be referred to the Assistant Secretary or designee for a decision as to the issues presented. All base period employers, as well as the most recent employer of a claimant on a temporary layoff, shall be notified upon the filing of a claim which establishes a benefit year.

At any time within one year from the date of the making of an initial determination, the Division on its own initiative may reconsider such determination if it finds that an error in computation or identity has occurred in connection therewith or that additional wages pertinent to the claimant's benefit status have become available, or if such determination of benefit status was made as a result of a nondisclosure or misrepresentation of a material fact.

(2)   Adjudication. - When a protest is made by the claimant to the initial or monetary determination, or a question or issue is raised or presented as to the eligibility of a claimant, or whether any disqualification should be imposed, or benefits denied or adjusted pursuant to G.S. 96-18, the matter shall be referred to an adjudicator. The adjudicator may consider any matter, document or statement deemed to be pertinent to the issues, including telephone conversations, and after such consideration shall render a conclusion as to the claimant's benefit entitlements. The adjudicator shall notify the claimant and all other interested parties of the conclusion reached. The conclusion of the adjudicator shall be deemed the final decision of the Division unless within 30 days after the date of notification or mailing of the conclusion, whichever is earlier, a written appeal is filed pursuant to rules adopted by the Division. The Division shall be deemed an interested party for such purposes and may remove to itself or transfer to an appeals referee the proceedings involving any claim pending before an adjudicator.

Provided, any interested employer shall be allowed 14 days from the mailing or delivery of the notice of the filing of a claim against the employer's account, whichever first occurs, to file with the Division its protest of the claim in order to have the claim referred to an adjudicator for a decision on the question or issue raised. Any protest filed must contain a basis for the protest and supporting statement of facts, and the protest may not be amended after the 14-day period from the mailing or delivery of the notice of filing of a claim has expired. A copy of the notice of the filing shall be sent contemporaneously to the employer by telefacsimile transmission if a fax number is on file. No payment of benefits shall be made by the Division to a claimant until one of the following occurs:

a.   The employer has filed a timely protest to the claim.

b.   The 14-day period for the filing of a protest by the employer has expired.

c. A determination under this subdivision has been made.

Provided further, no question or issue may be raised or presented by the Division as to the eligibility of a claimant, or whether any disqualification should be imposed, after 45 days from the first day of the first week after the question or issue occurs with respect to which week an individual filed a claim for benefits. None of the provisions of this subsection shall have the force and effect nor shall the same be construed or interested as repealing any other provisions of G.S. 96-18.

An employer shall receive written notice of the employer's appeal rights and any forms that are required to allow the employer to protest the claim. The forms shall include a section referencing the appropriate rules pertaining to appeals and the instructions on how to appeal.

(c) Appeals. - Unless an appeal from the adjudicator is withdrawn, an appeals referee or hearing officer shall set a hearing in which the parties are given reasonable opportunity to be heard. The conduct of hearings shall be governed by suitable rules adopted by the Division. The rules need not conform to common law or statutory rules of evidence or technical or formal rules of procedure but shall provide for the conduct of hearings in such manner as to ascertain the substantial rights of the parties. The hearings may be conducted by conference telephone call or other similar means provided that if any party files with the Division prior written objection to the telephone procedure, that party will be afforded an opportunity for an in-person hearing at such place in the State as the Division by rule shall provide. The hearing shall be scheduled for a time that, as much as practicable, least intrudes on and reasonably accommodates the ordinary business activities of an employer and the return to employment of a claimant. The appeals referee or hearing officer may affirm or modify the conclusion of the adjudicator or issue a new decision in which findings of fact and conclusions of law will be set out or dismiss an appeal when the appellant fails to appear at the appeals hearing to prosecute the appeal after having been duly notified of the appeals hearing. The evidence taken at the hearings before the appeals referee shall be recorded and the decision of the appeals referee shall be deemed to be the final decision of the Division unless within 10 days after the date of notification or mailing of the decision, whichever is earlier a written appeal is filed pursuant to such rules as the Board of Review and the Division may adopt. No person may be appointed as an appeals referee or hearing officer unless he or she possesses the minimum qualifications necessary to be a staff attorney eligible for designation by the Division as a hearing officer under G.S. 96-4(q). No appeals referee or hearing officer in full-time permanent status may engage in the private practice of law as defined in G.S. 84-2.1 while serving in office as appeals referee or hearing officer; violation of this prohibition shall be grounds for removal. Whenever an appeal is taken from a decision of the appeals referee or hearing officer; the appealing party shall submit a clear written statement containing the grounds for the appeal within the time allowed by law for taking the appeal, and if such timely statement is not submitted, the Board of Review may dismiss the appeal.

(c1) Unless required for disposition of an ex parte matter authorized by law, the Division, appeals referee, or employee assigned to make a decision or to make findings of facts and conclusions of law in a case shall not communicate, directly or indirectly, in connection with any issue of fact, or question of law, with any person or party or his representative, except on notice and opportunity for parties to participate.

(c2) Whenever a party is notified of the Board of Review's or a hearing officer's decision by mail, G.S. 1A-1, Rule 6(e) shall apply, and three days shall be added to the prescribed period to file a written appeal.

(d) Repealed by Session Laws 1977, c. 727, s. 54.

(d1) No continuance shall be granted except upon application to the Division, the appeals referee, or other authority assigned to make the decision in the matter to be continued. A continuance may be granted only for good cause shown and upon such terms and conditions as justice may require. Good cause for granting a continuance shall include, but not be limited to, those instances when a party to the proceeding, a witness, or counsel of record has an obligation of service to the State, such as service as a member of the North Carolina General Assembly, or an obligation to participate in a proceeding in a court of greater jurisdiction.

(e) Review by the Board of Review. - The Board of Review may on its own motion affirm, modify, or set aside any decision of an appeals referee, hearing officer, or other employee assigned to make a decision on the basis of the evidence previously submitted in such case, or direct the taking of additional evidence, or may permit any of the parties to such decision to initiate further appeals before it, or may provide for group hearings in such cases as the Board of Review finds appropriate. The Board of Review may remove itself or transfer to an appeals referee, hearing officer, or other employee assigned to make a decision the proceedings on any claim pending before an appeals referee, hearing officer, or other employee assigned to make a decision. Interested parties shall be promptly notified of the findings and decision of the Board of Review.

(f) Procedure. - The manner in which disputed claims shall be presented, the reports thereon required from the claimant and from employers, and the conduct of hearings and appeals shall be in accordance with rules adopted by the Division for determining the rights of the parties, whether or not such regulations conform to common-law or statutory rules of evidence and other technical rules of procedure.

All testimony at any hearing before an appeals referee upon a disputed claim shall be recorded unless the recording is waived by all interested parties. If the testimony is recorded, it need not be transcribed unless the disputed claim is further appealed and, one or more of the parties objects, under such rules as the Division may adopt, to being provided a copy of the tape recording of the hearing. Any other provisions of this Chapter notwithstanding, any individual receiving the transcript shall pay to the Division such reasonable fee for the transcript as the Division may by regulation provide. The fee so prescribed by the Division for a party shall not exceed the lesser of sixty-five cents (65¢) per page or sixty-five dollars ($65.00) per transcript. The Division may by regulation provide for the fee to be waived in such circumstances as it in its sole discretion deems appropriate but in the case of an appeal in forma pauperis supported by such proofs as are required in G.S. 1-110, the Division shall waive the fee.

The parties may enter into a stipulation of the facts. If the appeals referee, hearing officer, or other employee assigned to make the decision believes the stipulation provides sufficient information to make a decision, then the appeals referee, hearing officer, or other employee assigned to make the decision may accept the stipulation and render a decision based on the stipulation. If the appeals referee, hearing officer, or other employee assigned to make the decision does not believe the stipulation provides sufficient information to make a decision, then the appeals referee, hearing officer, or other employee assigned to make the decision must reject the stipulation. The decision to accept or reject a stipulation must occur in a recorded hearing.

(g) Witness Fees. - Witnesses subpoenaed pursuant to this section shall be allowed fees at a rate fixed by the Division. Such fees and all expenses of proceedings involving disputed claims shall be deemed a part of the expense of administering this Chapter.

(h) Judicial Review. - Any decision of the Division, in the absence of judicial review as herein provided, or in the absence of an interested party filing a request for reconsideration, shall become final 30 days after the date of notification or mailing thereof, whichever is earlier. Judicial review shall be permitted only after a party claiming to be aggrieved by the decision has exhausted his remedies before the Division as provided in this Chapter and has filed a petition for review in the superior court of the county in which he resides or has his principal place of business. The petition for review shall explicitly state what exceptions are taken to the decision or procedure of the Division and what relief the petitioner seeks. Within 10 days after the petition is filed with the court, the petitioner shall serve copies of the petition by personal service or by certified mail, return receipt requested, upon the Division and upon all parties of record to the Division proceedings. Names and addresses of the parties shall be furnished to the petitioner by the Division upon request. The Division shall be deemed to be a party to any judicial action involving any of its decisions and may be represented in the judicial action by any qualified attorney who has been designated by it for that purpose. Any questions regarding the requirements of this subsection concerning the service or filing of a petition shall be determined by the superior court. Any party to the Division proceeding may become a party to the review proceeding by notifying the court within 10 days after receipt of the copy of the petition. Any person aggrieved may petition to become a party by filing a motion to intervene as provided in G.S. 1A-1, Rule 24.

Within 45 days after receipt of the copy of the petition for review or within such additional time as the court may allow, the Division shall transmit to the reviewing court the original or a certified copy of the entire record of the proceedings under review. With the permission of the court the record may be shortened by stipulation of all parties to the review proceedings. Any party unreasonably refusing to stipulate to limit the record may be taxed by the court for such additional cost as is occasioned by the refusal. The court may require or permit subsequent corrections or additions to the record when deemed desirable.

(i) Review Proceedings. - If a timely petition for review has been filed and served as provided in G.S. 96-15(h), the court may make party defendant any other party it deems necessary or proper to a just and fair determination of the case. The Division may, in its discretion, certify to the reviewing court questions of law involved in any decision by it. In any judicial proceeding under this section, the findings of fact by the Division, if there is any competent evidence to support them and in the absence of fraud, shall be conclusive, and the jurisdiction of the court shall be confined to questions of law. Such actions and the questions so certified shall be heard in a summary manner and shall be given precedence over all civil cases. An appeal may be taken from the judgment of the superior court, as provided in civil cases. The Division shall have the right to appeal to the appellate division from a decision or judgment of the superior court and for such purpose shall be deemed to be an aggrieved party. No bond shall be required of the Division upon appeal. Upon the final determination of the case or proceeding, the Division shall enter an order in accordance with the determination. When an appeal has been entered to any judgment, order, or decision of the court below, no benefits shall be paid pending a final determination of the cause, except in those cases in which the final decision of the Division allowed benefits.

(j)   Repealed by Session Laws 1985, c. 197, s. 9.

(k)   Irrespective of any other provision of this Chapter, the Division may adopt minimum regulations necessary to provide for the payment of benefits to individuals promptly when due as required by section 303(a)(1) of the Social Security Act as amended (42 U.S.C.A., section 503(a)(1)). (Ex. Sess. 1936, c. 1, s. 6; 1937, c. 150; c. 448, s. 4; 1941, c. 108, s. 5; 1943, c. 377, ss. 9, 10; 1945, c. 522, ss. 30-32; 1947, c. 326, s. 23; 1951, c. 332, s. 15; 1953, c. 401, s. 19; 1959, c. 362, ss. 16, 17; 1961, c. 454, s. 21; 1965, c. 795, ss. 20-22; 1969, c. 575, ss. 13, 14; 1971, c. 673, ss. 30, 30.1; 1977, c. 727, s. 54; 1981, c. 160, ss. 27-32; 1983, c. 625, ss. 10-14; 1985, c. 197, s. 9; c. 552, ss. 18-20; 1987 (Reg. Sess., 1988), c. 999, s. 6; 1989, c. 583, ss. 11, 12; c. 707, s. 4; 1991, c. 723, ss. 1, 2; 1993, c. 343, ss. 4, 5; 1999-340, ss. 6, 7; 2004-124, s. 13.7B(c); 2005-122, s. 1; 2006-242, s. 1; 2011-401, s. 2.16; 2012-134, s. 2(c), (d); 2013-2, s. 7(b); 2013-224, ss. 16, 17, 19.)

§ 96-15.01. Establishing a benefit year.

(a)   Initial Unemployment. - An individual is unemployed for the purpose of establishing a benefit year if one of the following conditions is met:

(1)   Payroll attachment. - The individual has payroll attachment but because of lack of work during the payroll week for which the individual is requesting the establishment of a benefit year, the individual worked less than the equivalent of three customary scheduled full-time days in the establishment, plant, or industry in which the individual has payroll attachment as a regular employee.

(2) No payroll attachment. - The individual has no payroll attachment on the date the individual files a claim for unemployment benefits.

(b) Unemployed. - For benefit weeks within an established benefit year, a claimant is unemployed as provided in this subsection:

(1) Totally unemployed. - The claimant's earnings for the week, including payments in subsection (c) of this section, would not reduce the claimant's weekly benefit amount as calculated in G.S. 96-14.2.

(2) Partially unemployed. - The claimant is payroll attached and both of the following apply:

a. The claimant worked less than three customary scheduled full-time days in the establishment, plant, or industry in which the claimant is employed because of lack of work during the payroll week for which the claimant is requesting benefits.

b. The claimant's earnings for the payroll week for which the claimant is requesting benefits, including payments in subsection (c) of this section, would qualify the claimant for a reduced weekly benefit amount as calculated in G.S. 96-14.2.

(3) Part-totally unemployed. - The claimant has no payroll attachment during all or part of the week, and the claimant's earnings for odd jobs or subsidiary work would qualify the claimant for a reduced weekly benefit amount as calculated in G.S. 96-14.2.

(c) Separation Payments. - An individual is not unemployed if, with respect to the entire calendar week, the individual receives or will receive as a result of the individual's separation from work remuneration in one or more of the forms listed in this subsection. If the remuneration is given in a lump sum, the amount must be allocated on a weekly basis as if it had been earned by the individual during a week of employment. An individual may be unemployed, as provided in subsection (b) of this section, if the individual is receiving payment applicable to less than the entire week:

(1) Wages in lieu of notice.

(2) Accrued vacation pay.

(3) Terminal leave pay.

(4) Severance pay.

(5) Separation pay.

(6) Dismissal payments or wages by whatever name.

(d) Substitute School Personnel. - An individual that performs service in a school as a substitute is not unemployed for days or weeks when the individual is not called to work unless the individual was employed as a full-time substitute during the period of time for which the individual is requesting benefits. For purposes of this subsection, a full-time substitute is an employee that works for more than 30 hours a week for the school on a continual basis for a period of six months or more. (2013-2, s. 7(b); 2013-224, s. 19.)

§ 96-15.1. Protection of witnesses from discharge, demotion, or intimidation.

(a) No person may discharge, demote, or threaten any person because that person has testified or has been summoned to testify in any proceeding under the Employment Security Act.

(b) Any person who violates the provisions of this section shall be liable in a civil action for reasonable damages suffered by any person as a result of the violation, and an employee discharged or demoted in violation of this section shall be entitled to be reinstated to his former position. The burden of proof shall be upon the party claiming a violation to prove a claim under this section.

(c) The General Court of Justice shall have jurisdiction over actions under this section.

(d) The statute of limitations for actions under this section shall be one year pursuant to G.S. 1-54. (1987, c. 532, s. 1.)

§ 96-15.2. Protection of witness before the Employment Security Commission.

If any person shall by threats, menace, or in any other manner intimidate or attempt to intimidate any person who is summoned or acting as a witness in any proceeding brought under the Employment Security Act, or prevent or deter, or attempt to prevent or deter any person summoned or acting as such witness from attendance upon such proceeding, he shall be guilty of a Class 1 misdemeanor. (1987, c. 532, s. 2; 1993, c. 539, s. 673; 1994, Ex. Sess., c. 24, s. 14(c).)

§ 96-16. Seasonal pursuits.

(a) A seasonal pursuit is one which, because of seasonal conditions making it impracticable or impossible to do otherwise, customarily carries on production operations only within a regularly recurring active period or periods of less than an aggregate of 36 weeks in a calendar year. No pursuit shall be deemed seasonal unless and until so found by the Division; except that any successor under G.S. 96-11.7 to a seasonal pursuit shall be deemed seasonal unless such successor shall within 120 days after the acquisition request cancellation of the determination of status of such seasonal pursuit; provided further that this provision shall not be applicable to pending cases nor retroactive in effect.

(b) Upon application therefor by a pursuit, the Division shall determine or redetermine whether such pursuit is seasonal and, if seasonal, the active period or periods thereof. The Division may, on its own motion, redetermine the active period or periods of a seasonal pursuit. An application for a seasonal determination must be made on forms prescribed by the Division and must be made at least 20 days prior to the beginning date of the period of production operations for which a determination is requested.

(c) Whenever the Division has determined or redetermined a pursuit to be seasonal, such pursuit shall be notified immediately, and such notice shall contain the beginning and ending dates of the pursuit's active period or periods. Such pursuits shall display notices of its seasonal determination conspicuously on its premises in a sufficient number of places to be available for inspection by its workers. Such notices shall be furnished by the Division.

(d) A seasonal determination shall become effective unless an interested party files an application for review within 10 days after the beginning date of the first period of production operations to which it applies. Such an application for review shall be deemed to be an application for a determination of status, as provided in G.S. 96-4, subsections (q) through (u) of this Chapter, and shall be heard and determined in accordance with the provisions thereof.

(e) All wages paid to a seasonal worker during his base period shall be used in determining his weekly benefit amount; provided however, that all weekly benefit amounts so determined shall be rounded to the nearest lower full dollar amount (if not a full dollar amount).

(f) (1) A seasonal worker shall be eligible to receive benefits based on seasonal wages only for a week of unemployment which occurs, or the greater part of which occurs within the active period or periods of the seasonal pursuit or pursuits in which he earned base period wages.

(2) A seasonal worker shall be eligible to receive benefits based on nonseasonal wages for any week of unemployment which occurs during any active period or periods of the seasonal pursuit in which he has earned base period wages provided he has exhausted benefits based on seasonal wages. Such worker shall also be eligible to receive benefits based on nonseasonal wages for any week of unemployment which occurs during the inactive period or periods of the seasonal pursuit in which he earned base period wages irrespective as to whether he has exhausted benefits based on seasonal wages.

(3) The maximum amount of benefits which a seasonal worker shall be eligible to receive based on seasonal wages shall be an amount, adjusted to the nearest multiple of one dollar ($1.00), determined by multiplying the maximum benefits payable in his benefit year, as provided in G.S. 96-14.4, by the percentage obtained by dividing the seasonal wages in his base period by all of his base period wages.

(4) The maximum amount of benefits which a seasonal worker shall be eligible to receive based on nonseasonal wages shall be an amount, adjusted to the nearest multiple of one dollar ($1.00), determined by multiplying the maximum benefits payable in his benefit year, as provided in G.S. 96-14.4, by the percentage obtained by dividing the nonseasonal wages in his base period by all of his base period wages.

(5) In no case shall a seasonal worker be eligible to receive a total amount of benefits in a benefit year in excess of the maximum benefits payable for such benefit year, as provided in G.S. 96-14.4.

(g) All benefits paid to a seasonal worker shall be charged in accordance with G.S. 96-11.2.

(h) The benefits payable to any otherwise eligible individual shall be calculated in accordance with this section for any benefit year which is established on or after the beginning date of a seasonal determination applying to a pursuit by which such individual was employed during the base period applicable to such benefit year, as if such determination had been effective in such base period.

(i) Nothing in this section shall be construed to limit the right of any individual whose claim for benefits is determined in accordance herewith to appeal from such determination as provided in G.S. 96-15 of this Chapter.

(j) As used in this section:

(1) "Pursuit" means an employer or branch of an employer.

(2) "Branch of an employer" means a part of an employer's activities which is carried on or is capable of being carried on as a separate enterprise.

(3) "Production operations" mean all the activities of a pursuit which are primarily related to the production of its characteristic goods or services.

(4) "Active period or periods" of a seasonal pursuit means the longest regularly recurring period or periods within which production operations of the pursuit are customarily carried on.

(5) "Seasonal wages" mean the wages earned in a seasonal pursuit within its active period or periods. The Division may prescribe by regulation the manner in which seasonal wages shall be reported.

(6) "Seasonal worker" means a worker at least twenty-five percent (25%) of whose base period wages are seasonal wages.

(7) "Interested party" means any individual affected by a seasonal determination.

(8) "Inactive period or periods" of a seasonal pursuit means that part of a calendar year which is not included in the active period or periods of such pursuit.

(9) "Nonseasonal wages" mean the wages earned in a seasonal pursuit within the inactive period or periods of such pursuit, or wages earned at any time in a nonseasonal pursuit.

(10) "Wages" mean remuneration for employment. (1939, c. 28; 1941, c. 108, s. 7; 1943, c. 377, s. 141/2; 1945, c. 522, s. 33; 1953, c. 401, ss. 20, 21; 1957, c. 1059, s. 14; 1959, c. 362, s. 18; 1983, c. 585, s. 19; 2011-401, s. 2.17; 2013-2, s. 9(c); 2013-224, ss. 19, 20(k), (l); 2013-391, s. 7.)

§ 96-17. Protection of rights and benefits; attorney representation; prohibited fees; deductions for child support obligations.

(a) Waiver of Rights Void. - Any agreement by an individual to waive, release, or commute his rights to benefits or any other rights under this Chapter shall be void. Any agreement by any individual in the employ of any person or concern to pay all or any portion of an employer's contributions, required under this Chapter from such employer, shall be void. No employer shall directly or indirectly make or require or accept any deduction from the remuneration of individuals in his employ to finance the employer's contributions required from him, or require or accept any waiver of any right hereunder by any individual in his employ. Any employer or officer or agent of an employer who violates any provision of this subsection shall, for each offense, be fined not less than one hundred dollars ($100.00) nor more than one thousand dollars ($1,000) or be imprisoned for not more than six months, or both.

(b) Representation. - Any claimant or employer who is a party to any proceeding before the Division may be represented by (i) an attorney; or (ii) any person who is supervised by an attorney, however, the attorney need not be present at any proceeding before the Division.

(b1) Fees Prohibited. - Except as otherwise provided in this Chapter, no individual claiming benefits in any administrative proceeding under this Chapter shall be charged fees of any kind by the Division or its representative, and in any court proceeding under this Chapter each party shall bear its own costs and legal fees.

(c) No Assignment of Benefits; Exemptions. - Except as provided in subsection (d) of this section, any assignment, pledge, or encumbrance of any right to benefits which are or may become due or payable under this Chapter shall be void; and such rights to benefits shall be exempt from levy, execution, attachment, or any other remedy whatsoever provided for the collection of debts; and benefits received by any individual, so long as they are not mingled with other funds of the recipient, shall be exempt from any remedy whatsoever for the collection of all debts except debts incurred for necessaries furnished to such individual or his spouse or dependents during the time when such individual was unemployed. Any waiver of any exemption provided for in this subsection shall be void.

(d) (1) Definitions. - For the purpose of this subsection and when used herein:

a. "Unemployment compensation" means any compensation found by the Division to be payable to an unemployed individual under the Employment Security Law of North Carolina (including amounts payable by the Division pursuant to an agreement under any federal law providing for compensation, assistance or allowances with respect to unemployment) provided, that nothing in this subsection shall be construed to limit the Division's ability to reduce or withhold benefits, otherwise payable, under authority granted elsewhere in this Chapter including but not limited to reductions for wages or earnings while unemployed and for the recovery of previous overpayments of benefits.

b. "Child support obligation" includes only obligations which are being enforced pursuant to a plan described in section 454 of the Social Security Act which has been approved by the Secretary of Health and Human Services under Part D of Title IV of the Social Security Act.

c. "State or local child support enforcement agency" means any agency of this State or a political subdivision thereof operating pursuant to a plan described in subparagraph b. above.

(2) a. An individual filing a new claim for unemployment compensation shall, at the time of filing such claim, disclose whether the individual owes child support obligations, as defined under subparagraph (1)b. of this subsection. If any such individual discloses that he or she owes child support obligations and is determined by the Division to be eligible for payment of unemployment compensation, the Division shall notify the State or local child support enforcement agency enforcing such obligation that such individual has been determined to be eligible for payment of unemployment compensation.

b. Upon payment by the State or local child support enforcement agency of the processing fee provided for in paragraph (4) of this subsection and beginning with any payment of unemployment compensation that, except for the provisions of this subsection, would be made to the individual during the then current benefit year and more than five working days after the receipt of the processing fee by the Division, the Division shall deduct and withhold from any unemployment compensation otherwise payable to an individual who owes child support obligations:

1. The amount specified by the individual to the Division to be deducted and withheld under this paragraph if neither subparagraph 2. nor subparagraph 3. of this paragraph is applicable; or

2. The amount, if any, determined pursuant to an agreement submitted to the Division under section 454(20)(B)(i) of the Social Security Act by the State or local child support enforcement agency, unless subparagraph 3. of this paragraph is applicable; or

3. Any amount otherwise required to be so deducted and withheld from such unemployment compensation pursuant to properly served legal process, as that term is defined in section 462(e) of the Social Security Act.

c. Any amount deducted and withheld under paragraph b. of this subdivision shall be paid by the Division to the appropriate State or local child support enforcement agency.

d. The Department of Health and Human Services and the Division are hereby authorized to enter into one or more agreements which may provide for the payment to the Division of the processing fees referred to in subparagraph b. and the payment to the Department of Health and Human Services of unemployment compensation benefits withheld, referred to in subparagraph c., on an open account basis. Where such an agreement has been entered into, the processing fee shall be deemed to have been made and received (for the purposes of fixing the date on which the Division will begin withholding unemployment compensation benefits) on the date a written authorization from the Department of Health and Human Services to charge its account is received by the Division. Such an authorization shall apply to all processing fees then or thereafter (within the then current benefit year) chargeable with respect to any individual name in the authorization. Any agreement shall provide for the reimbursement to the Division of any start-up costs and the cost of providing notice to the Department of Health and Human Services of any disclosure required by subparagraph a. Such an agreement may dispense with the notice requirements of subparagraph a. by providing for a suitable substitute procedure, reasonably calculated to discover those persons owing child support obligations who are eligible for unemployment compensation payments.

(3)   Any amount deducted and withheld under paragraph (2) of this subdivision shall, for all purposes, be treated as if it were paid to the individual as unemployment compensation and then paid by such individual to the State or local child support enforcement agency in satisfaction of the individual's child support obligations.

(4)   a.   On or before April 1 of 1983 and each calendar year thereafter, the Division shall set and forward to the Secretary of Health and Human Services for use in the next fiscal year, a schedule of processing fees for the withholding and payment of unemployment compensation as provided for in this subsection, which fees shall reflect its best estimate of the administrative cost to the Division generated thereby.

b.   At least 20 days prior to September 25, 1982, the Division shall set and forward to the Secretary of Health and Human Services an interim schedule of fees which will be in effect until July 1, 1983.

c.   The provisions of this subsection apply only if arrangements are made for reimbursement by the State or local child support agency for all administrative costs incurred by the Division under this subsection attributable to child support obligations enforced by the agency. (Ex. Sess. 1936, c. 1, s. 15; 1937, c. 150; 1979, c. 660, s. 22; 1981, c. 762, ss. 1, 2; 1981 (Reg. Sess., 1982), c. 1178, ss. 1, 2; 1985, c. 552, s. 21; 1997-443, s. 11A.118(a); 1997-456, s. 27; 2011-401, s. 2.18.)

§ 96-18. Penalties.

(a)   (1)   It shall be unlawful for any person to make a false statement or representation knowing it to be false or to knowingly fail to disclose a material fact to obtain or increase any benefit under this Chapter or under an employment security law of any other state, the federal government, or of a foreign government, either for himself or any other person. Records, with any necessary authentication thereof, required in the prosecution of any criminal action brought by another state or foreign government for misrepresentation to obtain benefits under the law of this State shall be made available to the agency administering the employment security law of any such state or foreign government for the purpose of such prosecution. Photostatic copies of all records of agencies of other states or foreign governments required in the prosecution of any criminal action under this section shall be as competent evidence as the originals when certified under the seal of such agency, or when there is no seal, under the hand of the keeper of such records.

(2)   A person who violates this subsection shall be found guilty of a Class I felony if the value of the benefit wrongfully obtained is more than four hundred dollars ($400.00).

(3)   A person who violates this subsection shall be found guilty of a Class 1 misdemeanor if the value of the benefit wrongfully obtained is four hundred dollars ($400.00) or less.

(b)   Any employing unit or any officer or agent of an employing unit or any other person who makes a false statement or representation, knowing it to be false, or who knowingly fails to disclose a material fact to prevent or reduce the payment of benefits to any individual entitled thereto, or to avoid becoming or remaining subject hereto or to avoid or reduce any contributions or other payment required from an employing unit under this Chapter, or who willfully fails or refuses to furnish any reports required hereunder, or to produce or permit the inspection or copying of records as required hereunder, shall be guilty of a Class 1 misdemeanor; and each such false statement or representation or failure to disclose a material fact, and each day of such failure or refusal shall constitute a separate offense.

(b1)   Except as provided in this subsection, the penalties and other provisions in subdivisions (6), (7), (9a), and (11) of G.S. 105-236 apply to unemployment insurance contributions under this Chapter to the same extent that they apply to taxes as defined in G.S. 105-228.90(b)(7). The Division has the same powers under those subdivisions with respect to unemployment insurance contributions as does the Secretary of Revenue with respect to taxes as defined in G.S. 105-228.90(b)(7).

G.S. 105-236(9a) applies to a "contribution tax return preparer" to the same extent as it applies to an income tax preparer. As used in this subsection, a "contribution tax return preparer" is a person who prepares for compensation, or who employs one or more persons to prepare for compensation, any return of tax imposed by this Chapter or any claim for refund of tax imposed by this

Chapter. For purposes of this definition, the completion of a substantial portion of a return or claim for refund is treated as the preparation of the return or claim for refund. The term does not include a person merely because the person (i) furnishes typing, reproducing, or other mechanical assistance, (ii) prepares a return or claim for refund of the employer, or an officer or employee of the employer, by whom the person is regularly and continuously employed, (iii) prepares as a fiduciary a return or claim for refund for any person, or (iv) represents a taxpayer in a hearing regarding a proposed assessment.

The penalty in G.S. 105-236(7) applies with respect to unemployment insurance contributions under this Chapter only when one of the following circumstances exist in connection with the violation:

(1)   Any employing units employing more than 10 employees.

(2)   A contribution of more than two thousand dollars ($2,000) has not been paid.

(3)   An experience rating account balance is more than five thousand dollars ($5,000) overdrawn.

If none of the circumstances set forth in subdivision (1), (2), or (3) of this subsection exist in connection with a violation of G.S. 105-236(7) applied under this Chapter, the offender is guilty of a Class 1 misdemeanor and each day the violation continues constitutes a separate offense.

If the Division finds that any person violated G.S. 105-236(9a) and is not subject to a fraud penalty, the person shall pay a civil penalty of five hundred dollars ($500.00) per violation for each day the violations continue, plus the reasonable costs of investigation and enforcement.

(c)   Any person who shall willfully violate any provisions of this Chapter or any rule or regulation thereunder, the violation of which is made unlawful or the observance of which is required under the terms of this Chapter, or for which a penalty is neither prescribed herein nor provided by any other applicable statute, shall be guilty of a Class 1 misdemeanor, and each day such violation continues shall be deemed to be a separate offense.

(d)   Repealed by Session Laws 1983, c. 625, s. 15.

(e) An individual shall not be entitled to receive benefits for a period of 52 weeks beginning with the first day of the week following the date that notice of determination or decision is mailed finding that he, or another in his behalf with his knowledge, has been found to have knowingly made a false statement or misrepresentation, or who has knowingly failed to disclose a material fact to obtain or increase any benefit or other payment under this Chapter.

(f) Repealed by Session Laws 1983, c. 625, s. 15.

(g) (1) Repealed by Session Laws 2012-134, s. 4(b), effective October 1, 2012.

(2) Any person who has received any sum as benefits under this Chapter by reason of the nondisclosure or misrepresentation by him or by another of a material fact (irrespective of whether such nondisclosure or misrepresentation was known or fraudulent) or has been paid benefits to which he was not entitled for any reason (including errors on the part of any representative of the Division) shall be liable to repay such sum to the Division as provided in subdivision (3) of this subsection.

(3) The Division may collect the overpayments provided for in this subsection by one or more of the following procedures as the Division may, except as provided herein, in its sole discretion choose:

a. If, after due notice, any overpaid claimant shall fail to repay the sums to which he was not entitled, the amount due may be collected by civil action in the name of the Division, and the cost of such action shall be taxed to the claimant. Civil actions brought under this section to collect overpayments shall be heard by the court at the earliest possible date and shall be entitled to preference upon the calendar of the court over all other civil actions except petitions for judicial review under this Chapter.

b. If any overpayment recognized by this subsection shall not be repaid within 30 days after the claimant has received notice and demand for same, and after due notice and reasonable opportunity for hearing (if a hearing on the merits of the claim has not already been had) the Division, under the hand of the Assistant Secretary, may certify the same to the clerk of the superior court of the county in which the claimant resides or has property, and additional copies of said certificate for each county in which the Division has reason to believe such claimant has property located; such certificate and/or copies thereof so forwarded to the clerk of the superior court shall immediately be docketed and indexed on the cross index of judgments, and from the date of such docketing shall constitute a preferred lien upon any property which said claimant may own in said county, with the same force and effect as a judgment rendered by the superior court. The Division shall forward a copy of said certificate to the sheriff or sheriffs of such county or counties, or to a duly authorized agent of the Division, and when so forwarded and in the hands of such sheriff or agent of the Division, shall have all the force and effect of an execution issued to such sheriff or agent of the Division by the clerk of the superior court upon a judgment of the superior court duly docketed in said county. The Division is further authorized and empowered to issue alias copies of said certificate or execution to the sheriff or sheriffs of such county or counties, or a duly authorized agent of the Division in all cases in which the sheriff or duly authorized agent has returned an execution or certificate unsatisfied; when so issued and in the hands of the sheriff or duly authorized agent of the Division, such alias shall have all the force and effect of an alias execution issued to such sheriff or duly authorized agent of the Division by the clerk of the superior court upon a judgment of the superior court duly docketed in said county. Provided, however, that notwithstanding any provision of this subsection, upon filing one written notice with the Division, the sheriff of any county shall have the sole and exclusive right to serve all executions and make all collections mentioned in this subsection and in such case, no agent of the Division shall have the authority to serve any executions or make any collections therein in such county. A return of such execution or alias execution, shall be made to the Division, together with all monies collected thereunder, and when such order, execution or alias is referred to the agent of the Division for service, the said agent of the Division shall be vested with all the powers of the sheriff to the extent of serving such order, execution or alias and levying or collecting thereunder. The agent of the Division to whom such order or execution is referred shall give a bond not to exceed three thousand dollars ($3,000) approved by the Division for the faithful performance of such duties. The liability of said agent shall be in the same manner and to the same extent as is now imposed on sheriffs in the service of execution. If any sheriff of this State or any agent of the Division who is charged with the duty of serving executions shall willfully fail, refuse or neglect to execute any order directed to him by the said Division and within the time provided by law, the official bond of such sheriff or of such agent of the Division shall be liable for the overpayments and costs due by the claimant. Additionally, the Division or its designated representatives in the collection of overpayments shall have the powers enumerated in G.S. 96-10(b)(2) and (3).

c.   Any person who has been found by the Division to have been overpaid under subparagraph (2) above due to fraudulent nondisclosure or misrepresentation shall be liable to have the sums deducted from future benefits payable to the person under this Chapter. The amount deducted may be up to one hundred percent (100%) of that person's weekly benefit amount.

d. Any person who has been found by the Division to have been overpaid under subparagraph (2) above due to nonfraudulent reasons shall be liable to have the sums deducted from future benefits payable to the person under this Chapter but the amount deducted for any week shall be reduced by no more than fifty percent (50%) of that person's weekly benefit amount.

e. To the extent permissible under the laws and Constitution of the United States, the Division is authorized to enter into or cooperate in arrangements or reciprocal agreements with appropriate and duly authorized agencies of other states or the United States Secretary of Labor, or both, whereby: (1) Overpayments of unemployment benefits as determined under subparagraphs (1) and (2) above shall be recovered by offset from unemployment benefits otherwise payable under the unemployment compensation law of another state, and overpayments of unemployment benefits as determined under the unemployment compensation law of such other state shall be recovered by offset from unemployment benefits otherwise payable under this Chapter; and, (2) Overpayments of unemployment benefits as determined under applicable federal law, with respect to benefits or allowances for unemployment provided under a federal program administered by this State under an agreement with the United States Secretary of Labor, shall be recovered by offset from unemployment benefits otherwise payable under this Chapter or any such federal program, or under the unemployment compensation law of another state or any such federal unemployment benefit or allowance program administered by such other state under an agreement with the United States Secretary of Labor if such other state has in effect a reciprocal agreement with the United States Secretary of Labor as authorized by Section 303(g)(2) of the federal Social Security Act, if the United States agrees, as provided in the reciprocal agreement with this State entered into under such Section 303(g)(2) of the Social Security Act, that overpayments of unemployment benefits as determined under subparagraphs (1) and (2) above, and overpayment as determined under the unemployment compensation law of another state which has in effect a reciprocal agreement with the United States Secretary of Labor as authorized by Section 303(g)(2) of the Social Security Act, shall be recovered by offset from benefits or allowances for unemployment otherwise payable under a federal program administered by this State or such other state under an agreement with the United States Secretary of Labor.

f. The Division may in its discretion decline to collect overpayments to claimants if the claimant has deceased after the payment was made. In such a case the Division may remove the debt of the deceased claimant from its records.

(h) Mandatory Federal Penalty. - A person who has been held ineligible for benefits under subsection (e) of this section and who, because of those same acts or omissions, has received any sum as benefits under this Chapter to which the person is not entitled shall be assessed a penalty in an amount equal to fifteen percent (15%) of the amount of the erroneous payment. The penalty amount shall be payable to the Unemployment Insurance Fund. The penalty applies to an erroneous payment made under any State program providing for the payment of unemployment compensation as well as an erroneous payment made under any federal program providing for the payment of unemployment compensation. The notice of determination or decision advising the person that benefits have been denied or adjusted pursuant to subsection (e) of this section must include the reason for the finding of an erroneous payment, the penalty amount assessed under this subsection, and the reason the penalty has been applied.

The penalty amount may be collected in any manner allowed for the recovery of the erroneous payment, except that the penalty amount may not be recovered through offsets of future benefits. When a recovery with respect to an erroneous payment is made, any recovery applies first to the principal of the erroneous payment, then to the federally mandated penalty amount imposed under this subsection, and finally to any other amounts due. (Ex. Sess. 1936, c. 1, s. 16; 1943, c. 319; c. 377, ss. 29, 30; 1945, c. 552, s. 34; 1949, c. 424, s. 26; 1951, c. 332, s. 16; 1953, c. 401, ss. 1, 22; 1955, c. 385, s. 9; 1959, c. 362, ss. 19, 20; 1965, c. 795, ss. 23, 24; 1971, c. 673, s. 31; 1977, c. 727, s. 55; 1979, c. 660, ss. 23-25; 1981, c. 160, s. 33; 1983, c. 625, s. 15; 1985, c. 552, s. 22; 1987, c. 103, s. 4; 1989, c. 583, ss. 13, 14; 1993, c. 343, s. 7; c. 539, ss. 674-676; 1994, Ex. Sess., c. 24, s. 14(c); 2003-67, s. 2; 2005-410, s. 6; 2011-401, s. 2.19; 2012-134, ss. 3(d), 4(a)-(c); 2013-2, s. 9(d); 2013-224, s. 19.)

§ 96-18.1. Attachment and garnishment of fraudulent overpayment.

(a) Applicability. - This section applies to an individual who has been provided notice of a determination or an appeals decision finding that the individual, or another individual acting in the individual's behalf and with the individual's knowledge, has knowingly done one or more of the following to obtain or increase a benefit or other payment under this Chapter:

(1) Made a false statement or misrepresentation.

(2) Failed to disclose a material fact.

(b) Attachment and Garnishment. - Intangible property that belongs to an individual, is owed to an individual, or has been transferred by an individual under circumstances that would permit it to be levied upon if it were tangible property is subject to attachment and garnishment in payment of a fraudulent overpayment that is due from the individual and is collectible under this Article. Intangible personal property includes bank deposits, rent, salaries, wages, property held in the Escheat Fund, and any other property incapable of manual levy or delivery.

A person who is in possession of intangible property that is subject to attachment and garnishment is the garnishee and is liable for the amount the individual owes. The liability applies only to the amount of the individual's property in the garnishee's possession, reduced by any amount the individual owes the garnishee.

The Secretary may submit to a financial institution, as defined in G.S. 53B-2, information that identifies an individual who owes a fraudulent overpayment that is collectible under this section and the amount of the overpayment. The Secretary may submit the information on a quarterly basis or, with the agreement of the financial institution, on a more frequent basis. A financial institution that receives the information must determine the amount, if any, of intangible property it holds that belongs to the individual and must inform the Secretary of its determination. The Secretary must reimburse a financial institution for its costs in providing the information, not to exceed the amount payable to the financial institution under G.S. 110-139 for providing information for use in locating a noncustodial parent.

No more than ten percent (10%) of an individual's wages or salary is subject to attachment and garnishment. The wages or salary of an employee of the United States, the State, or a political subdivision of the State are subject to attachment and garnishment.

(c) Notice. - Before the Secretary attaches and garnishes intangible property in payment of a fraudulent overpayment, the Secretary must send the garnishee a notice of garnishment. The notice must be sent either in person, by certified mail with a return receipt requested, or with the agreement of the garnishee, by electronic means. The notice must contain all of the following information:

(1)   The individual's name.

(2)   The individual's social security number or federal identification number.

(3)   The amount of fraudulent overpaid benefits the individual owes.

(4)   An explanation of the liability of a garnishee for fraudulent overpayment of unemployment insurance benefits owed by an overpaid individual.

(5)   An explanation of the garnishee's responsibility concerning the notice.

(d)   Action. - A garnishee must comply with a notice of garnishment or file a written response to the notice within the time set in this subsection. A garnishee that is a financial institution must comply or file a response within 20 days after receiving a notice of garnishment. All other garnishees must comply or file a response within 30 days after receiving a notice of garnishment. A written response must explain why the garnishee is not subject to garnishment and attachment.

Upon receipt of a written response, the Department must contact the garnishee and schedule a conference to discuss the response or inform the garnishee of the Department's position concerning the response. If the Department does not agree with the garnishee on the garnishee's liability, the Department may proceed to enforce the garnishee's liability for the fraudulent overpayment of unemployment benefits by civil action. (2013-2, s. 7(b); 2013-224, s. 19.)

§ 96-19. Enforcement of Employment Security Law discontinued upon repeal or invalidation of federal acts; suspension of enforcement provisions contested.

(a)   It is the purpose of this Chapter to secure for employers and employees the benefits of Title III and Title IX of the Federal Social Security Act, approved August 14, 1935, as to credit on payment of federal taxes, of State contributions, the receipt of federal grants for administrative purposes, and all other provisions of the said Federal Social Security Act; and it is intended as a policy of the State that this Chapter and its requirements for contributions by employers shall continue in force only so long as such employers are required to pay the federal taxes imposed in said Federal Social Security Act by a valid act of Congress. Therefore, if Title III and Title IX of the said Federal Social Security Act shall be declared invalid by the United States Supreme Court, or if such law be repealed by congressional action so that the federal tax cannot be further levied, from and after the declaration of such invalidity by the United States Supreme Court, or the repeal of said law by congressional action, as the case may be, no further levy or collection of contributions shall be made hereunder. The enactment by the Congress of the United States of the Railroad Retirement Act and the Railroad Unemployment Insurance Act shall in no way affect the administration of this law except as herein expressly provided.

All federal grants and all contributions theretofore collected, and all funds in the treasury by virtue of this Chapter, shall, nevertheless, be disbursed and expended, as far as may be possible, under the terms of this Chapter: Provided, however, that contributions already due from any employer shall be collected and paid into the said fund, subject to such distribution; and provided further, that the personnel of the Division of Employment Security shall be reduced as rapidly as possible.

The funds remaining available for use by the Division of Employment Security shall be expended, as necessary, in making payment of all such awards as have been made and are fully approved at the date aforesaid, and the payment of the necessary costs for the further administration of this Chapter, and the final settlement of all affairs connected with same. After complete payment of all administrative costs and full payment of all awards made as aforesaid, any and all moneys remaining to the credit of any employer shall be refunded to such employer, or his duly authorized assignee: Provided, that the State employment service, created by Chapter 106, Public Laws of 1935, and transferred by Chapter 1, Public Laws of 1936, Extra Session, and made a part of the former Employment Security Commission of North Carolina, and that is now part of the Division of Employment Security of the North Carolina Department of Commerce, shall in such event return to and have the same status as it had prior to enactment of Chapter 1, Public Laws of 1936, Extra Session, and under authority of Chapter 106, Public Laws of 1935, shall carry on the duties therein prescribed; but, pending a final settlement of the affairs of the Division, the said State employment service shall render such service in connection therewith as shall be demanded or required under the provisions of this Chapter or the provisions of Chapter 1, Public Laws of 1936, Extra Session.

(b) The Division of Employment Security may, upon receiving notification from the U.S. Department of Labor that any provision of this Chapter is out of conformity with the requirements of the federal law or of the U.S. Department of Labor, suspend the enforcement of the contested section or provision until the North Carolina Legislature next has an opportunity to make changes in the North Carolina law. The Division shall, in order to implement the above suspension:

(1) Notify the Governor's office and provide that office with a copy of the determination or notification of the U.S. Department of Labor;

(2) Advise the Governor's office as to whether the contested portion or provision of the law would, if not enforced, so seriously hamper the operations of the agency as to make it advisable that a special session of the legislature be called;

(3) Take all reasonable steps available to obtain a reprieval from the implementation of any federal conformity failure sanctions until the State legislature has been afforded an opportunity to consider the existing conflict. (1937, c. 363; 1939, c. 52, s. 8; 1947, c. 598, s. 1; 1977, c. 727, s. 56; 2011-401, s. 2.20.)

Article 3.

Employment Service Division.

§ 96-20. Duties of Division; conformance to Wagner-Peyser Act; organization; director; employees.

The Employment Security Section of the Division of Employment Security, Department of Commerce, shall establish and maintain free public employment offices in such number and in such places as may be necessary for the proper administration of this Chapter, and for the purpose of performing such duties as are within the purview of the act of Congress entitled "An act to provide for the establishment of a national employment system and for cooperation with the states in the promotion of such system and for other purposes," approved June 6, 1933, (48 Stat., 113; U.S.C., Title 29, section 49(c), as amended). The said

Division shall be administered by a full-time salaried director. The Division shall be charged with the duty to cooperate with any official or agency of the United States having powers or duties under the provisions of the said act of Congress, as amended, and to do and perform all things necessary to secure to this State the benefits of the said act of Congress, as amended, in the promotion and maintenance of a system of public employment offices. The provisions of the said act of Congress, as amended, are hereby accepted by this State, in conformity with section 4 of said act, and this State will observe and comply with the requirements thereof. The Division is hereby designated and constituted the agency of this State for the purpose of said act. The Secretary is directed to appoint the head, other officers, and employees of the Employment Security Section. (Ex. Sess. 1936, c. 1, s. 12; 1941, c. 108, s. 11; 1947, c. 326, s. 24; 2011-401, s. 2.21.)

§ 96-21. Duties concerning veterans and worker profiling.

The duties of the Employment Security Section include the following:

(1)   To cooperate with all State and federal agencies in attempting to secure suitable employment and fair treatment for military veterans and disabled veterans.

(2)   To establish and use a worker profiling system that complies with 42 U.S.C. § 503(a)(10) to identify claimants for benefits whom the Section must refer to reemployment services in accordance with that law. (1921, c. 131, s. 3; C.S., s. 7312(c); Ex. Sess. 1936, c. 1, s. 12; 1979, c. 660, s. 26; 1993 (Reg. Sess., 1994), c. 680, s. 6; 2011-401, s. 2.22.)

§ 96-22. Employment of and assistance to minors.

The Employment Security Section shall have jurisdiction over all matters contemplated in this Article pertaining to securing employment for all minors who avail themselves of the free employment service. The Employment Security Section shall have power to so conduct its affairs that at all times it shall be in harmony with laws relating to child labor and compulsory education; to aid in inducing minors over 16, who cannot or do not for various reasons attend day school, to undertake promising skilled employment; to aid in influencing minors who do not come within the purview of compulsory education laws, and who do not attend day school, to avail themselves of continuation or special courses in existing night schools, vocational schools, part-time schools, trade schools, business schools, library schools, university extension courses, etc., so as to become more skilled in such occupation or vocation to which they are respectively inclined or particularly adapted, including assisting those minors who are interested in securing vocational employment in agriculture and to aid in the development of good citizenship and in the study and development of vocational rehabilitation capabilities for handicapped minors. (1921, c. 131, s. 4; C.S., s. 7312(d); Ex. Sess. 1936, c. 1, s. 12; 1979, c. 660, s. 27; 2011-401, s. 2.23.)

§ 96-23: Repealed by Session Laws 1985, c. 197, s. 8.

§ 96-24. Local offices; cooperation with United States service; financial aid from United States.

(a) Agreement. - The Department of Commerce is authorized to enter into agreement with the governing authorities of any municipality, county, township, or school corporation in the State for such period of time as may be deemed desirable for the purpose of establishing and maintaining local free employment offices, and for the extension of vocational guidance in cooperation with the United States Employment Service, and under and by virtue of any such agreement as aforesaid to pay, from any funds appropriated by the State for the purposes of this Article, any part or the whole of the salaries, expenses or rent, maintenance, and equipment of offices and other expenses.

(b) Location. - The Department of Commerce must take into consideration all of the following factors when determining the appropriate number and location of local offices:

(1) Location of the population served.

(2) Staff availability.

(3) Proximity of local offices to each other.

(4)   Use of automation products to provide services.

(5)   Services and procedural efficiencies.

(6)   Any other factors the Division considers necessary in determining the appropriate number and location of local offices. (1921, c. 131, s. 6; C.S., s. 7312(f); 1931, c. 312, s. 3; 1935, c. 106, s. 4; Ex. Sess. 1936, c. 1, s. 12; 2011-401, s. 2.24; 2013-2, s. 8; 2013-224, s. 19.)

§ 96-25. Acceptance and use of donations.

It shall be lawful for the Employment Security Section to receive, accept, and use, in the name of the people of the State, or any community or municipal corporation, as the donor may designate, by gift or devise, any moneys, buildings, or real estate for the purpose of extending the benefits of this Article and for the purpose of giving assistance to handicapped citizens through vocational rehabilitation. (1921, c. 131, s. 7; C.S., s. 7312(g); 1931, c. 312, s. 3; Ex. Sess. 1936, c. 1, s. 12; 1979, c. 660, s. 28; 2011-401, s. 2.25.)

§ 96-26. Cooperation of towns, townships, and counties with Division.

It shall be lawful for the governing authorities of any municipality, county, township, or school corporation in the State to enter into cooperative agreement with the Employment Security Section and to appropriate and expend the necessary money upon such conditions as may be approved by the Employment Security Section and to permit the use of public property for the joint establishment and maintenance of such offices as may be mutually agreed upon, and which will further the purpose of this Article. (1921, c. 131, s. 8; C.S., s. 7312(h); 1931, c. 312, s. 3; 1935, c. 106, s. 5; Ex. Sess. 1936, c. 1, s. 12; 2011-401, s. 2.26.)

§ 96-27. Method of handling employment service funds.

All federal funds received by this State under the Wagner-Peyser Act (48 Stat. 113; Title 29, U.S.C., section 49) as amended, and all State funds appropriated or made available to the Employment Security Section shall be paid into the Employment Security Administration Fund, and said moneys are hereby made available to the State employment service to be expended as provided in this Article and by said act of Congress. For the purpose of establishing and maintaining free public employment offices, the Section is authorized to enter into agreements with any political subdivision of this State or with any private, nonprofit organization, and as a part of any such agreement the Division may accept moneys, services, or quarters as a contribution to the Employment Security Administration Fund. (1935, c. 106, s. 7; Ex. Sess. 1936, c. 1, s. 12; 1941, c. 108, s. 11; 1947, c. 598, s. 1; 2011-401, s. 2.27.)

§ 96-28. Repealed by Session Laws 1951, c. 332, s. 17.

§ 96-29. Openings listed by State agencies.

Every State agency shall list with the Division of Employment Security every job opening occurring within the agency which opening the agency wishes filled and which will not be filled solely by promotion or transfer from within the existing State government work force. The listing shall include a brief description of the duties and salary range and shall be filed with the Division within 30 days after the occurrence of the opening. The State agency may not fill the job opening for at least 21 days after the listing has been filed with the Division. The listing agency shall report to the Division the filling of any listed opening within 15 days after the opening has been filled.

The Division may act to waive the 21-day listing period for job openings in job classifications declared to be in short supply by the State Human Resources Commission, upon the request of a State agency, if the 21-day listing requirement for these classifications hinders the agency in providing essential services. (1973, c. 715, s. 1; c. 1341; 1985, c. 358; 1989, c. 583, s. 16; 1991, c. 357, s. 1; 2011-401, s. 2.28; 2013-382, s. 9.1(c).)

Article 4.

Labor and Economic Analysis Division: Job Training, Education, and Placement Information Management.

§ 96-30. Findings and purpose.

The General Assembly finds it in the best interests of this State that the establishment, maintenance, and funding of State job training, education, and placement programs be based on current, comprehensive information on the effectiveness of these programs in securing employment for North Carolina citizens and providing a well-trained workforce for business and industry in this State. To this end, it is the purpose of this Article to require the establishment of an information system that maintains up-to-date job-related information on current and former participants in State job training and education programs. (1995, c. 507, s. 25.6(a).)

§ 96-31. Definitions.

As used in this Article, unless the context clearly requires otherwise, the term:

(1)   "CFS" means the common follow-up information management system developed by the Labor and Economic Analysis Division under this Article.

(2)   Repealed by Session Laws 2012-134, s. 5(b), effective June 29, 2012.

(3)   Repealed by Session Laws 2000, c. 140, s. 93.1(d).

(4)   "State job training, education, and placement program" or "State-funded program" means a program operated by a State or local government agency or entity and supported in whole or in part by State or federal funds, that provides job training and education or job placement services to program participants. The term does not include on-the-job training provided to current employees of the agency or entity for the purposes of professional development. (1995, c. 507, s. 25.6(a); 2000-140, s. 93.1(d); 2011-401, s. 2.29; 2012-134, s. 5(b).)

§ 96-32. Common follow-up information management system created.

(a) The Department of Commerce, Labor and Economic Analysis Division (LEAD), shall develop, implement, and maintain a common follow-up information management system for tracking the performance measures related to current and former participants in State job training, education, and placement programs. The system shall provide for the automated collection, organization, dissemination, and analysis of data obtained from State-funded programs that provide job training and education and job placement services to program participants. In developing the system, LEAD shall ensure that data and information collected from State agencies is confidential, not open for general public inspection, and maintained and disseminated in a manner that protects the identity of individual persons from general public disclosure.

(b) LEAD shall adopt procedures and guidelines for the development and implementation of the CFS authorized under this section.

(c) Based on data collected under the CFS, the LEAD shall evaluate the effectiveness of job training, education, and placement programs to determine if specific program goals and objectives are attained, to determine placement and completion rates for each program, and to make recommendations regarding the continuation of State funding for programs evaluated.

(d) The LEAD shall do the following:

(1) Collaborate with the Commission on Workforce Development to develop common performance measures across workforce programs in the Department of Commerce, the Department of Health and Human Services, the Community Colleges System Office, the Department of Administration, and the Department of Public Instruction that can be tracked through the CFS in order to assess and report on workforce development program performance.

(2) Determine whether other workforce development programs not participating in CFS should be required to report information and data.

(3) Provide information from CFS to reporting agencies annually.

(4) Provide training for participating agencies to ensure data quality and consistency.

(5) Develop common data definitions that are shared across agencies contributing information to the system.

(e) The Department of Commerce shall ensure that funding and staff resources for the CFS are not diverted to other programs or systems managed by the Department of Commerce. (1995, c. 507, s. 25.6(a); 2000-140, s. 93.1(e); 2001-424, ss. 12.2(b), 20.17(a); 2011-401, s. 2.30; 2012-131, s. 4(a); 2012-134, s. 5(c); 2013-391, s. 8.)

§ 96-33. State agencies required to provide information and data.

(a) Every State agency and local government agency or entity that receives State or federal funds for the direct or indirect support of State job training, education, and placement programs shall provide to the Labor and Economic Analysis Division all data and information available to or within the agency or entity's possession requested by the Division for input into the common follow-up information management system authorized under this Article and for such other official functions as are performed by the Division. The Division of Employment Security shall provide all information in its possession and control requested by the Division in order for the Division to accomplish the purpose set forth in this Article and such other official functions performed by it.

(a1) Local school administrative units shall not be required to report directly to the Labor and Economic Analysis Division. The Department of Public Instruction shall be responsible for the collection of information from local school administrative units for input into the common follow-up information management system authorized under this Article and for such other official functions as are performed by the Division.

(b) Each agency or entity required to report information and data to the Labor and Economic Analysis Division under this Article shall maintain true and accurate records of the information and data requested by the Division. The records shall be open to the Division for inspection and copying at reasonable times and as often as necessary. Each agency or entity shall further provide, upon request by the Division, sworn or unsworn reports with respect to persons employed or trained by the agency or entity, as deemed necessary by the Division to carry out the purposes of this Article. Information obtained by the Division from the agency, entity, or the Division of Employment Security shall be held by the Division as confidential, subject to the State and federal laws governing treatment of such information, and shall not be published or open to public inspection other than in a manner that protects the identity of individual persons and employers. (1995, c. 507, s. 25.6(a); 2011-401, s. 2.31; 2012-134, s. 5(d); 2013-226, s. 7.)

§ 96-34. Prohibitions on use of information collected.

Data and information reported, collected, maintained, disseminated, and analyzed may not be used by any State or local government agency or entity for purposes of making personal contacts with current or former students or their employers or trainers. (1995, c. 507, s. 25.6(a).)

§ 96-35. Reports on common follow-up system activities.

(a) The Secretary shall present annually by May 1 to the General Assembly and to the Governor a report of CFS activities for the preceding calendar year. The report shall include information on and evaluation of job training, education, and placement programs for which data was reported by State and local agencies subject to this Article. Evaluation of the programs shall be on the basis of fiscal year data.

(b) The Secretary shall report to the Governor and to the General Assembly upon the convening of each biennial session, its evaluation of and recommendations regarding job training, education, and placement programs for which data was provided to the CFS. (1995, c. 507, s. 25.6(a); 2000-140, s. 93.1(a); 2001-424, ss. 12.2(b), 20.17(b); 2011-401, s. 2.32; 2012-134, s. 5(e).)

Chapter 97.

Workers' Compensation Act.

Article 1.

Workers' Compensation Act.

§ 97-1. Short title.

This Article shall be known and cited as The North Carolina Workers' Compensation Act. (1929, c. 120, s. 1; 1979, c. 714, s. 1.)

§ 97-1.1. References to workmen's compensation.

Any reference in any act, public or local, to the "Workmen's Compensation Act," "Workmen's Compensation," or "workmen's compensation" shall be deemed to refer respectively to "Workers' Compensation Act," "Workers' Compensation" or "workers' compensation." (1979, c. 714, s. 4.)

§ 97-2. Definitions.

When used in this Article, unless the context otherwise requires:

(1)   Employment. - The term "employment" includes employment by the State and all political subdivisions thereof, and all public and quasi-public corporations therein and all private employments in which three or more employees are regularly employed in the same business or establishment or in which one or more employees are employed in activities which involve the use or presence of radiation, except agriculture and domestic services, unless 10 or more full-time nonseasonal agricultural workers are regularly employed by the employer and an individual sawmill and logging operator with less than 10 employees, who saws and logs less than 60 days in any six consecutive months and whose principal business is unrelated to sawmilling or logging.

(2)   Employee. - The term "employee" means every person engaged in an employment under any appointment or contract of hire or apprenticeship, express or implied, oral or written, including aliens, and also minors, whether lawfully or unlawfully employed, but excluding persons whose employment is both casual and not in the course of the trade, business, profession, or occupation of his employer, and as relating to those so employed by the State, the term "employee" shall include all officers and employees of the State, including such as are elected by the people, or by the General Assembly, or appointed by the Governor to serve on a per diem, part-time or fee basis, either with or without the confirmation of the Senate; as relating to municipal corporations and political subdivisions of the State, the term "employee" shall include all officers and employees thereof, including such as are elected by the

people. The term "employee" shall include members of the North Carolina National Guard while on State active duty under orders of the Governor and members of the North Carolina State Defense Militia while on State active duty under orders of the Governor. The term "employee" shall include deputy sheriffs and all persons acting in the capacity of deputy sheriffs, whether appointed by the sheriff or by the governing body of the county and whether serving on a fee basis or on a salary basis, or whether deputy sheriffs serving upon a full-time basis or a part-time basis, and including deputy sheriffs appointed to serve in an emergency, but as to those so appointed, only during the continuation of the emergency. The sheriff shall furnish to the board of county commissioners a complete list of all deputy sheriffs named or appointed by him immediately after their appointment and notify the board of commissioners of any changes made therein promptly after such changes are made. Any reference to an employee who has been injured shall, when the employee is dead, include also the employee's legal representative, dependents, and other persons to whom compensation may be payable: Provided, further, that any employee, as herein defined, of a municipality, county, or of the State of North Carolina, while engaged in the discharge of the employee's official duty outside the jurisdictional or territorial limits of the municipality, county, or the State of North Carolina and while acting pursuant to authorization or instruction from any superior officer, shall have the same rights under this Article as if such duty or activity were performed within the territorial boundary limits of their employer.

Every executive officer elected or appointed and empowered in accordance with the charter and bylaws of a corporation shall be considered as an employee of such corporation under this Article.

Any such executive officer of a corporation may, notwithstanding any other provision of this Article, be exempt from the coverage of the corporation's insurance contract by such corporation's specifically excluding such executive officer in such contract of insurance, and the exclusion to remove such executive officer from the coverage shall continue for the period such contract of insurance is in effect, and during such period such executive officers thus exempted from the coverage of the insurance contract shall not be employees of such corporation under this Article.

All county agricultural extension service employees who do not receive official federal appointments as employees of the United States Department of Agriculture and who are field faculty members with professional rank as designated in the memorandum of understanding between the North Carolina Agricultural Extension Service, North Carolina State University, A & T State

University, and the boards of county commissioners shall be deemed to be employees of the State of North Carolina. All other county agricultural extension service employees paid from State or county funds shall be deemed to be employees of the county board of commissioners in the county in which the employee is employed for purposes of workers' compensation.

The term "employee" shall also include members of the Civil Air Patrol currently certified pursuant to G.S. 143B-1031(a) when performing duties in the course and scope of a State-approved mission pursuant to Subpart C of Part 5 of Article 13 of Chapter 143B of the General Statutes.

"Employee" shall not include any person performing voluntary service as a ski patrolman who receives no compensation for such services other than meals or lodging or the use of ski tow or ski lift facilities or any combination thereof.

Any sole proprietor or partner of a business or any member of a limited liability company may elect to be included as an employee under the workers' compensation coverage of such business if he is actively engaged in the operation of the business and if the insurer is notified of his election to be so included. Any such sole proprietor or partner or member of a limited liability company shall, upon such election, be entitled to employee benefits and be subject to employee responsibilities prescribed in this Article.

"Employee" shall include an authorized pickup firefighter of the North Carolina Forest Service of the Department of Agriculture and Consumer Services when that individual is engaged in emergency fire suppression activities for the North Carolina Forest Service. As used in this section, "authorized pickup firefighter" means an individual who has completed required fire suppression training as a wildland firefighter and who is available as needed by the North Carolina Forest Service for emergency fire suppression activities, including immediate dispatch to wildfires and standby for initial attack on fires during periods of high fire danger.

It shall be a rebuttable presumption that the term "employee" shall not include any person performing services in the sale of newspapers or magazines to ultimate consumers under an arrangement whereby the newspapers or magazines are to be sold by that person at a fixed price and the person's compensation is based on the retention of the excess of the fixed price over the amount at which the newspapers or magazines are charged to the person.

(3) Employer. - The term "employer" means the State and all political subdivisions thereof, all public and quasi-public corporations therein, every person carrying on any employment, and the legal representative of a deceased person or the receiver or trustee of any person. The board of commissioners of each county of the State, for the purposes of this law, shall be considered as "employer" of all deputy sheriffs serving within such county, or persons serving or performing the duties of a deputy sheriff, whether such persons are appointed by the sheriff or by the board of commissioners and whether serving on a fee basis or salary basis. Each county is authorized to insure its compensation liability for deputy sheriffs to the same extent it is authorized to insure other compensation liability for employees thereof. For purposes of this Chapter, when an authorized pickup firefighter of the North Carolina Forest Service of the Department of Agriculture and Consumer Services is engaged in emergency fire suppression activities for the North Carolina Forest Service, that individual's employer is the North Carolina Forest Service.

(4) Person. - The term "person" means individual, partnership, association or corporation.

(5) Average Weekly Wages. - "Average weekly wages" shall mean the earnings of the injured employee in the employment in which the employee was working at the time of the injury during the period of 52 weeks immediately preceding the date of the injury, including the subsistence allowance paid to veteran trainees by the United States government, provided the amount of said allowance shall be reported monthly by said trainee to the trainee's employer, divided by 52; but if the injured employee lost more than seven consecutive calendar days at one or more times during such period, although not in the same week, then the earnings for the remainder of such 52 weeks shall be divided by the number of weeks remaining after the time so lost has been deducted. Where the employment prior to the injury extended over a period of fewer than 52 weeks, the method of dividing the earnings during that period by the number of weeks and parts thereof during which the employee earned wages shall be followed; provided, results fair and just to both parties will be thereby obtained. Where, by reason of a shortness of time during which the employee has been in the employment of his employer or the casual nature or terms of his employment, it is impractical to compute the average weekly wages as above defined, regard shall be had to the average weekly amount which during the 52 weeks previous to the injury was being earned by a person of the same grade and character employed in the same class of employment in the same locality or community.

But where for exceptional reasons the foregoing would be unfair, either to the employer or employee, such other method of computing average weekly wages may be resorted to as will most nearly approximate the amount which the injured employee would be earning were it not for the injury.

Wherever allowances of any character made to an employee in lieu of wages are specified part of the wage contract, they shall be deemed a part of his earnings.

Where a minor employee, under the age of 18 years, sustains a permanent disability or dies leaving dependents surviving, the compensation payable for permanent disability or death shall be calculated, first, upon the average weekly wage paid to adult employees employed by the same employer at the time of the accident in a similar or like class of work which the injured minor employee would probably have been promoted to if not injured, or, second, upon a wage sufficient to yield the maximum weekly compensation benefit. Compensation for temporary total disability or for the death of a minor without dependents shall be computed upon the average weekly wage at the time of the accident, unless the total disability extends more than 52 weeks, and then the compensation may be increased in proportion to the employee's expected earnings.

In case of disabling injury or death to a volunteer fireman; member of an organized rescue squad; an authorized pickup firefighter, as defined in subdivision (2) of this section, when that individual is engaged in emergency fire suppression activities for the North Carolina Forest Service; a duly appointed and sworn member of an auxiliary police department organized pursuant to G.S. 160A-282; or senior members of the State Civil Air Patrol functioning under Subpart C of Part 5 of Article 13 of Chapter 143B of the General Statutes, under compensable circumstances, compensation payable shall be calculated upon the average weekly wage the volunteer fireman, member of an organized rescue squad, authorized pickup firefighter of the North Carolina Forest Service; when that individual is engaged in emergency fire suppression activities for the North Carolina Forest Service, member of an auxiliary police department, or senior member of the State Civil Air Patrol was earning in the employment wherein he principally earned his livelihood as of the date of injury. Provided, however, that the minimum compensation payable to a volunteer fireman, member of an organized rescue squad, an authorized pickup firefighter of the North Carolina Forest Service of the Department of Agriculture and Consumer Services, when that individual is engaged in emergency fire suppression activities for the North Carolina Forest Service, a sworn member of an auxiliary police department organized pursuant to G.S. 160A-282, or senior members of the State Civil Air Patrol shall be sixty-six and two-thirds percent (66 2/3%) of the maximum weekly benefit established in G.S. 97-29.

(6) Injury. - "Injury and personal injury" shall mean only injury by accident arising out of and in the course of the employment, and shall not include a disease in any form, except where it results naturally and unavoidably from the accident. With respect to back injuries, however, where injury to the back arises out of and in the course of the employment and is the direct result of a specific traumatic incident of the work assigned, "injury by accident" shall be construed to include any disabling physical injury to the back arising out of and causally related to such incident. Injury shall include breakage or damage to eyeglasses, hearing aids, dentures, or other prosthetic devices which function as part of the body; provided, however, that eyeglasses and hearing aids will not be replaced, repaired, or otherwise compensated for unless injury to them is incidental to a compensable injury.

(7) Carrier. - The term "carrier" or "insurer" means any person or fund authorized under G.S. 97-93 to insure under this Article, and includes self-insurers.

(8) Commission. - The term "Commission" means the North Carolina Industrial Commission, to be created under the provisions of this Article.

(9) Disability. - The term "disability" means incapacity because of injury to earn the wages which the employee was receiving at the time of injury in the same or any other employment.

(10) Death. - The term "death" as a basis for a right to compensation means only death resulting from an injury.

(11) Compensation. - The term "compensation" means the money allowance payable to an employee or to his dependents as provided for in this Article, and includes funeral benefits provided herein.

(12) Child, Grandchild, Brother, Sister. - The term "child" shall include a posthumous child, a child legally adopted prior to the injury of the employee, and a stepchild or acknowledged child born out of wedlock dependent upon the deceased, but does not include married children unless wholly dependent upon him. "Grandchild" means a child, as defined in this subdivision, of a child, as defined in this subdivision. "Brother" and "sister" include stepbrothers and stepsisters, half brothers and half sisters, and brothers and sisters by adoption,

but does not include married brothers nor married sisters unless wholly dependent on the employee. "Child," "grandchild," "brother," and "sister" include only persons who at the time of the death of the deceased employee are under 18 years of age.

(13) Parent. - The term "parent" includes stepparents and parents by adoption, parents-in-law, and any person who for more than three years prior to the death of the deceased employee stood in the place of a parent to him, if dependent on the injured employee.

(14) Widow. - The term "widow" includes only the decedent's wife living with or dependent for support upon him at the time of his death; or living apart for justifiable cause or by reason of his desertion at such time.

(15) Widower. - The term "widower" includes only the decedent's husband living with or dependent for support upon her at the time of her death or living apart for justifiable cause or by reason of her desertion at such time.

(16) Adoption. - The term "adoption" or "adopted" means legal adoption prior to the time of the injury.

(17) Singular. - The singular includes the plural and the masculine includes the feminine and neuter.

(18) Hernia. - In all claims for compensation for hernia or rupture, resulting from injury by accident arising out of and in the course of the employee's employment, it must be definitely proven to the satisfaction of the Industrial Commission:

a. That there was an injury resulting in hernia or rupture.

b. That the hernia or rupture appeared suddenly.

c. Repealed by Session Laws 1987, c. 729, s. 2.

d. That the hernia or rupture immediately followed an accident. Provided, however, a hernia shall be compensable under this Article if it arises out of and in the course of the employment and is the direct result of a specific traumatic incident of the work assigned.

e. That the hernia or rupture did not exist prior to the accident for which compensation is claimed.

All hernia or rupture, inguinal, femoral or otherwise, so proven to be the result of an injury by accident arising out of and in the course of employment, shall be treated in a surgical manner by a radical operation. If death results from such operation, the death shall be considered as a result of the injury, and compensation paid in accordance with the provisions of G.S. 97-38. In nonfatal cases, if it is shown by special examination, as provided in G.S. 97-27, that the injured employee has a disability resulting after the operation, compensation for such disability shall be paid in accordance with the provisions of this Article.

In case the injured employee refuses to undergo the radical operation for the cure of said hernia or rupture, no compensation will be allowed during the time such refusal continues. If, however, it is shown that the employee has some chronic disease, or is otherwise in such physical condition that the Commission considers it unsafe for the employee to undergo said operation, the employee shall be paid compensation in accordance with the provisions of this Article.

(19)   Medical Compensation. - The term "medical compensation" means medical, surgical, hospital, nursing, and rehabilitative services, including, but not limited to, attendant care services prescribed by a health care provider authorized by the employer or subsequently by the Commission, vocational rehabilitation, and medicines, sick travel, and other treatment, including medical and surgical supplies, as may reasonably be required to effect a cure or give relief and for such additional time as, in the judgment of the Commission, will tend to lessen the period of disability; and any original artificial members as may reasonably be necessary at the end of the healing period and the replacement of such artificial members when reasonably necessitated by ordinary use or medical circumstances.

(20)   Health care provider. - The term "health care provider" means physician, hospital, pharmacy, chiropractor, nurse, dentist, podiatrist, physical therapist, rehabilitation specialist, psychologist, and any other person providing medical care pursuant to this Article.

(21)   Managed care organization. - The term "managed care organization" means a preferred provider organization or a health maintenance organization regulated under Chapter 58 of the General Statutes. "Managed care organization" also means a preferred provider benefit plan of an insurance company, hospital, or medical service corporation in which utilization review or

quality management programs are used to manage the provision of health care services and benefits under this Chapter.

(22) Suitable employment. - The term "suitable employment" means employment offered to the employee or, if prohibited by the Immigration and Nationality Act, 8 U.S.C. § 1324a, employment available to the employee that (i) prior to reaching maximum medical improvement is within the employee's work restrictions, including rehabilitative or other noncompetitive employment with the employer of injury approved by the employee's authorized health care provider or (ii) after reaching maximum medical improvement is employment that the employee is capable of performing considering the employee's preexisting and injury-related physical and mental limitations, vocational skills, education, and experience and is located within a 50-mile radius of the employee's residence at the time of injury or the employee's current residence if the employee had a legitimate reason to relocate since the date of injury. No one factor shall be considered exclusively in determining suitable employment. (1929, c. 120, s. 2; 1933, c. 448; 1939, c. 277, s. 1; 1943, c. 543; c. 672, s. 1; 1945, c. 766; 1947, c. 698; 1949, c. 399; 1953, c. 619; 1955, c. 644; c. 1026, s. 1; c. 1055; 1957, c. 95; 1959, c. 289; 1961, cc. 231, 235; 1967, c. 1229, s. 1; 1969, c. 206, s. 2; c. 707; 1971, c. 284, s. 1; c. 1231, s. 1; 1973, c. 521, ss. 1, 2; c. 763, ss. 1-3; c. 1291, s. 14; 1975, c. 266, s. 1; c. 284, ss. 2, 3; c. 288; c. 718, s. 3; c. 817, s. 1; 1977, c. 419; c. 893, s. 1; 1979, cc. 86, 374; c. 516, ss. 4, 5; c. 714, s. 3; 1981, c. 421, ss. 1, 2; 1983, c. 833; 1983 (Reg. Sess., 1984), c. 1042, s. 1; 1985, cc. 133, 144; 1987, c. 729, ss. 1, 2; 1991, c. 703, s. 1; 1993, c. 389, s. 3; 1993 (Reg. Sess., 1994), c. 679, ss. 2.6, 10.7; 1995, c. 517, s. 35; 1999-219, s. 4.2; 1999-418, s. 1; 1999-456, s. 33(c); 2001-204, ss. 1, 1.1, 2; 2003-156, s. 1; 2009-281, s. 1; 2011-145, s. 13.25(mm), (xx); 2011-287, s. 2; 2013-155, s. 5; 2013-198, s. 25.)

§ 97-3. Presumption that all employers and employees have come under provisions of Article.

From and after January 1, 1975, every employer and employee, as hereinbefore defined and except as herein stated, shall be presumed to have accepted the provisions of this Article respectively to pay and accept compensation for personal injury or death by accident arising out of and in the course of his employment and shall be bound thereby. (1929, c. 120, s. 4; 1973, c. 1291, s. 1.)

§ 97-4: Repealed by Session Laws 1973, c. 1291, s. 2.

§ 97-5. Presumption as to contract of service.

Every contract of service between any employer and employee covered by this Article, written or implied, now in operation or made or implied prior to July 1, 1929, shall, after that date, be presumed to continue, subject to the provisions of this Article; and every such contract made subsequent to that date shall be presumed to have been made subject to the provisions of this Article. (1929, c. 120, s. 6; 1973, c. 1291, s. 3.)

§ 97-5.1. Presumption that taxicab drivers are independent contractors.

(a) It shall be a rebuttable presumption under this Chapter that any person who operates, and who has an ownership or leasehold interest in, a passenger motor vehicle that is operated as a taxicab is an independent contractor for the purposes of this Chapter and not an employee as defined in G.S. 97-2. The presumption is not rebutted solely (i) because the operator is required to comply with rules and regulations imposed on taxicabs by the local governmental unit that licenses companies, taxicabs, or operators or (ii) because a taxicab accepts a trip request to be at a specific place at a specific time, but the presumption may be rebutted by application of the common law test for determining employment status.

(b) The following definitions apply in this section:

(1) Lease. - A contract under which the lessor provides a vehicle to a lessee for consideration.

(2) Leasehold. - Includes, but is not limited to, a lease for a shift or a longer period.

(3) Passenger motor vehicle that is operated as a taxicab. - Any vehicle that:

a. Has a passenger seating capacity that does not exceed seven persons; and

b. Is transporting persons, property, or both on a route that begins or ends in this State and either:

1. Carries passengers for hire when the destination and route traveled may be controlled by a passenger and the fare is calculated on the basis of any combination of an initial fee, distance traveled, or waiting time; or

2. Is in use under a contract between the operator and a third party to provide specific service to transport designated passengers or to provide errand services to locations selected by the third party. (2013-413, s. 17(a).)

§ 97-6. No special contract can relieve an employer of obligations.

No contract or agreement, written or implied, no rule, regulation, or other device shall in any manner operate to relieve an employer in whole or in part, of any obligation created by this Article, except as herein otherwise expressly provided. (1929, c. 120, s. 7.)

§ 97-6.1: Repealed by 1991 (Regular Session, 1992), c. 1021, s. 4.

§ 97-7. State or subdivision and employees thereof.

Neither the State nor any municipal corporation within the State, nor any political subdivision thereof, nor any employee of the State or of any such corporation or subdivision, shall have the right to reject the provisions of this Article relative to payment and acceptance of compensation, and G.S. 97-100(c) does not apply to them: Provided, that all such corporations or subdivisions are hereby authorized to self-insure or purchase insurance to secure its liability under this Article and to include thereunder the liability of such subordinate governmental agencies as the county board of health, the school board, and other political and quasi-political subdivisions supported in whole or in part by the municipal corporation or political subdivision of the State. Each municipality is authorized to make appropriations for these purposes and to fund them by levy of property taxes pursuant to G.S. 153A-149 and G.S. 160A-209 and by the allocation of other revenues whose use is not otherwise restricted by law. (1929, c. 120, s. 8;

1931, c. 274, s. 1; 1945, c. 766; 1957, c. 1396, s. 1; 1961, c. 1200; 1973, c. 803, s. 34; c. 1291, s. 4; 2006-105, s. 1.10.)

§ 97-8. Prior injuries and deaths unaffected.

The provisions of this Article shall not apply to injuries or deaths, nor to accidents which occurred prior to July 1, 1929. (1929, c. 120, s. 9.)

§ 97-9. Employer to secure payment of compensation.

Every employer subject to the compensation provisions of this Article shall secure the payment of compensation to his employees in the manner hereinafter provided; and while such security remains in force, he or those conducting his business shall only be liable to any employee for personal injury or death by accident to the extent and in the manner herein specified. (1929, c. 120, s. 10; 1973, c. 1291, s. 5.)

§ 97-10. Repealed by Session Laws 1959, c. 1324.

§ 97-10.1. Other rights and remedies against employer excluded.

If the employee and the employer are subject to and have complied with the provisions of this Article, then the rights and remedies herein granted to the employee, his dependents, next of kin, or personal representative shall exclude all other rights and remedies of the employee, his dependents, next of kin, or representative as against the employer at common law or otherwise on account of such injury or death. (1929, c. 120, s. 11; 1933, c. 449, s. 1; 1943, c. 622; 1959, c. 1324; 1973, c. 1291, s. 6.)

§ 97-10.2. Rights under Article not affected by liability of third party; rights and remedies against third parties.

(a) The right to compensation and other benefits under this Article for disability, disfigurement, or death shall not be affected by the fact that the injury or death was caused under circumstances creating a liability in some person other than the employer to pay damages therefor, such person hereinafter being referred to as the "third party." The respective rights and interests of the employee-beneficiary under this Article, the employer, and the employer's insurance carrier, if any, in respect of the common-law cause of action against such third party and the damages recovered shall be as set forth in this section.

(b) The employee, or his personal representative if he be dead, shall have the exclusive right to proceed to enforce the liability of the third party by appropriate proceedings if such proceedings are instituted not later than 12 months after the date of injury or death, whichever is later. During said 12-month period, and at any time thereafter if summons is issued against the third party during said 12-month period, the employee or his personal representative shall have the right to settle with the third party and to give a valid and complete release of all claims to the third party by reason of such injury or death, subject to the provisions of (h) below.

(c) If settlement is not made and summons is not issued within said 12-month period, and if employer shall have filed with the Industrial Commission a written admission of liability for the benefits provided by this Chapter, then either the employee or the employer shall have the right to proceed to enforce the liability of the third party by appropriate proceedings; either shall have the right to settle with the third party and to give a valid and complete release of all claims to the third party by reason of such injury or death, subject to the provisions of (h) below. Provided that 60 days before the expiration of the period fixed by the applicable statute of limitations if neither the employee nor the employer shall have settled with or instituted proceedings against the third party, all such rights shall revert to the employee or his personal representative.

(d) The person in whom the right to bring such proceeding or make settlement is vested shall, during the continuation thereof, also have the exclusive right to make settlement with the third party and the release of the person having the right shall fully acquit and discharge the third party except as provided by (h) below. A proceeding so instituted by the person having the right shall be brought in the name of the employee or his personal representative and the employer or the insurance carrier shall not be a necessary or proper party thereto. If the employee or his personal representative shall refuse to cooperate with the employer by being the party plaintiff, then the action shall be brought in the name of the employer and the employee or his personal representative shall be made a party plaintiff or party defendant by order of court.

(e) The amount of compensation and other benefits paid or payable on account of such injury or death shall be admissible in evidence in any proceeding against the third party. In the event that said amount of compensation and other benefits is introduced in such a proceeding the court shall instruct the jury that said amount will be deducted by the court from any amount of damages awarded to the plaintiff. If the third party defending such proceeding, by answer duly served on the employer, sufficiently alleges that actionable negligence of the employer joined and concurred with the negligence of the third party in producing the injury or death, then an issue shall be submitted to the jury in such case as to whether actionable negligence of employer joined and concurred with the negligence of the third party in producing the injury or death. The employer shall have the right to appear, to be represented, to introduce evidence, to cross-examine adverse witnesses, and to argue to the jury as to this issue as fully as though he were a party although not named or joined as a party to the proceeding. Such issue shall be the last of the issues submitted to the jury. If the verdict shall be that actionable negligence of the employer did join and concur with that of the third party in producing the injury or death, then the court shall reduce the damages awarded by the jury against the third party by the amount which the employer would otherwise be entitled to receive therefrom by way of subrogation hereunder and the entire amount recovered, after such reduction, shall belong to the employee or his personal representative free of any claim by the employer and the third party shall have no further right by way of contribution or otherwise against the employer, except any right which may exist by reason of an express contract of indemnity between the employer and the third party, which was entered into prior to the injury to the employee. In the event that the court becomes aware that there is an express contract of indemnity between the employer and the third party the court may in the interest of justice exclude the employer from the trial of the claim against the third party and may meet the issue of the actionable negligence of the employer to the jury in a separate hearing.

(f) (1) If the employer has filed a written admission of liability for benefits under this Chapter with, or if an award final in nature in favor of the employee has been entered by the Industrial Commission, then any amount obtained by any person by settlement with, judgment against, or otherwise from the third party by reason of such injury or death shall be disbursed by order of the Industrial Commission for the following purposes and in the following order of priority:

a. First to the payment of actual court costs taxed by judgment and/or reasonable expenses incurred by the employee in the litigation of the third-party claim.

b. Second to the payment of the fee of the attorney representing the person making settlement or obtaining judgment, and except for the fee on the subrogation interest of the employer such fee shall not be subject to the provisions of G.S. 97-90 but shall not exceed one third of the amount obtained or recovered of the third party.

c. Third to the reimbursement of the employer for all benefits by way of compensation or medical compensation expense paid or to be paid by the employer under award of the Industrial Commission.

d. Fourth to the payment of any amount remaining to the employee or his personal representative.

(2) The attorney fee paid under (f)(1) shall be paid by the employee and the employer in direct proportion to the amount each shall receive under (f)(1)c and (f)(1)d hereof and shall be deducted from such payments when distribution is made.

(g) The insurance carrier affording coverage to the employer under this Chapter shall be subrogated to all rights and liabilities of the employer hereunder but this shall not be construed as conferring any other or further rights upon such insurance carrier than those herein conferred upon the employer, anything in the policy of insurance to the contrary notwithstanding.

(h) In any proceeding against or settlement with the third party, every party to the claim for compensation shall have a lien to the extent of his interest under (f) hereof upon any payment made by the third party by reason of such injury or death, whether paid in settlement, in satisfaction of judgment, as consideration for covenant not to sue, or otherwise and such lien may be enforced against any person receiving such funds. Neither the employee or his personal representative nor the employer shall make any settlement with or accept any payment from the third party without the written consent of the other and no release to or agreement with the third party shall be valid or enforceable for any purpose unless both employer and employee or his personal representative join therein; provided, that this sentence shall not apply:

(1) If the employer is made whole for all benefits paid or to be paid by him under this Chapter less attorney's fees as provided by (f)(1) and (2) hereof and the release to or agreement with the third party is executed by the employee; or

(2) If either party follows the provisions of subsection (j) of this section.

(i) Institution of proceedings against or settlement with the third party, or acceptance of benefits under this Chapter, shall not in any way or manner affect any other remedy which any party to the claim for compensation may have except as otherwise specifically provided in this Chapter, and the exercise of one remedy shall not in any way or manner be held to constitute an election of remedies so as to bar the other.

(j) Notwithstanding any other subsection in this section, in the event that a judgment is obtained by the employee in an action against a third party, or in the event that a settlement has been agreed upon by the employee and the third party, either party may apply to the resident superior court judge of the county in which the cause of action arose or where the injured employee resides, or to a presiding judge of either district, to determine the subrogation amount. After notice to the employer and the insurance carrier, after an opportunity to be heard by all interested parties, and with or without the consent of the employer, the judge shall determine, in his discretion, the amount, if any, of the employer's lien, whether based on accrued or prospective workers' compensation benefits, and the amount of cost of the third-party litigation to be shared between the employee and employer. The judge shall consider the anticipated amount of prospective compensation the employer or workers' compensation carrier is likely to pay to the employee in the future, the net recovery to plaintiff, the likelihood of the plaintiff prevailing at trial or on appeal, the need for finality in the litigation, and any other factors the court deems just and reasonable, in determining the appropriate amount of the employer's lien. If the matter is pending in the federal district court such determination may be made by a federal district court judge of that division. (1929, c. 120, s. 11; 1933, c. 449, s. 1; 1943, c. 622; 1959, c. 1324; 1963, c. 450, s. 1; 1971, c. 171, s. 1; 1979, c. 865, s. 1; 1983, c. 645, ss. 1, 2; 1991, c. 408, s. 1; c. 703, s. 2; 1999-194, s. 1; 2004-199, s. 13(b).)

§ 97-10.3. Minors illegally employed.

In any case where an employer and employee are subject to the provisions of this Chapter, any injury to a minor while employed contrary to the laws of this State shall be compensable under this Chapter as if said minor were an adult, subject to the other provisions of this Chapter. (1929, c. 120, s. 11; 1933, c. 449, s. 1; 1943, c. 622; 1959, c. 1324.)

§ 97-11. Employer not relieved of statutory duty.

Nothing in this Article shall be construed to relieve any employer or employee from penalty for failure or neglect to perform any statutory duty. (1929, c. 120, s. 12.)

§ 97-12. Use of intoxicant or controlled substance; willful neglect; willful disobedience of statutory duty, safety regulation or rule.

No compensation shall be payable if the injury or death to the employee was proximately caused by:

(1)   His intoxication, provided the intoxicant was not supplied by the employer or his agent in a supervisory capacity to the employee; or

(2)   His being under the influence of any controlled substance listed in the North Carolina Controlled Substances Act, G.S. 90-86, et seq., where such controlled substance was not by prescription by a practitioner; or

(3)   His willful intention to injure or kill himself or another.

When the injury or death is caused by the willful failure of the employer to comply with any statutory requirement or any lawful order of the Commission, compensation shall be increased ten percent (10%). When the injury or death is caused by the willful failure of the employee to use a safety appliance or perform a statutory duty or by the willful breach of any rule or regulation adopted by the employer and approved by the Commission and brought to the knowledge of the employee prior to the injury compensation shall be reduced ten percent (10%). The burden of proof shall be upon him who claims an exemption or forfeiture under this section.

"Intoxication" and "under the influence" shall mean that the employee shall have consumed a sufficient quantity of intoxicating beverage or controlled substance to cause the employee to lose the normal control of his or her bodily or mental faculties, or both, to such an extent that there was an appreciable impairment of either or both of these faculties at the time of the injury.

A result consistent with "intoxication" or being "under the influence" from a blood or other medical test conducted in a manner generally acceptable to the scientific community and consistent with applicable State and federal law, if any, shall create a rebuttable presumption of impairment from the use of alcohol or a controlled substance. (1929, c. 120, s. 13; 1975, c. 740; 2005-448, s. 2.)

§ 97-12.1. Willful misrepresentation in applying for employment.

No compensation shall be allowed under this Article for injury by accident or occupational disease if the employer proves that (i) at the time of hire or in the course of entering into employment, (ii) at the time of receiving notice of the removal of conditions from a conditional offer of employment, or (iii) during the course of a post-offer medical examination:

(1)   The employee knowingly and willfully made a false representation as to the employee's physical condition;

(2)   The employer relied upon one or more false representations by the employee, and the reliance was a substantial factor in the employer's decision to hire the employee; and

(3)   There was a causal connection between false representation by the employee and the injury or occupational disease. (2011-287, s. 3.)

§ 97-13. Exceptions from provisions of Article.

(a)   Employees of Certain Railroads. - This Article shall not apply to railroads or railroad employees nor in any way repeal, amend, alter or affect Article 8 of Chapter 60 or any section thereof relating to the liability of railroads for injuries to employees, nor upon the trial of any action in tort for injuries not coming under the provisions of this Article, shall any provision herein be placed in evidence or be permitted to be argued to the jury. Provided, however, that the foregoing exemption to railroads and railroad employees shall not apply to employees of a State-owned railroad company, as defined in G.S. 124-11, or to electric street railroads or employees thereof; and this Article shall apply to electric street railroads and employees thereof and to this extent the provisions of Article 8 of Chapter 60 are hereby amended.

(b) Casual Employment, Domestic Servants, Farm Laborers, Federal Government, Employer of Less than Three Employees. - This Article shall not apply to casual employees, farm laborers when fewer than 10 full-time nonseasonal farm laborers are regularly employed by the same employer, federal government employees in North Carolina, and domestic servants, nor to employees of such persons, nor to any person, firm or private corporation that has regularly in service less than three employees in the same business within this State, except that any employer without regard to number of employees, including an employer of domestic servants, farm laborers, or one who previously had exempted himself, who has purchased workers' compensation insurance to cover his compensation liability shall be conclusively presumed during life of the policy to have accepted the provisions of this Article from the effective date of said policy and his employees shall be so bound unless waived as provided in this Article; provided however, that this Article shall apply to all employers of one or more employees who are employed in activities which involve the use or presence of radiation.

(c) Prisoners. - This Article shall not apply to prisoners being worked by the State or any subdivision thereof, except to the following extent: Whenever any prisoner assigned to the Division of Adult Correction of the Department of Public Safety shall suffer accidental injury or accidental death arising out of and in the course of the employment to which he had been assigned, if there be death or if the results of such injury continue until after the date of the lawful discharge of such prisoner to such an extent as to amount to a disability as defined in this Article, then such discharged prisoner or the dependents or next of kin of such discharged prisoner may have the benefit of this Article by applying to the Industrial Commission as any other employee; provided, such application is made within 12 months from the date of the discharge; and provided further that the maximum compensation to any prisoner or to the dependents or next of kin of any deceased prisoner shall not exceed thirty dollars ($30.00) per week and the period of compensation shall relate to the date of his discharge rather than the date of the accident. If any person who has been awarded compensation under the provisions of this subsection shall be recommitted to prison upon conviction of an offense committed subsequent to the award, such compensation shall immediately cease. Any awards made under the terms of this subsection shall be paid by the Department of Public Safety from the funds available for the operation of the Division of Adult Correction of the Department of Public Safety. The provisions of G.S. 97-10.1 and 97-10.2 shall apply to prisoners and discharged prisoners entitled to compensation under this subsection and to the State in the same manner as said section applies to employees and employers.

(d) Sellers of Agricultural Products. - This Article shall not apply to persons, firms or corporations engaged in selling agricultural products for the producers thereof on commission or for other compensation, paid by the producers, provided the product is prepared for sale by the producer. (1929, c. 120, s. 14; 1933, c. 401; 1935, c. 150; 1941, c. 295; 1943, c. 543; 1945, c. 766; 1957, c. 349, s. 10; c. 809; 1967, c. 996, s. 13; 1971, c. 284, s. 2; c. 1176; 1975, c. 718, s. 3; 1979, c. 247, s. 1; c. 714, s. 2; 1981, c. 378, s. 1; 1983 (Reg. Sess., 1984), c. 1042, s. 2; 1987, c. 729, s. 3; 2000-146, s. 11; 2011-145, s. 19.1(h); 2012-83, s. 34.)

§§ 97-14 through 97-16. Repealed by Session Laws 1973, c. 1291, ss. 7-9.

§ 97-17. Settlements allowed in accordance with Article.

(a) This article does not prevent settlements made by and between the employee and employer so long as the amount of compensation and the time and manner of payment are in accordance with the provisions of this Article. A copy of a settlement agreement shall be filed by the employer with and approved by the Commission. No party to any agreement for compensation approved by the Commission shall deny the truth of the matters contained in the settlement agreement, unless the party is able to show to the satisfaction of the Commission that there has been error due to fraud, misrepresentation, undue influence or mutual mistake, in which event the Commission may set aside the agreement. Except as provided in this subsection, the decision of the Commission to approve a settlement agreement is final and is not subject to review or collateral attack.

(b) The Commission shall not approve a settlement agreement under this section, unless all of the following conditions are satisfied:

(1) The settlement agreement is deemed by the Commission to be fair and just, and that the interests of all of the parties and of any person, including a health benefit plan that paid medical expenses of the employee have been considered.

(2) The settlement agreement contains a list of all of the known medical expenses of the employee related to the injury to the date of the settlement agreement, including medical expenses that the employer or carrier disputes, and a list of medical expenses, if any, that will be paid by the employer under the settlement agreement.

(3) The settlement agreement contains a finding that the positions of all of the parties to the agreement are reasonable as to the payment of medical expenses.

It is not necessary, however, to satisfy the condition in subdivision (2) of this subsection when in the settlement agreement the employer agrees to pay all medical expenses of the employee related to the injury to the date of the settlement agreement.

(c) In determining whether the positions of all of the parties to the agreement are reasonable as to the payment of medical expenses under subdivision (3) of subsection (b) of this section, the Commission shall consider all of the following:

(1) Whether the employer admitted or reasonably denied the employee's claim for compensation.

(2) The amount of all of the known medical expenses of the employee related to the injury to the date of the settlement agreement, including medical expenses that the employer or carrier disputes.

(3) The need for finality in the litigation.

(d) Nothing in this section shall be construed to limit the application of G.S. 44-49 and G.S. 44-50 to funds in compensation for settlement under this section.

(e) Nothing in this section prevents the parties from reaching a separate contemporaneous agreement resolving issues not covered by this Article.

(1929, c. 120, s. 18; 1963, c. 436; 2001-216, s. 2; 2001-487, s. 102(b); 2005-448, s. 3; 2011-287, s. 4.)

§ 97-18. Prompt payment of compensation required; installments; payment without prejudice; notice to Commission; penalties.

(a) Compensation under this Article shall be paid periodically, promptly and directly to the person entitled thereto unless otherwise specifically provided.

(b) When the employer or insurer admits the employee's right to compensation, the first installment of compensation payable by the employer shall become due on the fourteenth day after the employer has written or actual notice of the injury or death, on which date all compensation then due shall be paid. Compensation thereafter shall be paid in installments weekly except where the Commission determines that payment in installments should be made monthly or at some other period. Upon paying the first installment of compensation and upon suspending, reinstating, changing, or modifying such compensation for any cause, the insurer shall immediately notify the Commission, on a form prescribed by the Commission, that compensation has begun, or has been suspended, reinstated, changed, or modified. A copy of each notice shall be provided to the employee. The first notice of payment to the Commission shall contain the date and nature of the injury, the average weekly wages of the employee, the weekly compensation rate, the date the disability resulting from the injury began, and the date compensation commenced.

(c) If the employer or insurer denies the employee's right to compensation, the employer or insurer shall notify the Commission, on or before the fourteenth day after it has written or actual notice of the injury or death, or within such reasonable additional time as the Commission may allow, and advise the employee in writing of its refusal to pay compensation on a form prescribed by the Commission. This notification shall (i) include the name of the employee, the name of the employer, the date of the alleged injury or death, the insurer on the risk, if any, and a detailed statement of the grounds upon which the right to compensation is denied, and (ii) advise the employee of the employee's right to request a hearing pursuant to G.S. 97-83. If the employer or insurer, in good faith, is without sufficient information to admit the employee's right to compensation, the employer or insurer may deny the employee's right to compensation.

(d) In any claim for compensation in which the employer or insurer is uncertain on reasonable grounds whether the claim is compensable or whether it has liability for the claim under this Article, the employer or insurer may initiate compensation payments without prejudice and without admitting liability. The initial payment shall be accompanied by a form prescribed by and filed with the Commission, stating that the payments are being made without prejudice. Payments made pursuant to this subsection may continue until the employer or insurer contests or accepts liability for the claim or 90 days from the date the employer has written or actual notice of the injury or death, whichever occurs first, unless an extension is granted pursuant to this section. Prior to the expiration of the 90-day period, the employer or insurer may upon reasonable grounds apply to the Commission for an extension of not more than 30 days. The initiation of payment does not affect the right of the employer or insurer to continue to investigate or deny the compensability of the claim or its liability therefor during this period. If at any time during the 90-day period or extension thereof, the employer or insurer contests the compensability of the claim or its liability therefor, it may suspend payment of compensation and shall promptly notify the Commission and the employee on a form prescribed by the Commission. The employer or insurer must provide on the prescribed form a detailed statement of its grounds for denying compensability of the claim or its liability therefor. If the employer or insurer does not contest the compensability of the claim or its liability therefor within 90 days from the date it first has written or actual notice of the injury or death, or within such additional period as may be granted by the Commission, it waives the right to contest the compensability of and its liability for the claim under this Article. However, the employer or insurer may contest the compensability of or its liability for the claim after the 90-day period or extension thereof when it can show that material evidence was discovered after that period that could not have been reasonably discovered earlier, in which event the employer or insurer may terminate or suspend compensation subject to the provisions of G.S. 97-18.1.

(e) The first installment of compensation payable under the terms of an award by the Commission, or under the terms of a judgment of the court upon an appeal from such an award, shall become due 10 days from the day following expiration of the time for appeal from the award or judgment or the day after notice waiving the right of appeal by all parties has been received by the Commission, whichever is sooner. Thereafter compensation shall be paid in installments weekly, except where the Commission determines that payment in installments shall be made monthly or in some other manner.

(f) The employer's or insurer's grounds for contesting the employee's claim or its liability therefor as specified in the notice suspending compensation under subsection (d) of this section are the only bases for the employer's or insurer's defense on the issue of compensability in a subsequent proceeding, unless the defense is based on newly discovered material evidence that could not reasonably have been discovered prior to the notice suspending compensation.

(g) If any installment of compensation is not paid within 14 days after it becomes due, there shall be added to such unpaid installment an amount equal to ten per centum (10%) thereof, which shall be paid at the same time as, but in addition to, such installment, unless such nonpayment is excused by the Commission after a showing by the employer that owing to conditions over which he had no control such installment could not be paid within the period prescribed for the payment.

(h) Within 16 days after final payment of compensation has been made, the employer or insurer shall send to the Commission and the employee a notice, in accordance with a form prescribed by the Commission, stating that such final payment has been made, the total amount of compensation paid, the name of the employee and of any other person to whom compensation has been paid, the date of the injury or death, and the date to which compensation has been paid. If the employer or insurer fails to so notify the Commission or the employee within such time, the Commission shall assess against such employer or insurer a civil penalty in the amount of twenty-five dollars ($25.00). The clear proceeds of civil penalties assessed pursuant to this section shall be remitted to the Civil Penalty and Forfeiture Fund in accordance with G.S. 115C-457.2.

(i) If any bill for services rendered under G.S. 97-25 by any provider of health care is not paid within 60 days after it has been approved by the Commission and returned to the responsible party, or within 60 days after it was properly submitted, in accordance with the provisions of this Article, to an insurer or managed care organization responsible for direct reimbursement pursuant to G.S. 97-26(g), there shall be added to such unpaid bill an amount equal to ten per centum (10%) thereof, which shall be paid at the same time as, but in addition to, such medical bill, unless such late payment is excused by the Commission.

(j) The employer or insurer shall promptly investigate each injury reported or known to the employer and at the earliest practicable time shall admit or deny the employee's right to compensation or commence payment of compensation as provided in subsections (b), (c), or (d) of this section. When an employee files a claim for compensation with the Commission, the Commission may order reasonable sanctions against an employer or insurer which does not, within 30 days following notice from the Commission of the filing of a claim, or within such reasonable additional time as the Commission may allow, do one of the following:

(1) Notify the Commission and the employee in writing that it is admitting the employee's right to compensation and, if applicable, satisfy the requirements for payment of compensation under subsection (b) of this section.

(2) Notify the Commission and the employee that it denies the employee's right to compensation consistent with subsection (c) of this section.

(3) Initiate payments without prejudice and without liability and satisfy the requirements of subsection (d) of this section.

For purposes of this subsection, reasonable sanctions shall not prohibit the employer or insurer from contesting the compensability of or its liability for the claim.

(k) In addition to any other methods for reinstatement of compensation available under the Act, whenever the employer or insurer has admitted the employee's right to compensation, or liability has been established, the employee may move for reinstatement of compensation on a form prescribed by the Commission. The form prescribed by the Commission shall contain the reasons for the proposed reinstatement of compensation, be supported by available documentation, and inform the employer of the employer's right to contest the reinstatement of compensation by filing an objection in writing with the Commission within 14 days of the date the employee's notice is filed with the Commission or within such additional reasonable time as the Commission may allow. If the employer or insurer contests the employee's request for reinstatement, the Commission shall conduct an informal hearing by telephone with the parties or their counsel. If either party objects to conducting the hearing by telephone, the Commission may conduct the hearing in person in Raleigh or at another location selected by the Commission. The parties shall be afforded an opportunity to state their position and to submit documentary evidence at the informal hearing. The employee may waive the right to an informal hearing and proceed to the formal hearing. The Commission's decision in the informal hearing is not binding in the subsequent hearings. If the application for Reinstatement of Payment of Disability Compensation is approved or not contested, then compensation shall be reinstated immediately and continue until further order of the Commission. The employer or employee may request a formal hearing pursuant to G.S. 97-83 on the Commission's decision approving or denying the employee's application for reinstatement. A formal hearing under G.S. 97-83 ordered or requested pursuant to this subsection shall be a hearing de novo on the employee's application for reinstatement of compensation and may be scheduled by the Commission on a preemptive basis. This subsection shall not apply to a request for a review of an award on the grounds of a change in condition pursuant to G.S. 97-47. (1929, c. 120, s. 181/2; 1967, c. 1229, s. 2; 1979, c. 249, ss. 1, 2; c. 599; 1993 (Reg. Sess., 1994), c. 679, s. 3.1; 1998-215, s. 114; 2005-448, s. 4; 2006-264, s. 91.7; 2011-287, s. 5; 2013-294, s. 3.)

§ 97-18.1. Termination or suspension of compensation benefits.

(a) Payments of compensation pursuant to an award of the Commission shall continue until the terms of the award have been fully satisfied.

(b) An employer may terminate payment of compensation for total disability being paid pursuant to G.S. 97-29 when the employee has returned to work for the same or a different employer, subject to the provisions of G.S. 97-32.1, or when the employer contests a claim pursuant to G.S. 97-18(d) within the time allowed thereunder. The employer shall promptly notify the Commission and the employee, on a form prescribed by the Commission, of the termination of compensation and the availability of trial return to work and additional compensation due the employee for any partial disability.

(c) An employer seeking to terminate or suspend compensation being paid pursuant to G.S. 97-29 for a reason other than those specified in subsection (b) of this section shall notify the employee and the employee's attorney of record in writing of its intent to do so on a form prescribed by the Commission. A copy of the notice shall be filed with the Commission. This form shall contain the reasons for the proposed termination or suspension of compensation, be supported by available documentation, and inform the employee of the employee's right to contest the termination or suspension by filing an objection in writing with the Commission within 14 days of the date the employer's notice is filed with the Commission or within such additional reasonable time as the Commission may allow.

(d) If the employee fails to object to the employer's notice of proposed termination or suspension within the time provided, the Commission may enter an appropriate order terminating or suspending the compensation if it finds that there is a sufficient basis under this Article for this action. If the employee files a timely objection to the employer's notice, the Commission shall conduct an informal hearing by telephone with the parties or their counsel. If either party objects to conducting the hearing by telephone, the Commission may conduct the hearing in person in Raleigh or at another location selected by the Commission. The parties shall be afforded an opportunity to state their position and to submit documentary evidence at the informal hearing. The employer may waive the right to an informal hearing and proceed to the formal hearing. The informal hearing, whether by telephone or in person, shall be conducted only on the issue of termination or suspension of compensation and shall be conducted within 25 days of the receipt by the Commission of the employer's notice to the employee unless this time is extended by the Commission for good cause. The Commission shall issue a decision on the employer's application for termination of compensation within five days after completion of the informal hearing. The decision shall (i) approve the application, (ii) disapprove the application, or (iii) state that the Commission is unable to reach a decision on the application in an informal hearing, in which event the Commission shall schedule a formal hearing pursuant to G.S. 97-83 on the employer's application for termination of compensation. Compensation may be terminated or suspended by the employer following an informal hearing only if its application is approved. If the Commission was unable to reach a decision in the informal hearing, the employee's compensation shall continue pending a decision by the Commission in the formal hearing. The Commission's decision in the informal hearing is not binding in subsequent hearings.

The employer or the employee may request a formal hearing pursuant to G.S. 97-83 on the Commission's decision approving or denying the employer's application for termination of compensation. A formal hearing under G.S. 97-83 ordered or requested pursuant to this section shall be a hearing de novo on the employer's application for termination or suspension of compensation and may be scheduled by the Commission on a preemptive basis.

(e) At an informal hearing on the issue of termination or suspension of compensation, and at any subsequent hearing, the Commission may address related issues regarding the selection of medical providers or treatment under G.S. 97-25, subject to exhaustion of the dispute resolution procedures of a managed care organization pursuant to G.S. 97-25.2. (1993 (Reg. Sess., 1994), c. 679, ss. 3.6, 10.9.)

§ 97-19. Liability of principal contractors; certificate that subcontractor has complied with law; right to recover compensation of those who would have been liable; order of liability.

Any principal contractor, intermediate contractor, or subcontractor who shall sublet any contract for the performance of any work without obtaining from such subcontractor or obtaining from the Industrial Commission a certificate, issued by a workers' compensation insurance carrier, or a certificate of compliance issued by the Department of Insurance to a self-insured subcontractor, stating that such subcontractor has complied with G.S. 97-93 for a specified term, shall be liable, irrespective of whether such subcontractor has regularly in service fewer than three employees in the same business within this State, to the same extent as such subcontractor would be if he were subject to the provisions of this Article for the payment of compensation and other benefits under this Article on account of the injury or death of any employee of such subcontractor due to an accident arising out of and in the course of the performance of the work covered by such subcontract. If the principal contractor, intermediate contractor or subcontractor shall obtain such certificate at any time before subletting such contract to the subcontractor, he shall not thereafter be held liable to any employee of such subcontractor for compensation or other benefits under this Article and within the term specified by the certificate.

Notwithstanding the provisions of this section, any principal contractor, intermediate contractor, or subcontractor who shall sublet any contract for the performance of work shall not be held liable to any employee of such subcontractor if either (i) the subcontractor has a workers' compensation insurance policy in compliance with G.S. 97-93 in effect on the date of injury regardless of whether the principal contractor, intermediate contractor, or subcontractor failed to timely obtain a certificate from the subcontractor; or (ii) the policy expired or was cancelled prior to the date of injury provided the principal contractor, intermediate contractor, or subcontractor obtained a certificate at any time before subletting such contract to the subcontractor and was unaware of the expiration or cancellation.

Any principal contractor, intermediate contractor, or subcontractor paying compensation or other benefits under this Article, under the foregoing provisions of this section, may recover the amount so paid from any person, persons, or corporation who independently of such provision, would have been liable for the payment thereof.

Every claim filed with the Industrial Commission under this section shall be instituted against all parties liable for payment, and said Commission, in its award, shall fix the order in which said parties shall be exhausted, beginning with the immediate employer.

The principal or owner may insure any or all of his contractors and their employees in a blanket policy, and when so insured such contractor's employees will be entitled to compensation benefits regardless of whether the relationship of employer and employee exists between the principal and the contractor. (1929, c. 120, s. 19; 1941, c. 358, s. 1; 1945, c. 766; 1973, c. 1291, s. 10; 1979, c. 247, s. 2; 1987, c. 729, s. 4; 1989, c. 637; 1991, c. 703, s. 7; 1993 (Reg. Sess., 1994), c. 679, s. 10.6; 1995, c. 517, s. 36; 1995 (Reg. Sess., 1996), c. 555, s. 1; 2013-413, s. 13(c).)

§ 97-19.1. Truck, tractor, or truck tractor trailer driver's status as employee or independent contractor.

(a) An individual in the interstate or intrastate carrier industry who operates a truck, tractor, or truck tractor trailer licensed by a governmental motor vehicle regulatory agency may be an employee or an independent contractor under this Article dependent upon the application of the common law test for determining employment status.

Any principal contractor, intermediate contractor, or subcontractor, irrespective of whether such contractor regularly employs three or more employees, who contracts with an individual in the interstate or intrastate carrier industry who operates a truck, tractor, or truck tractor trailer licensed by the United States Department of Transportation and who has not secured the payment of compensation in the manner provided for employers set forth in G.S. 97-93 for himself personally and for his employees and subcontractors, if any, shall be liable as an employer under this Article for the payment of compensation and other benefits on account of the injury or death of the independent contractor and his employees or subcontractors due to an accident arising out of and in the course of the performance of the work covered by such contract.

(b) Notwithstanding subsection (a) of this section, a principal contractor, intermediate contractor, or subcontractor shall not be liable as an employer under this Article for the payment of compensation on account of the injury or death of the independent contractor if the principal contractor, intermediate contractor, or subcontractor (i) contracts with an independent contractor who is an individual licensed by the United States Department of Transportation and (ii) the independent contractor personally is operating the vehicle solely pursuant to that license.

(c)   The principal contractor, intermediate contractor, or subcontractor may insure any and all of his independent contractors and their employees or subcontractors in a blanket policy, and when insured, the independent contractors, subcontractors, and employees will be entitled to compensation benefits under the blanket policy.

A principal contractor, intermediate contractor, or subcontractor may include in the governing contract with an independent contractor in the interstate or intrastate carrier industry who operates a truck, tractor, or truck tractor trailer licensed by a governmental motor vehicle regulatory agency an agreement for the independent contractor to reimburse the cost of covering that independent contractor under the principal contractor's, intermediate contractor's, or subcontractor's coverage of his business. (2003-235, s. 1; 2006-26, s. 1; 2006-259, s. 19.)

§ 97-20. Priority of compensation claims against assets of employer.

All rights of compensation granted by this Article shall have the same preference or priority for the whole thereof against the assets of the employer as is allowed by law for any unpaid wages for labor. (1929, c. 120, s. 20.)

§ 97-21. Claims unassignable and exempt from taxes and debts; agreement of employee to contribute to premium or waive right to compensation void; unlawful deduction by employer.

No claim for compensation under this Article shall be assignable, and all compensation and claims therefor shall be exempt from all claims of creditors and from taxes.

No agreement by an employee to pay any portion of premium paid by his employer to a carrier or to contribute to a benefit fund or department maintained by such employer for the purpose of providing compensation or medical services and supplies as required by this Article shall be valid, and any employer who makes a deduction for such purpose from the pay of any employee entitled to the benefits of this Article shall be guilty of a Class 3 misdemeanor and upon conviction thereof shall be punished only by a fine of not more than five hundred dollars ($500.00). No agreement by an employee to waive his right to compensation under this Chapter shall be valid. (1929, c. 120, s. 21; 1993, c. 539, s. 677; 1994, Ex. Sess., c. 24, s. 14(c).)

§ 97-22. Notice of accident to employer.

Every injured employee or his representative shall immediately on the occurrence of an accident, or as soon thereafter as practicable, give or cause to be given to the employer a written notice of the accident, and the employee shall not be entitled to physician's fees nor to any compensation which may have accrued under the terms of this Article prior to the giving of such notice, unless it can be shown that the employer, his agent or representative, had knowledge of the accident, or that the party required to give such notice had been prevented from doing so by reason of physical or mental incapacity, or the fraud or deceit of some third person; but no compensation shall be payable unless such written notice is given within 30 days after the occurrence of the accident or death, unless reasonable excuse is made to the satisfaction of the Industrial Commission for not giving such notice and the Commission is satisfied that the employer has not been prejudiced thereby. (1929, c. 120, s. 22.)

§ 97-23. What notice is to contain; defects no bar; notice personally or by registered letter or certified mail.

The notice provided in the foregoing section [G.S. 97-22] shall state in ordinary language the name and address of the employee, the time, place, nature, and cause of the accident, and of the resulting injury or death; and shall be signed by the employee or by a person on his behalf, or, in the event of his death, by any one or more of his dependents, or by a person in their behalf.

No defect or inaccuracy in the notice shall be a bar to compensation unless the employer shall prove that his interest was prejudiced thereby, and then only to such extent as the prejudice.

Said notice shall be given personally to the employer or any of his agents upon whom a summons in civil action may be served under the laws of the State, or may be sent by registered letter or certified mail addressed to the employer at his last known residence or place of business. (1929, c. 120, s. 23; 1959, c. 863, s. 1.)

§ 97-24. Right to compensation barred after two years; destruction of records.

(a)   The right to compensation under this Article shall be forever barred unless (i) a claim or memorandum of agreement as provided in G.S. 97-82 is filed with the Commission or the employee is paid compensation as provided under this Article within two years after the accident or (ii) a claim or memorandum of agreement as provided in G.S. 97-82 is filed with the Commission within two years after the last payment of medical compensation when no other compensation has been paid and when the employer's liability has not otherwise been established under this Article. The provisions of this subsection shall not limit the time otherwise allowed for the filing of a claim for compensation for occupational disease in G.S. 97-58, but in no event shall the time for filing a claim for compensation for occupational disease be less than the times provided herein for filing a claim for an injury by accident.

(b)   If any claim for compensation is hereafter made upon the theory that such claim or the injury upon which said claim is based is within the jurisdiction of the Industrial Commission under the provisions of this Article, and if the Commission, or the appellate courts on appeal, shall adjudge that such claim is not within the Article, the claimant, or if he dies, his personal representative, shall have one year after the rendition of a final judgment in the case within which to commence an action at law.

(c)   When all claims and reports required by this Article have been filed, and the cases and records of which they are a part have been closed by proper reports, receipts, awards or orders, these records, may after five years in the discretion of the Commission, with and by the authorization and approval of the Department of Cultural Resources, be destroyed by burning or otherwise. (1929, c. 120, s. 24; 1933, c. 449, s. 2; 1945, c. 766; 1955, c. 1026, s. 12; 1973, c. 476, s. 48; c. 1060, s. 1; 1991, c. 703, s. 8; 1993 (Reg. Sess., 1994), c. 679, s. 3.4.)

§ 97-25. Medical treatment and supplies.

(a)   Medical compensation shall be provided by the employer.

(b)   Upon the written request of the employee to the employer, the employer may agree to authorize and pay for a second opinion examination with a duly qualified physician licensed to practice in North Carolina, or licensed in another state if agreed to by the parties or ordered by the Commission. If, within 14 calendar days of the receipt of the written request, the request is denied or the parties, in good faith, are unable to agree upon a health care provider to perform a second opinion examination, the employee may request that the Industrial Commission order a second opinion examination. The expense thereof shall be borne by the employer upon the same terms and conditions as provided in this section for medical compensation.

(c)   Provided, however, if the employee so desires, an injured employee may select a health care provider of the employee's own choosing to attend, prescribe, and assume the care and charge of the employee's case subject to the approval of the Industrial Commission. In addition, in case of a controversy arising between the employer and the employee, the Industrial Commission may order necessary treatment. In order for the Commission to grant an employee's request to change treatment or health care provider, the employee must show by a preponderance of the evidence that the change is reasonably necessary to effect a cure, provide relief, or lessen the period of disability. When deciding whether to grant an employee's request to change treatment or health care provider, the Commission may disregard or give less weight to the opinion of a health care provider from whom the employee sought evaluation, diagnosis, or treatment before the employee first requested authorization in writing from the employer, insurer, or Commission.

(d)   The refusal of the employee to accept any medical compensation when ordered by the Industrial Commission shall bar the employee from further compensation until such refusal ceases, and no compensation shall at any time be paid for the period of suspension unless in the opinion of the Industrial Commission the circumstances justified the refusal. Any order issued by the Commission suspending compensation pursuant to G.S. 97-18.1 shall specify what action the employee should take to end the suspension and reinstate the compensation.

(e)   If in an emergency on account of the employer's failure to provide medical compensation, a physician other than provided by the employer is called to treat the injured employee, the reasonable cost of such service shall be paid by the employer if so ordered by the Industrial Commission.

(f) In claims subject to G.S. 97-18(b) and (d), a party may file an expedited, emergency, or other medical motion with the Office of the Chief Deputy Commissioner. The nonmoving party shall have the right to contest the motion. Motions and responses shall be submitted via electronic mail to the Commission, the opposing party and the opposing party's attorney, simultaneously. The Commission shall conduct an informal telephonic pretrial conference to determine if the motion warrants an expedited or emergency hearing. If the Commission determines that the motion does not warrant an expedited or emergency hearing, the motion shall be decided administratively within 60 days of the date the motion was filed pursuant to rules governing motions practices in contested cases. If the Commission determines that any party has acted unreasonably by initiating or objecting to a medical motion, the Commission may assess costs associated with any proceeding, including reasonable attorneys' fees and deposition costs, against the offending party.

(g) If the Commission determines that a medical motion should be expedited, each party shall be afforded an opportunity to state its position and to submit documentary evidence at an informal telephonic hearing. The medical motion shall contain documentation and support of the request, including the most relevant medical records and a representation that informal means of resolving the issue have been attempted in good faith, and the opposing parties' position, if known. The Commission shall determine whether deposition testimony of medical and other experts is necessary and if so shall order that the testimony be taken within 35 days of the date the motion is filed. For good cause shown, the Commission may reduce or enlarge the time to complete depositions of medical and other experts. Transcripts of depositions shall be expedited and paid for by the administrator, carrier, or employer. Transcripts shall be submitted electronically to the Commission within 40 days of the date the motion is filed unless the Commission has reduced or enlarged the time to complete the depositions. The Commission shall render a decision on the motion within five days of the date transcripts are due to the Commission.

(h) If the Commission determines that a medical motion is an emergency, the Commission shall make a determination on the motion within five days of receipt by the Commission of the medical motion. Motions requesting emergency medical relief shall contain the following:

(1) An explanation of the medical diagnosis and treatment recommendation of the health care provider that requires emergency attention.

(2) A specific statement detailing the time-sensitive nature of the request to include relevant dates and the potential for adverse consequences to the employee if the recommended treatment is not provided emergently.

(3) An explanation of opinions known and in the possession of the employee of additional medical or other relevant experts, independent medical examiners, and second opinion examiners.

(4) Documentation known and in the possession of the employee in support of the request, including relevant medical records.

(5) A representation that informal means of resolving the issue have been attempted. (1929, c. 120, s. 25; 1931, c. 274, s. 4; 1933, c. 506; 1955, c. 1026, s. 2; 1973, c. 520, s. 1; 1991, c. 703, s. 3; 1997-308, s. 1; 1999-150, s. 1; 2005-448, s. 6.2; 2011-287, s. 6; 2013-294, s. 4.)

§ 97-25.1. Limitation of duration of medical compensation.

The right to medical compensation shall terminate two years after the employer's last payment of medical or indemnity compensation unless, prior to the expiration of this period, either: (i) the employee files with the Commission an application for additional medical compensation which is thereafter approved by the Commission, or (ii) the Commission on its own motion orders additional medical compensation. If the Commission determines that there is a substantial risk of the necessity of future medical compensation, the Commission shall provide by order for payment of future necessary medical compensation. (1993 (Reg. Sess., 1994), c. 679, s. 2.5.)

§ 97-25.2. Managed care organizations.

The requirements of G.S. 97-25 may be satisfied by contracting with a managed care organization. Notwithstanding any other provision of this Article, if an employer or carrier contracts with a managed care organization for medical services pursuant to this Article, those employees who are covered by the contract with the managed care organization shall receive medical services for a condition for which the employer has accepted liability or authorized treatment under this Article in the manner prescribed by the contract and in accordance with the managed care organization's certificate of authority; provided that the contract complies with rules adopted by the Commission, consistent with this Article, governing managed care organizations. An employee must exhaust all dispute resolution procedures of a managed care organization before applying to the Commission for review of any issue related to medical services compensable under this Article. Once application to the Commission has been made, the employee shall be entitled to an examination by a duly qualified physician or surgeon in the same manner as provided by G.S. 97-27.

If an employee's medical services are provided through a managed care organization pursuant to this section, subject to the rules of the managed care organization, the employee shall select the attending physician from those physicians who are members of the managed care organization's panel, and may subsequently change attending physicians once within the group of physicians who are members of the managed care organization's panel without approval from the employer or insurer. Additional changes in the attending physician or any change to a physician or examination by a physician not a member of the insurer's managed care organization's panel shall only be made pursuant to the organization's contract or upon reasonable grounds by order of the Commission. (1993 (Reg. Sess., 1994), c. 679, s. 2.1.)

§ 97-25.3. Preauthorization.

(a) An insurer may require preauthorization for inpatient admission to a hospital, inpatient admission to a treatment center, and inpatient or outpatient surgery. The insurer's preauthorization requirement must adhere to the following standards:

(1) The insurer may require no more than 10 days advance notice of the inpatient admission or surgery.

(2) The insurer must respond to a request for preauthorization within two business days of the request.

(3) The insurer shall review the need for the inpatient admission or surgery and may require the employee to submit to an independent medical examination

as provided in G.S. 97-27(a). This examination must be completed and the insurer must make its determination on the request for preauthorization within seven days of the date of the request unless this time is extended by the Commission for good cause.

(4)   The insurer shall document its review findings and determination in writing and shall provide a copy of the findings and determination to the employee and the employee's attending physician, and, if applicable, to the hospital or treatment center.

(5)   The insurer shall authorize the inpatient admission or surgery when it requires the employee to submit to a medical examination as provided in G.S. 97-27(a) and the examining physician concurs with the original recommendation for the inpatient admission or surgery. The insurer shall also authorize the inpatient admission or surgery when the employee obtains a second opinion from a physician approved by the insurer or the Commission, and the second physician concurs with the original recommendation for the inpatient admission or surgery. However, the insurer shall not be required by this subdivision to authorize the inpatient admission or surgery if it denies liability under this Article for the particular medical condition for which the services are sought.

(6)   Except as provided in subsection (c) of this section, the insurer may reduce its reimbursement of the provider's eligible charges under this Article by up to fifty percent (50%) if the insurer has notified the provider in writing of its preauthorization requirement and the provider failed to timely obtain preauthorization. The employee shall not be liable for the balance of the charges.

(7)   The insurer shall adhere to all other procedures for preauthorization prescribed by the Commission.

(b)   An insurer may not impose a preauthorization requirement for the following:

(1)   Emergency services;

(2)   Services rendered in the diagnosis or treatment of an injury or illness for which the insurer has not admitted liability or authorized payment for treatment pursuant to this Article; and

(3) Services rendered in the diagnosis and treatment of a specific medical condition for which the insurer has not admitted liability or authorized payment for treatment although the insurer admits the employee has suffered a compensable injury or illness.

(c) The Commission may, upon reasonable grounds, upon the request of the employee or provider, authorize treatment for which preauthorization is otherwise required by this section but was not obtained if the Commission determines that the treatment is or was reasonably required to effect a cure or give relief.

(d) The Commission may adopt procedures governing the use of preauthorization requirements and expeditious review of preauthorization denials.

(e) A managed care organization may impose preauthorization requirements consistent with the provisions of Chapter 58 of the General Statutes.

(f) A provider that refuses to treat an employee for other than an emergency medical condition because preauthorization has not been obtained shall be immune from liability in any civil action for the refusal to treat the employee because of lack of preauthorization. (1993 (Reg. Sess., 1994), c. 679, s. 2.2.)

§ 97-25.4. Utilization guidelines for medical treatment.

(a) The Commission may adopt utilization rules and guidelines, consistent with this Article, for medical care and medical rehabilitation services, other than those services provided by managed care organizations pursuant to G.S. 97-25.2, including, but not limited to, necessary palliative care, physical therapy treatment, psychological therapy, chiropractic services, medical rehabilitation services, and attendant care. The Commission's rules and guidelines shall ensure that injured employees are provided the services and care intended by this Article and that medical costs are adequately contained. In developing the rules and guidelines, the Commission may consider, among other factors, the practice guidelines adopted by the boards and associations representing medical and rehabilitation professionals.

(b) Palliative care rules or guidelines adopted by the Commission may require that the provider (i) supply to the employer a treatment plan, including a schedule of measurable objectives, a projected termination date for treatment, and an estimated cost of services, and (ii) obtain preauthorization from the employer, not inconsistent with the provisions of G.S. 97-25.3. (1993 (Reg. Sess., 1994), c. 679, s. 2.4.)

§ 97-25.5. Utilization guidelines for vocational and other rehabilitation.

The Commission may adopt utilization rules and guidelines, consistent with this Article, for vocational rehabilitation services and other types of rehabilitation services. In developing the rules and guidelines, the Commission may consider, among other factors, the practice and treatment guidelines adopted by professional rehabilitation associations and organizations. (1993 (Reg. Sess., 1994), c. 679, s. 2.4.)

§ 97-25.6. Reasonable access to medical information.

(a) Notwithstanding any provision of G.S. 8-53 to the contrary, and because discovery is limited pursuant to G.S. 97-80, it is the policy of this State to protect the employee's right to a confidential physician-patient relationship while allowing the parties to have reasonable access to all relevant medical information, including medical records, reports, and information necessary to the fair and swift administration and resolution of workers' compensation claims, while limiting unnecessary communications with and administrative requests to health care providers.

(b) As used in this section, "relevant medical information" means any medical record, report, or information that is any of the following:

(1) Restricted to the particular evaluation, diagnosis, or treatment of the injury or disease for which compensation, including medical compensation, is sought.

(2) Reasonably related to the injury or disease for which the employee claims compensation.

(3) Related to an assessment of the employee's ability to return to work as a result of the particular injury or disease.

(c) Relevant medical information shall be requested and provided subject to the following provisions:

(1) Medical records. - An employer is entitled, without the express authorization of the employee, to obtain the employee's medical records containing relevant medical information from the employee's health care providers. In a claim in which the employer is not paying medical compensation to a health care provider from whom the medical records are sought, or in a claim denied pursuant to G.S. 97-18(c), the employer shall provide the employee with contemporaneous written notice of the request for medical records. Upon the request of the employee, the employer shall provide the employee with a copy of any records received in response to this request within 30 days of its receipt by the employer.

(2) Written communications with health care providers. - An employer may communicate with the employee's authorized health care provider in writing, without the express authorization of the employee, to obtain relevant medical information not available in the employee's medical records. The employer shall provide the employee with contemporaneous written notice of the written communication. The employer may request the following additional information:

a. The diagnosis of the employee's condition.

b. The appropriate course of treatment.

c. The anticipated time that the employee will be out of work.

d. The relationship, if any, of the employee's condition to the employment.

e. Work restrictions resulting from the condition, including whether the employee is able to return to the employee's employment with the employer of injury as provided in an attached job description.

f. The kind of work for which the employee may be eligible.

g. The anticipated time the employee will be restricted.

h. Any permanent impairment as a result of the condition.

The employer shall provide a copy of the health care provider's response to the employee within 10 business days of its receipt by the employer.

(3) Oral communications with health care providers. - An employer may communicate with the employee's authorized health care provider by oral communication to obtain relevant medical information not contained in the employee's medical records, not available through written communication, and not otherwise available to the employer, subject to the following:

a. The employer must give the employee prior notice of the purpose of the intended oral communication and an opportunity for the employee to participate in the oral communication at a mutually convenient time for the employer, employee, and health care provider.

b. The employer shall provide the employee with a summary of the communication with the health care provider within 10 business days of any oral communication in which the employee did not participate.

(d) Additional Information Submitted by the Employer. - Notwithstanding subsection (c) of this section, an employer may submit additional relevant medical information not already contained in the employee's medical records to the employee's authorized health care provider and may communicate in writing with the health care provider about the additional information in accordance with the following procedure:

(1) The employer shall first notify the employee in writing that the employer intends to communicate additional information about the employee to the employee's health care provider. The notice shall include the employer's proposed written communication to the health care provider and the additional information to be submitted.

(2) The employee shall have 10 business days from the postmark or verifiable facsimile or electronic mail either to consent or object to the employer's proposed written communication.

(3) Upon consent of the employee or in the absence of the employee's timely objection, the employer may submit the additional information directly to the health care provider.

(4) Upon making a timely objection, the employee may request a protective order to prevent the written communication, in which case the employer shall refrain from communicating with the health care provider until the Commission has ruled upon the employee's request. If the employee does not file with the Industrial Commission a request for a protective order within the time period set forth in subdivision (2) of subsection (d) of this section, the employer may submit the additional information directly to the health care provider. In deciding whether to allow the submission of additional information to the health care provider, in part or in whole, the Commission shall determine whether the proposed written communication and additional information are pertinent to and necessary for the fair and swift administration and resolution of the workers' compensation claim and whether there is an alternative method to discover the information. If the Industrial Commission determines that any party has acted unreasonably by initiating or objecting to the submission of additional information to the health care provider, the Commission may assess costs associated with any proceeding, including reasonable attorneys' fees and deposition costs, against the offending party.

(e) Any medical records or reports that reflect evaluation, diagnosis, or treatment of the particular injury or disease for which compensation is sought or are reasonably related to the injury or disease for which the employee seeks compensation that are in the possession of a party shall be furnished to the requesting party by the opposing party when requested in writing, except for records or reports generated by a retained expert.

(f) Upon motion by an employee or the health care provider from whom medical records, reports, or information are sought, or with whom oral communication is sought, or upon its own motion, for good cause shown, the Commission may make any order which justice requires to protect an employee, health care provider, or other person from unreasonable annoyance, embarrassment, oppression, or undue burden or expense.

(g) Other forms of communication with a health care provider may be authorized by any of the following:

(1) A valid written authorization voluntarily given and signed by the employee.

(2) An agreement of the parties.

(3)   An order of the Industrial Commission issued upon a showing that the information sought is necessary for the administration of the employee's claim and is not otherwise reasonably obtainable under this section or through other discovery authorized by the rules of the Commission.

(h)   The employer may communicate with the health care provider to request medical bills or a response to a pending written request, or about nonsubstantive administrative matters without the express authorization of the employee.

(i)   The Commission shall establish an appropriate fee to compensate health care providers for time spent communicating with the employer or employee. Each party shall bear its own costs for said communication.

(j)   No cause of action shall arise and no health care provider shall incur any liability as a result of the release of medical records, reports, or information pursuant to this Article.

(k)   For purposes of this section, the term "employer" means the employer, the employer's attorney, and the employer's insurance carrier or third-party administrator; and the term "employee" means the employee, legally appointed guardian, or any attorney representing the employee. (2005-448, s. 6.1; 2011-287, s. 7; 2012-135, s. 2.)

§ 97-26. Fees allowed for medical treatment; malpractice of physician.

(a)   Fee Schedule. - The Commission shall adopt by rule a schedule of maximum fees for medical compensation and shall periodically review the schedule and make revisions.

The fees adopted by the Commission in its schedule shall be adequate to ensure that (i) injured workers are provided the standard of services and care intended by this Chapter, (ii) providers are reimbursed reasonable fees for providing these services, and (iii) medical costs are adequately contained.

The Commission may consider any and all reimbursement systems and plans in establishing its fee schedule, including, but not limited to, the State Health Plan for Teachers and State Employees (hereinafter, "State Plan"), Blue Cross and Blue Shield, and any other private or governmental plans. The Commission may also consider any and all reimbursement methodologies, including, but not limited to, the use of current procedural terminology ("CPT") codes, diagnostic-related groupings ("DRGs"), per diem rates, capitated payments, and resource-based relative-value system ("RBRVS") payments. The Commission may consider statewide fee averages, geographical and community variations in provider costs, and any other factors affecting provider costs.

(b) Hospital Fees. - Each hospital subject to the provisions of this section shall be reimbursed the amount provided for in this section unless it has agreed under contract with the insurer, managed care organization, employer (or other payor obligated to reimburse for inpatient hospital services rendered under this Chapter) to accept a different amount or reimbursement methodology.

The explanation of the fee schedule change that is published pursuant to G.S. 150B-21.2(c)(2) shall include a summary of the data and calculations on which the fee schedule rate is based.

A hospital's itemized charges on the UB-92 claim form for workers' compensation services shall be the same as itemized charges for like services for all other payers.

(c) Maximum Reimbursement for Providers Under Subsection (a). - Each health care provider subject to the provisions of subsection (a) of this section shall be reimbursed the amount specified under the fee schedule unless the provider has agreed under contract with the insurer or managed care organization to accept a different amount or reimbursement methodology. In any instance in which neither the fee schedule nor a contractual fee applies, the maximum reimbursement to which a provider under subsection (a) is entitled under this Article is the usual, customary, and reasonable charge for the service or treatment rendered. In no event shall a provider under subsection (a) charge more than its usual fee for the service or treatment rendered.

(d) Information to Commission. - Each health care provider seeking reimbursement for medical compensation under this Article shall provide the Commission information requested by the Commission for the development of fee schedules and the determination of appropriate reimbursement.

(e) When Charges Submitted. - Health care providers shall submit charges to the insurer or managed care organization within 30 days of treatment, within 30 days after the end of the month during which multiple treatments were provided, or within such other reasonable period of time as allowed by the

Commission. If an insurer or managed care organization disputes a portion of a health care provider's bill, it shall pay the uncontested portion of the bill and shall resolve disputes regarding the balance of the charges in accordance with this Article or its contractual arrangement.

(f) Repeating Diagnostic Tests. - A health care provider shall not authorize a diagnostic test previously conducted by another provider, unless the health care provider has reasonable grounds to believe a change in patient condition may have occurred or the quality of the prior test is doubted. The Commission may adopt rules establishing reasonable requirements for reports and records to be made available to other health care providers to prevent unnecessary duplication of tests and examinations. A health care provider that violates this subsection shall not be reimbursed for the costs associated with administering or analyzing the test.

(g) Direct Reimbursement. - The Commission may adopt rules to allow insurers and managed care organizations to review and reimburse charges for medical compensation without submitting the charges to the Commission for review and approval.

(g1) Administrative Simplification. - The applicable administrative standards for code sets, identifiers, formats, and electronic transactions to be used in processing electronic medical bills under this Article shall comply with 45 C.F.R. § 162. The Commission shall adopt rules to require electronic medical billing and payment processes, to standardize the necessary medical documentation for billing adjudication, to provide for effective dates and compliance, and for further implementation of this subsection.

(h) Malpractice. - The employer shall not be liable in damages for malpractice by a physician or surgeon furnished by him pursuant to the provisions of this section, but the consequences of any such malpractice shall be deemed part of the injury resulting from the accident, and shall be compensated for as such.

(i) Resolution of Dispute. - The employee or health care provider may apply to the Commission by motion or for a hearing to resolve any dispute regarding the payment of charges for medical compensation in accordance with this Article. (1929, c. 120, s. 26; 1955, c. 1026, s. 3; 1993 (Reg. Sess., 1994), c. 679, s. 2.3; 1995 (Reg. Sess., 1996), c. 548, s. 1; 1997-145, s. 1; 2001-410, s. 3; 2001-413, s. 8.2(a); 2005-448, s. 5; 2007-323, s. 28.22A(o); 2007-345, s. 12; 2011-287, s. 8; 2012-135, s. 3; 2013-410, s. 33(b).)

§ 97-26.1. Fees for medical records and reports; expert witnesses; communications with health care providers.

The Commission may establish maximum fees for the following when related to a claim under this Article: (i) the searching, handling, copying, and mailing of medical records, (ii) the preparation of medical reports and narratives, (iii) the presentation of expert testimony in a Commission proceeding, and (iv) the time spent communicating with the employer or employee pursuant to G.S. 97-25.6(i). (1993 (Reg. Sess., 1994), c. 679, s. 5.6; 2012-135, s. 4.)

§ 97-27. Medical examination; facts not privileged; refusal to be examined suspends compensation; other medical opinions; autopsy.

(a)   After an injury, and so long as the employee claims compensation, the employee, if so requested by his or her employer or ordered by the Industrial Commission, shall submit to independent medical examinations, at reasonable times and places, by a duly qualified physician who is licensed and practicing in North Carolina and is designated and paid by the employer or the Industrial Commission, even if the employee's claim has been denied pursuant to G.S. 97-18(c). The independent medical examination shall be subject to the following provisions:

(1)   The injured employee has the right to have present at the independent medical examination any physician provided and paid by the employee.

(2)   Notwithstanding the provisions of G.S. 8-53, no fact communicated to or otherwise learned by any physician who may have attended or examined the employee, or who may have been present at any examination, shall be privileged with respect to a claim before the Industrial Commission.

(3)   Notwithstanding the provisions of G.S. 97-25.6 to the contrary, an employer or its agent shall be allowed to openly communicate either orally or in writing with an independent medical examiner chosen by the employer regardless of whether the examiner physically examined the employee.

(4)   If the examiner physically examined the employee, the employer must produce the examiner's report to the employee within 10 business days of receipt by the employer, along with a copy of all documents and written

communication sent to the independent medical examiner pertaining to the employee.

(5) If the employee refuses to submit to or in any way obstructs an independent medical examination requested and provided by the employer, the employee's right to compensation and to take or prosecute any proceedings under this Article shall be suspended pursuant to G.S. 97-18.1 until the refusal or objection ceases, and no compensation shall at any time be payable for the period of obstruction, unless in the opinion of the Industrial Commission the circumstances justify the refusal or obstruction. When the employer seeks to suspend compensation under this subdivision, it shall not be necessary for the employer to have first obtained an order compelling the employee to submit to the proposed independent medical examination. Any order issued by the Commission suspending compensation pursuant to G.S. 97-18.1 shall specify what action the employee should take to end the suspension and reinstate the compensation.

(b) In any case arising under this Article in which the employee is dissatisfied with the percentage of permanent disability as provided by G.S. 97-31 and determined by the authorized health care provider, the employee is entitled to have another examination solely on the percentage of permanent disability provided by a duly qualified physician of the employee's choosing who is licensed to practice in North Carolina, or licensed in another state if agreed to by the parties or ordered by the Commission, and designated by the employee. That physician shall be paid by the employer in the same manner as health care providers designated by the employer or the Industrial Commission are paid. The Industrial Commission must either disregard or give less weight to the opinions of the duly qualified physician chosen by the employee pursuant to this subsection on issues outside the scope of the G.S. 97-27(b) examination. No fact that is communicated to or otherwise learned by any physician who attended or examined the employee, or who was present at any examination, shall be privileged with respect to a claim before the Industrial Commission. Provided, however, that all travel expenses incurred in obtaining the examination shall be paid by the employee.

(c) The employer, or the Industrial Commission, has the right in any case of death to require an autopsy at its expense. (1929, c. 120, s. 27; 1959, c. 732; 1969, c. 135; 1973, c. 520, s. 2; 1977, c. 511; 1991, c. 636, s. 3; 2011-287, s. 9; 2012-135, s. 5.)

§ 97-28. Seven-day waiting period; exceptions.

No compensation, as defined in G.S. 97-2(11), shall be allowed for the first seven calendar days of disability resulting from an injury, except the benefits provided for in G.S. 97-25. Provided however, that in the case the injury results in disability of more than 21 days, the compensation shall be allowed from the date of the disability. Nothing in this section shall prevent an employer from allowing an employee to use paid sick leave, vacation or annual leave, or disability benefits provided directly by the employer during the first seven calendar days of disability. (1929, c. 120, s. 28; 1983, c. 599; 1987, c. 729, s. 5.)

§ 97-29. Rates and duration of compensation for total incapacity.

(a) When an employee qualifies for total disability, the employer shall pay or cause to be paid, as hereinafter provided by subsections (b) through (d) of this section, to the injured employee a weekly compensation equal to sixty-six and two-thirds percent (662/3%) of his average weekly wages, but not more than the amount established annually to be effective January 1 as provided herein, nor less than thirty dollars ($30.00) per week.

(b) When a claim is compensable pursuant to G.S. 97-18(b), paid without prejudice pursuant to G.S. 97-18(d), agreed by the parties pursuant to G.S. 97-82, or when a claim has been deemed compensable following a hearing pursuant to G.S. 97-84, the employee qualifies for temporary total disability subject to the limitations noted herein. The employee shall not be entitled to compensation pursuant to this subsection greater than 500 weeks from the date of first disability unless the employee qualifies for extended compensation under subsection (c) of this section.

(c) An employee may qualify for extended compensation in excess of the 500-week limitation on temporary total disability as described in subsection (b) of this section only if (i) at the time the employee makes application to the Commission to exceed the 500-week limitation on temporary total disability as described in subsection (b) of this section, 425 weeks have passed since the date of first disability and (ii) pursuant to the provisions of G.S. 97-84, unless agreed to by the parties, the employee shall prove by a preponderance of the evidence that the employee has sustained a total loss of wage-earning capacity. If an employee makes application for extended compensation pursuant to this subsection and is awarded extended compensation by the Commission, the award shall not be stayed pursuant to G.S. 97-85 or G.S. 97-86 until the full Commission or an appellate court determines otherwise. Upon its own motion or upon the application of any party in interest, the Industrial Commission may review an award for extended compensation in excess of the 500-week limitation on temporary total disability described in subsection (b) of this section, and, on such review, may make an award ending or continuing extended compensation. When reviewing a prior award to determine if the employee remains entitled to extended compensation, the Commission shall determine if the employer has proven by a preponderance of the evidence that the employee no longer has a total loss of wage-earning capacity. When an employee is receiving full retirement benefits under section 202(a) of the Social Security Act, after attainment of retirement age, as defined in section 216(l) of the Social Security Act, the employer may reduce the extended compensation by one hundred percent (100%) of the employee's retirement benefit. The reduction shall consist of the employee's primary benefit paid pursuant to section 202(a) of the Social Security Act but shall not include any dependent or auxiliary benefits paid pursuant to any other section of the Social Security Act, if any, or any cost-of-living increases in benefits made pursuant to section 215(i) of the Social Security Act.

(d) An injured employee may qualify for permanent total disability only if the employee has one or more of the following physical or mental limitations resulting from the injury:

(1) The loss of both hands, both arms, both feet, both legs, both eyes, or any two thereof, as provided by G.S. 97-31(17).

(2) Spinal injury involving severe paralysis of both arms, both legs, or the trunk.

(3) Severe brain or closed head injury as evidenced by severe and permanent:

a. Sensory or motor disturbances;

b. Communication disturbances;

c. Complex integrated disturbances of cerebral function; or

d. Neurological disorders.

(4) Second-degree or third-degree burns to thirty-three percent (33%) or more of the total body surface.

An employee who qualifies for permanent total disability pursuant to this subsection shall be entitled to compensation, including medical compensation, during the lifetime of the injured employee, unless the employer shows by a preponderance of the evidence that the employee is capable of returning to suitable employment as defined in G.S. 97-2(22). Provided, however, the termination or suspension of compensation because the employee is capable of returning to suitable employment as defined in G.S. 97-2(22) does not affect the employee's entitlement to medical compensation. An employee who qualifies for permanent total disability under subdivision (1) of this subsection is entitled to lifetime compensation, including medical compensation, regardless of whether or not the employee has returned to work in any capacity. In no other case shall an employee be eligible for lifetime compensation for permanent total disability.

(e) An employee shall not be entitled to benefits under this section or G.S. 97-30 and G.S. 97-31 at the same time.

(f) Where an employee can show entitlement to compensation pursuant to this section or G.S. 97-30 and a specific physical impairment pursuant to G.S. 97-31, the employee shall not collect benefits concurrently pursuant to both this section or G.S. 97-30 and G.S. 97-31, but rather is entitled to select the statutory compensation which provides the more favorable remedy.

(g) The weekly compensation payment for members of the North Carolina National Guard and the North Carolina State Defense Militia shall be the maximum amount established annually in accordance with subsection (i) of this section per week as fixed herein. The weekly compensation payment for deputy sheriffs, or those acting in the capacity of deputy sheriffs, who serve upon a fee basis, shall be thirty dollars ($30.00) a week as fixed herein.

(h) An officer or member of the State Highway Patrol shall not be awarded any weekly compensation under the provisions of this section for the first two years of any incapacity resulting from an injury by accident arising out of and in the course of the performance by him of his official duties if, during such incapacity, he continues to be an officer or member of the State Highway Patrol, but he shall be awarded any other benefits to which he may be entitled under the provisions of this Article.

(i) Notwithstanding any other provision of this Article, on July 1 of each year, a maximum weekly benefit amount shall be computed. The amount of this maximum weekly benefit shall be derived by obtaining the average weekly insured wage, as defined in G.S. 96-1, by multiplying such average weekly insured wage by 1.10, and by rounding such figure to its nearest multiple of two dollars ($2.00), and this said maximum weekly benefit shall be applicable to all injuries and claims arising on and after January 1 following such computation. Such maximum weekly benefit shall apply to all provisions of this Chapter and shall be adjusted July 1 and effective January 1 of each year as herein provided.

(j) If death results from the injury or occupational disease, then the employer shall pay compensation in accordance with the provisions of G.S. 97-38. (1929, c. 120, s. 29; 1939, c. 277, s. 1; 1943, c. 502, s. 3; c. 543; c. 672, s. 2; 1945, c. 766; 1947, c. 823; 1949, c. 1017; 1951, c. 70, s. 1; 1953, c. 1135, s. 1; c. 1195, s. 2; 1955, c. 1026, s. 5; 1957, c. 1217; 1963, c. 604, s. 1; 1967, c. 84, s. 1; 1969, c. 143, s. 1; 1971, c. 281, s. 1; c. 321, s. 1; 1973, c. 515, s. 1; c. 759, s. 1; c. 1103, s. 1; c. 1308, ss. 1, 2; 1975, c. 284, s. 4; 1979, c. 244; 1981, c. 276, s. 2; c. 378, s. 1; c. 421, s. 3; c. 521, s. 2; c. 920, s. 1; 1987, c. 729, s. 6; 1991, c. 703, s. 4; 1999-456, s. 33(d); 2009-281, s. 1; 2011-287, s. 10; 2012-135, s. 6; 2013-2, s. 9(e); 2013-224, s. 19; 2013-410, s. 19.)

§ 97-29.1. Increase in payments in cases for total and permanent disability occurring prior to July 1, 1973.

In all cases of total and permanent disability occurring prior to July 1, 1973, weekly compensation payments shall be increased effective July 1, 1977, to an amount computed by multiplying the number of calendar years prior to July 1, 1973, that the case arose by five percent (5%). Payments made by the employer or its insurance carrier by reason of such increase in weekly benefits may be deducted by such employer or insurance carrier from the tax levied on such employer or carrier pursuant to G.S. 105-228.5 or G.S. 97-100. Every employer or insurance carrier claiming such deduction or credit shall verify such claim to the Secretary of Revenue or the Industrial Commission by affidavit or by such other method as may be prescribed by the Secretary of Revenue or the Industrial Commission. (1977, c. 651.)

§ 97-30. Partial incapacity.

Except as otherwise provided in G.S. 97-31, where the incapacity for work resulting from the injury is partial, the employer shall pay, or cause to be paid, as hereinafter provided, to the injured employee during such disability, a weekly compensation equal to sixty-six and two-thirds percent (66 2/3%) of the difference between his average weekly wages before the injury and the average weekly wages which he is able to earn thereafter, but not more than the amount established annually to be effective January 1 as provided in G.S. 97-29 a week, and in no case shall the employee receive more than 500 weeks of payments under this section. Any weeks of payments made pursuant to G.S. 97-29 shall be deducted from the 500 weeks of payments available under this section. An officer or member of the State Highway Patrol shall not be awarded any weekly compensation under the provisions of this section for the first two years of any incapacity resulting from an injury by accident arising out of and in the course of the performance by him of his official duties if, during such incapacity, he continues to be an officer or member of the State Highway Patrol, but he shall be awarded any other benefits to which he may be entitled under the provisions of this Article. (1929, c. 120, s. 30; 1943, c. 502, s. 4; 1947, c. 823; 1951, c. 70, s. 2; 1953, c. 1195, s. 3; 1955, c. 1026, s. 6; 1957, c. 1217; 1963, c. 604, s. 2; 1967, c. 84, s. 2; 1969, c. 143, s. 2; 1971, c. 281, s. 2; 1973, c. 515, s. 2; c. 759, s. 2; 1981, c. 276, s. 1; 2011-287, s. 11.)

§ 97-31. Schedule of injuries; rate and period of compensation.

In cases included by the following schedule the compensation in each case shall be paid for disability during the healing period and in addition the disability shall be deemed to continue for the period specified, and shall be in lieu of all other compensation, including disfigurement, to wit:

(1)   For the loss of a thumb, sixty-six and two-thirds percent (66 2/3%) of the average weekly wages during 75 weeks.

(2)   For the loss of a first finger, commonly called the index finger, sixty-six and two-thirds percent (66 2/3%) of the average weekly wages during 45 weeks.

(3)   For the loss of a second finger, sixty-six and two-thirds percent (66 2/3%) of the average weekly wages during 40 weeks.

(4) For the loss of a third finger, sixty-six and two-thirds percent (66 2/3%) of the average weekly wages during 25 weeks.

(5) For the loss of a fourth finger, commonly called the little finger, sixty-six and two-thirds percent (66 2/3%) of the average weekly wages during 20 weeks.

(6) The loss of the first phalange of the thumb or any finger shall be considered to be equal to the loss of one half of such thumb or finger, and the compensation shall be for one half of the periods of time above specified.

(7) The loss of more than one phalange shall be considered the loss of the entire finger or thumb: Provided, however, that in no case shall the amount received for more than one finger exceed the amount provided in this schedule for the loss of a hand.

(8) For the loss of a great toe, sixty-six and two-thirds percent (66 2/3%) of the average weekly wages during 35 weeks.

(9) For the loss of one of the toes other than a great toe, sixty-six and two-thirds percent (66 2/3%) of the average weekly wages during 10 weeks.

(10) The loss of the first phalange of any toe shall be considered to be equal to the loss of one half of such toe, and the compensation shall be for one half of the periods of time above specified.

(11) The loss of more than one phalange shall be considered as the loss of the entire toe.

(12) For the loss of a hand, sixty-six and two-thirds percent (66 2/3%) of the average weekly wages during 200 weeks.

(13) For the loss of an arm, sixty-six and two-thirds percent (66 2/3%) of the average weekly wages during 240 weeks.

(14) For the loss of a foot, sixty-six and two-thirds percent (66 2/3%) of the average weekly wages during 144 weeks.

(15) For the loss of a leg, sixty-six and two-thirds percent (66 2/3%) of the average weekly wages during 200 weeks.

(16) For the loss of an eye, sixty-six and two-thirds percent (66 2/3%) of the average weekly wages during 120 weeks.

(17) The loss of both hands, or both arms, or both feet, or both legs, or both eyes, or any two thereof, shall constitute total and permanent disability, to be compensated according to the provisions of G.S. 97-29. The employee shall have a vested right in a minimum amount of compensation for the total number of weeks of benefits provided under this section for each member involved. When an employee dies from any cause other than the injury for which he is entitled to compensation, payment of the minimum amount of compensation shall be payable as provided in G.S. 97-37.

(18) For the complete loss of hearing in one ear, sixty-six and two-thirds percent (66 2/3%) of the average weekly wages during 70 weeks; for the complete loss of hearing in both ears, sixty-six and two-thirds percent (66 2/3%) of the average weekly wages during 150 weeks.

(19) Total loss of use of a member or loss of vision of an eye shall be considered as equivalent to the loss of such member or eye. The compensation for partial loss of or for partial loss of use of a member or for partial loss of vision of an eye or for partial loss of hearing shall be such proportion of the periods of payment above provided for total loss as such partial loss bears to total loss, except that in cases where there is eighty-five per centum (85%), or more, loss of vision in any eye, this shall be deemed "industrial blindness" and compensated as for total loss of vision of such eye.

(20) The weekly compensation payments referred to in this section shall all be subject to the same limitations as to maximum and minimum as set out in G.S. 97-29.

(21) In case of serious facial or head disfigurement, the Industrial Commission shall award proper and equitable compensation not to exceed twenty thousand dollars ($20,000). In case of enucleation where an artificial eye cannot be fitted and used, the Industrial Commission may award compensation as for serious facial disfigurement.

(22) In case of serious bodily disfigurement for which no compensation is payable under any other subdivision of this section, but excluding the disfigurement resulting from permanent loss or permanent partial loss of use of any member of the body for which compensation is fixed in the schedule

contained in this section, the Industrial Commission may award proper and equitable compensation not to exceed ten thousand dollars ($10,000).

(23) For the total loss of use of the back, sixty-six and two-thirds percent (66 2/3%) of the average weekly wages during 300 weeks. The compensation for partial loss of use of the back shall be such proportion of the periods of payment herein provided for total loss as such partial loss bears to total loss, except that in cases where there is seventy-five per centum (75%) or more loss of use of the back, in which event the injured employee shall be deemed to have suffered "total industrial disability" and compensated as for total loss of use of the back.

(24) In case of the loss of or permanent injury to any important external or internal organ or part of the body for which no compensation is payable under any other subdivision of this section, the Industrial Commission may award proper and equitable compensation not to exceed twenty thousand dollars ($20,000). (1929, c. 120, s. 31; 1931, c. 164; 1943, c. 502, s. 2; 1955, c. 1026, s. 7; 1957, c. 1221; c. 1396, ss. 2, 3; 1963, c. 424, ss. 1, 2; 1967, c. 84, s. 3; 1969, c. 143, s. 3; 1973, c. 515, s. 3; c. 759, s. 3; c. 761, ss. 1, 2; 1975, c. 164, s. 1; 1977, c. 892, s. 1; 1979, c. 250; 1987, c. 729, ss. 7, 8.)

§ 97-31.1. Effective date of legislative changes in benefits.

Every act of the General Assembly that changes the benefits enumerated in this Chapter shall become law no later than June 1 and shall have an effective date of no earlier than January 1 of the year after which it is ratified. (1981, c. 521, s. 3; 1995, c. 20, s. 11.)

§ 97-32. Refusal of injured employee to accept suitable employment as suspending compensation.

If an injured employee refuses suitable employment as defined by G.S. 97-2(22), the employee shall not be entitled to any compensation at any time during the continuance of such refusal, unless in the opinion of the Industrial Commission such refusal was justified. Any order issued by the Commission suspending compensation pursuant to G.S. 97-18.1 on the ground of an unjustified refusal of an offer of suitable employment shall specify what actions the employee should take to end the suspension and reinstate the compensation. Nothing in this Article prohibits an employer from contacting the employee directly about returning to suitable employment with contemporaneous notice to the employee's counsel, if any. (1929, c. 120, s. 32; 2011-287, s. 12.)

§ 97-32.1. Trial return to work.

Notwithstanding the provisions of G.S. 97-32, an employee may attempt a trial return to work for a period not to exceed nine months. During a trial return to work period, the employee shall be paid any compensation which may be owed for partial disability pursuant to G.S. 97-30. If the trial return to work is unsuccessful, the employee's right to continuing compensation under G.S. 97-29 shall be unimpaired unless terminated or suspended thereafter pursuant to the provisions of this Article. (1993 (Reg. Sess., 1994), c. 679, s. 4.1.)

§ 97-32.2. Vocational rehabilitation.

(a)   In a compensable claim, the employer may engage vocational rehabilitation services at any point during a claim, regardless of whether the employee has reached maximum medical improvement to include, among other services, a one-time assessment of the employee's vocational potential, except vocational rehabilitation services may not be required if the employee is receiving benefits pursuant to G.S. 97-29(c) or G.S. 97-29(d). If the employee (i) has not returned to work or (ii) has returned to work earning less than seventy-five percent (75%) of the employee's average weekly wages and is receiving benefits pursuant to G.S. 97-30, the employee may request vocational rehabilitation services, including education and retraining in the North Carolina community college or university systems so long as the education and retraining are reasonably likely to substantially increase the employee's wage-earning capacity following completion of the education or retraining program. Provided, however, the seventy-five percent (75%) threshold is for the purposes of qualification for vocational rehabilitation benefits only and shall not impact a decision as to whether a job is suitable per G.S. 97-2(22). The expense of vocational rehabilitation services provided pursuant to this section shall be borne by the employer in the same manner as medical compensation.

(b) Vocational rehabilitation services shall be provided by either a qualified or conditional rehabilitation professional approved by the Industrial Commission. Unless the parties mutually agree to a vocational rehabilitation professional, the employer may make the initial selection. At any point during the vocational rehabilitation process, either party may request that the Industrial Commission order a change of vocational rehabilitation professional for good cause.

(c) Vocational rehabilitation services shall include a vocational assessment and the formulation of an individualized written rehabilitation plan with the goal of substantially increasing the employee's wage-earning capacity, and subject to the following provisions:

(1) When performing a vocational assessment, the vocational rehabilitation professional should evaluate the employee's medical and vocational circumstances, the employee's expectations and specific requests for vocational training, benefits expected from vocational services, and other information significant to the employee's employment potential. The assessment should also involve a face-to-face interview between the employee and the vocational rehabilitation professional to identify the specific type and sequence of appropriate services. If, at any point during vocational rehabilitation services, the vocational rehabilitation professional determines that the employee will not benefit from vocational rehabilitation services, the employer may terminate said services unless the Commission orders otherwise.

(2) Following assessment, and after receiving input from the employee, the vocational rehabilitation professional shall draft an individualized written rehabilitation plan. The plan should be individually tailored to the employee based on the employee's education, skills, experience, and aptitudes, with appropriate recommendations for vocational services, which may include appropriate retraining, education, or job placement. The plan may be changed or updated by mutual consent at any time during rehabilitation services. A written plan is not necessary if the vocational rehabilitation professional has been retained to perform a one-time assessment.

(d) Specific vocational rehabilitation services may include, but are not limited to, vocational assessment, vocational exploration, sheltered workshop or community supported employment training, counseling, job analysis, job modification, job development and placement, labor market survey, vocational or psychometric testing, analysis of transferable skills, work adjustment counseling, job seeking skills training, on-the-job training, or training or education through the North Carolina community college or university systems.

(e) Vocational rehabilitation services may be terminated by agreement of the parties or by order of the Commission.

(f) Job placement activities may commence after completion of an individualized written rehabilitation plan. Return-to-work options should be considered, with order of priority given to returning the employee to suitable employment with the current employer, returning the employee to suitable employment with a new employer, and, if appropriate, formal education or vocational training to prepare the employee for suitable employment with the current employer or a new employer.

(g) The refusal of the employee to accept or cooperate with vocational rehabilitation services when ordered by the Industrial Commission shall bar the employee from further compensation until such refusal ceases, and no compensation shall at any time be paid for the period of suspension, unless in the opinion of the Industrial Commission the circumstances justified the refusal. Any order issued by the Commission suspending compensation per G.S. 97-18.1 shall specify what action the employee should take to end the suspension and reinstate the compensation. (2011-287, s. 13; 2012-135, s. 7.)

§ 97-33. Prorating in event of earlier disability or injury.

If any employee is an epileptic, or has a permanent disability or has sustained a permanent injury in service in the United States Army or Navy, or in another employment other than that in which he received a subsequent permanent injury by accident, such as specified in G.S. 97-31, he shall be entitled to compensation only for the degree of disability which would have resulted from the later accident if the earlier disability or injury had not existed. (1929, c. 120, s. 33; 1975, c. 832; 2011-183, s. 127(b).)

§ 97-34. Employee receiving an injury when being compensated for former injury.

If an employee receives an injury for which compensation is payable, while he is still receiving or entitled to compensation for a previous injury in the same employment, he shall not at the same time be entitled to compensation for both injuries, unless the later injury be a permanent injury such as specified in G.S.

97-31; but he shall be entitled to compensation for that injury and from the time of that injury which will cover the longest period and the largest amount payable under this Article. (1929, c. 120, s. 34.)

§ 97-35. How compensation paid for two injuries; employer liable only for subsequent injury.

If any employee receives a permanent injury as specified in G.S. 97-31 after having sustained another permanent injury in the same employment, he shall be entitled to compensation for both injuries, but the total compensation shall be paid by extending the period and not by increasing the amount of weekly compensation, and in no case exceeding 500 weeks.

If an employee has previously incurred permanent partial disability through the loss of a hand, arm, foot, leg, or eye, and by subsequent accident incurs total permanent disability through the loss of another member, the employer's liability is for the subsequent injury only. (1929, c. 120, s. 35.)

§ 97-36. Accidents taking place outside State; employees receiving compensation from another state.

Where an accident happens while the employee is employed elsewhere than in this State and the accident is one which would entitle him or his dependents or next of kin to compensation if it had happened in this State, then the employee or his dependents or next of kin shall be entitled to compensation (i) if the contract of employment was made in this State, (ii) if the employer's principal place of business is in this State, or (iii) if the employee's principal place of employment is within this State; provided, however, that if an employee or his dependents or next of kin shall receive compensation or damages under the laws of any other state nothing herein contained shall be construed so as to permit a total compensation for the same injury greater than is provided for in this Article. (1929, c. 120, s. 36; 1963, c. 450, s. 2; 1967, c. 1229, s. 3; 1973, c. 1059; 1991, c. 284.)

§ 97-37. Where injured employee dies before total compensation is paid.

When an employee receives or is entitled to compensation under this Article for an injury covered by G.S. 97-31 and dies from any other cause than the injury for which he was entitled to compensation, payment of the unpaid balance of compensation shall be made: First, to the surviving whole dependents; second, to partial dependents, and, if no dependents, to the next of kin as defined in the Article; if there are no whole or partial dependents or next of kin as defined in the Article, then to the personal representative, in lieu of the compensation the employee would have been entitled to had he lived.

Provided, however, that if the death is due to a cause that is compensable under this Article, and the dependents of such employee are awarded compensation therefor, all right to unpaid compensation provided by this section shall cease and determine. (1929, c. 120, s. 37; 1947, c. 823; 1971, c. 322.)

§ 97-38. Where death results proximately from compensable injury or occupational disease; dependents; burial expenses; compensation to aliens; election by partial dependents.

If death results proximately from a compensable injury or occupational disease and within six years thereafter, or within two years of the final determination of disability, whichever is later, the employer shall pay or cause to be paid, subject to the provisions of other sections of this Article, weekly payments of compensation equal to sixty-six and two-thirds percent (66 2/3%) of the average weekly wages of the deceased employee at the time of the accident, but not more than the amount established annually to be effective October 1 as provided in G.S. 97-29, nor less than thirty dollars ($30.00), per week, and burial expenses not exceeding ten thousand dollars ($10,000), to the person or persons entitled thereto as follows:

(1) Persons wholly dependent for support upon the earnings of the deceased employee at the time of the accident shall be entitled to receive the entire compensation payable share and share alike to the exclusion of all other persons. If there be only one person wholly dependent, then that person shall receive the entire compensation payable.

(2) If there is no person wholly dependent, then any person partially dependent for support upon the earnings of the deceased employee at the time of the accident shall be entitled to receive a weekly payment of compensation computed as hereinabove provided, but such weekly payment shall be the same

proportion of the weekly compensation provided for a whole dependent as the amount annually contributed by the deceased employee to the support of such partial dependent bears to the annual earnings of the deceased at the time of the accident.

(3)   If there is no person wholly dependent, and the person or all persons partially dependent is or are within the classes of persons defined as "next of kin" in G.S. 97-40, whether or not such persons or such classes of persons are of kin to the deceased employee in equal degree, and all so elect, he or they may take, share and share alike, the commuted value of the amount provided for whole dependents in (1) above instead of the proportional payment provided for partial dependents in (2) above; provided, that the election herein provided may be exercised on behalf of any infant partial dependent by a duly qualified guardian; provided, further, that the Industrial Commission may, in its discretion, permit a parent or person standing in loco parentis to such infant to exercise such option in its behalf, the award to be payable only to a duly qualified guardian except as in this Article otherwise provided; and provided, further, that if such election is exercised by or on behalf of more than one person, then they shall take the commuted amount in equal shares.

When weekly payments have been made to an injured employee before his death, the compensation to dependents shall begin from the date of the last of such payments. Compensation payments due on account of death shall be paid for a period of 500 weeks from the date of the death of the employee; provided, however, after said 500-week period in case of a widow or widower who is unable to support herself or himself because of physical or mental disability as of the date of death of the employee, compensation payments shall continue during her or his lifetime or until remarriage and compensation payments due a dependent child shall be continued until such child reaches the age of 18.

Compensation payable under this Article to aliens not residents (or about to become nonresidents) of the United States or Canada, shall be the same in amounts as provided for residents, except that dependents in any foreign country except Canada shall be limited to surviving spouse and child or children, or if there be no surviving spouse or child or children, to the surviving father or mother. (1929, c. 120, s. 38; 1943, c. 163; c. 502, s. 5; 1947, c. 823; 1951, c. 70, s. 3; 1953, c. 53, s. 1; 1955, c. 1026, s. 8; 1957, c. 1217; 1963, c. 604, s. 3; 1967, c. 84, s. 4; 1969, c. 143, s. 4; 1971, c. 281, s. 3; 1973, c. 515, s. 4; c. 759, s. 4; c. 1308, ss. 3, 4; c. 1357, ss. 1, 2; 1977, c. 409; 1981, c. 276, s. 1; c. 378, s. 1; c. 379; 1983, c. 772, s. 1; 1987, c. 729, s. 9; 1997-301, s. 1; 2001-232, s. 1; 2011-287, s. 14.)

§ 97-39. Widow, widower, or child to be conclusively presumed to be dependent; other cases determined upon facts; division of death benefits among those wholly dependent; when division among partially dependent.

A widow, a widower and/or a child shall be conclusively presumed to be wholly dependent for support upon the deceased employee. In all other cases questions of dependency, in whole or in part shall be determined in accordance with the facts as the facts may be at the time of the accident, but no allowance shall be made for any payment made in lieu of board and lodging or services, and no compensation shall be allowed unless the dependency existed for a period of three months or more prior to the accident. If there is more than one person wholly dependent, the death benefit shall be divided among them, the persons partly dependent, if any, shall receive no part thereof. If there is no one wholly dependent, and more than one person partially dependent, the death benefit shall be divided among them according to the relative extent of their dependency.

The widow, or widower and all children of deceased employees shall be conclusively presumed to be dependents of deceased and shall be entitled to receive the benefits of this Article for the full periods specified herein. (1929, c. 120, s. 39.)

§ 97-40. Commutation and payment of compensation in absence of dependents; "next of kin" defined; commutation and distribution of compensation to partially dependent next of kin; payment in absence of both dependents and next of kin.

Subject to the provisions of G.S. 97-38, if the deceased employee leaves neither whole nor partial dependents, then the compensation which would be payable under G.S. 97-38 to whole dependents shall be commuted to its present value and paid in a lump sum to the next of kin as herein defined. For purposes of this section and G.S. 97-38, "next of kin" shall include only child, father, mother, brother or sister of the deceased employee, including adult children or adult brothers or adult sisters of the deceased, but excluding a parent who has willfully abandoned the care and maintenance of his or her child and who has not resumed its care and maintenance at least one year prior to the first occurring of the majority or death of the child and continued its care and maintenance until its death or majority. For all such next of kin who are neither wholly nor partially dependent upon the deceased employee and who take under this section, the order of priority among them shall be governed by the general law applicable to the distribution of the personal estate of persons dying intestate. In the event of exclusion of a parent based on abandonment, the claim for compensation benefits shall be treated as though the abandoning parent had predeceased the employee. For all such next of kin who were also partially dependent on the deceased employee but who exercise the election provided for partial dependents by G.S. 97-38, the general law applicable to the distribution of the personal estate of persons dying intestate shall not apply and such person or persons upon the exercise of such election, shall be entitled, share and share alike, to the compensation provided in G.S. 97-38 for whole dependents commuted to its present value and paid in a lump sum.

If the deceased employee leaves neither whole dependents, partial dependents, nor next of kin as hereinabove defined, then no compensation shall be due or payable on account of the death of the deceased employee, except that the employer shall pay or cause to be paid the burial expenses of the deceased employee not exceeding ten thousand dollars ($10,000) to the person or persons entitled thereto. (1929, c. 120, s. 40; 1931, c. 274, s. 5; c. 319; 1945, c. 766; 1953, c. 53, s. 2; c. 1135, s. 2; 1963, c. 604, s. 4; 1965, c. 419; 1967, c. 84, s. 5; 1971, c. 1179; 1981, c. 379; 1987, c. 729, s. 10; 2001-232, s. 3.1; 2011-287, s. 15.)

§ 97-40.1. Second Injury Fund.

(a) There is hereby created a fund to be known as the "Second Injury Fund," to be held and disbursed by the Industrial Commission as hereinafter provided.

For the purpose of providing money for said fund the Industrial Commission may assess against the employer or its insurance carrier the payment of not to exceed two hundred fifty dollars ($250.00) for the loss, or loss of use, of each minor member in every case of a permanent partial disability where there is such loss, and shall assess not to exceed seven hundred fifty dollars ($750.00) for fifty percent (50%) or more loss or loss of use of each major member, defined as back, foot, leg, hand, arm, eye, or hearing.

(b) The Industrial Commission shall disburse moneys from the Second Injury Fund in unusual cases of second injuries as follows:

(1) To pay additional compensation in cases of second injuries referred to in G.S. 97-33; provided, however, that the original injury and the subsequent injury were each at least twenty percent (20%) of the entire member; and, provided further, that such additional compensation, when added to the compensation awarded under said section, shall not exceed the amount which would have been payable for both injuries had both been sustained in the subsequent accident.

(2) To pay additional compensation to an injured employee who has sustained permanent total disability in the manner referred to in the second paragraph of G.S. 97-35, which shall be in addition to the compensation awarded under said section; provided, however, that such additional compensation, when added to the compensation awarded under said section, shall not exceed the compensation for permanent total disability as provided for in G.S. 97-29.

(3) To pay compensation and medical expense in cases of permanent and total disability resulting from an injury to the brain or spinal cord in the manner and to the extent hereinafter provided.

The additional compensation and treatment expenses herein provided for shall be paid out of the Second Injury Fund exclusively and only to the extent to which the assets of such fund shall permit.

(c) In addition to payments for the purposes hereinabove set forth, the Industrial Commission may, in its discretion, make payments from said fund for the following purposes and under the following conditions:

(1) In any case in which total and permanent disability due to paralysis or loss of mental capacity has resulted from an injury to the brain or spinal cord, the Industrial Commission may, in its discretion enter an award and pay compensation and reasonable and necessary medical, nursing, hospital, institutional, equipment, and other treatment expenses from the Second Injury Fund during the life of the injured employee in cases where the injury giving rise to such disability occurred prior to July 1, 1953, and the last payment of compensation has been made subsequent to January 1, 1941. Such compensation and medical expense shall be paid only from April 4, 1947, and after the employer's liability for compensation and treatment expense has ended, and in every case in which the injury resulting in paralysis due to injury to the spinal cord occurred subsequent to April 4, 1947, and prior to July 1, 1953, the liability of the employer and his insurance carrier to pay compensation

and medical expense during the life of the injured employee shall not be affected by this section.

(2) When compensation is allowed from the fund in any case under subdivision (1) of subsection (c), the Commission may in its discretion authorize payment of medical, nursing, hospital, equipment, and other treatment expenses incurred prior to the date compensation is allowed and after the employer's liability has ended if funds are reasonably available in the Second Injury Fund for such purpose after paying claims in cases of second injuries as specified in G.S. 97-33 and 97-35. Should the fund be insufficient to pay both compensation and treatment expenses, then the said expenses may, in the discretion of the Commission, be paid first and compensation thereafter according to the reasonable availability of funds in the fund. (1953, c. 1135, s. 2; 1957, c. 1396, s. 4; 1963, c. 450, s. 3; 1977, c. 457; 1991, c. 703, s. 11; 1993 (Reg. Sess., 1994), c. 679, s. 6.1.)

§ 97-41. Repealed by Session Laws 1973, c. 1308, s. 5.

§ 97-42. Deduction of payments.

Payments made by the employer to the injured employee during the period of his disability, or to his dependents, which by the terms of this Article were not due and payable when made, may, subject to the approval of the Commission be deducted from the amount to be paid as compensation. Provided, that in the case of disability such deductions shall be made by shortening the period during which compensation must be paid, and not by reducing the amount of the weekly payment. Unless otherwise provided by the plan, when payments are made to an injured employee pursuant to an employer-funded salary continuation, disability or other income replacement plan, the deduction shall be calculated from payments made by the employer in each week during which compensation was due and payable, without any carry-forward or carry-back of credit for amounts paid in excess of the compensation rate in any given week. (1929, c. 120, s. 42; 1993 (Reg. Sess., 1994), c. 679, s. 3.7.)

§ 97-42.1. Credit for unemployment benefits.

If an injured employee has received unemployment benefits under the Employment Security Law for any week with respect to which he is entitled to workers' compensation benefits for temporary total or permanent and total disability, the employment benefits paid for such weeks may be deducted from the award to be paid as compensation. If an injured employee has received unemployment benefits for any week with respect to which he is entitled to workers' compensation benefits for partial disability as provided in G.S. 97-30, the unemployment benefits paid for such weeks may be deducted from the award to be paid only to the extent that the sum of the unemployment benefits and workers' compensation payable for such week exceeds two-thirds of the injured employee's average weekly wages as determined by the Commission in accordance with G.S. 97-2(5). Benefits payable under G.S. 97-31 for permanent partial disability or other permanent injury shall not be subject to reduction because of the receipt of unemployment benefits. (1985, c. 616, s. 1.)

§ 97-43. Commission may prescribe monthly or quarterly payments.

The Industrial Commission, upon application of either party, may, in its discretion, having regard to the welfare of the employee and the convenience of the employer, authorize compensation to be paid monthly or quarterly instead of weekly. (1929, c. 120, s. 43.)

§ 97-44. Lump sums.

Whenever any weekly payment has been continued for not less than six weeks, the liability therefor may, in unusual cases, where the Industrial Commission deems it to be to the best interest of the employee or his dependents, or where it will prevent undue hardships on the employer or his insurance carrier, without prejudicing the interests of the employee or his dependents, be redeemed, in whole or in part, by the payment by the employer of a lump sum which shall be fixed by the Commission, but in no case to exceed the uncommuted value of the future installments which may be due under this Article. The Commission, however, in its discretion, may at any time in the case of a minor who has received permanently disabling injuries either partial or total provide that he be compensated, in whole or in part, by the payment of a lump sum, the amount of which shall be fixed by the Commission, but in no case to exceed the uncommuted value of the future installments which may be due under this Article. (1929, c. 120, s. 44; 1963, c. 450, s. 4; 1975, c. 255.)

§ 97-45. Reducing to judgment outstanding liability of insurance carriers withdrawing from State.

Upon the withdrawal of any insurance carrier from doing business in the State that has any outstanding liability under the Workers' Compensation Act, the Insurance Commissioner shall immediately notify the North Carolina Industrial Commission, and thereupon the said North Carolina Industrial Commission shall issue an award against said insurance carrier and commute the installments due the injured employee or employees, and immediately have said award docketed in the superior court of the county in which the claimant resides, and the said North Carolina Industrial Commission shall then cause suit to be brought on said judgment in the state of the residence of any such insurance carrier, and the proceeds from said judgment after deducting the cost, if any, of the proceeding, shall be turned over to the injured employee, or employees, taking from such employee, or employees, the proper receipt in satisfaction of his claim. (1933, c. 474; 1979, c. 714, s. 2.)

§ 97-46. Lump sum payments to trustee; receipt to discharge employer.

Whenever the Industrial Commission deems it expedient any lump sum, subject to the provisions of G.S. 97-44, shall be paid by the employer to some suitable person or corporation appointed by the superior court in the county wherein the accident occurred, as trustee, to administer the same for the benefit of the person entitled thereto, in the manner provided by the Commission. The receipt of such trustee for the amount as paid shall discharge the employer or anyone else who is liable therefor. (1929, c. 120, s. 45.)

§ 97-47. Change of condition; modification of award.

Upon its own motion or upon the application of any party in interest on the grounds of a change in condition, the Industrial Commission may review any award, and on such review may make an award ending, diminishing, or increasing the compensation previously awarded, subject to the maximum or minimum provided in this Article, and shall immediately send to the parties a copy of the award. No such review shall affect such award as regards any moneys paid but no such review shall be made after two years from the date of the last payment of compensation pursuant to an award under this Article, except that in cases in which only medical or other treatment bills are paid, no such review shall be made after 12 months from the date of the last payment of bills for medical or other treatment, paid pursuant to this Article. (1929, c. 120, s. 46; 1931, c. 274, s. 6; 1947, c. 823; 1973, c. 1060, s. 2.)

§ 97-47.1. Payment without prejudice; limitations period.

When the employer has paid compensation without prejudice but timely contested liability as provided in G.S. 97-18(d), the right, if any, to further indemnity compensation and medical compensation shall terminate two years after the employer's last payment of medical or indemnity compensation, whichever last occurs, unless the employee files with the Commission a claim for further compensation prior to the expiration of this period. (1993 (Reg. Sess., 1994), c. 679, s. 3.5.)

§ 97-48. Receipts relieving employer; payment to minors; when payment of claims to dependents subsequent in right discharges employer.

(a) Whenever payment of compensation is made to a widow or widower for her or his use, or for her or his use and the use of the child or children, the written receipt thereof of such widow or widower shall acquit the employer: Provided, however, that in order to protect the interests of minors or incompetents the Industrial Commission may at its discretion change the terms of any award with respect to whom compensation for the benefit of such minors or incompetents shall be paid.

(b) Whenever payment is made to any person 18 years of age or over, the written receipt of such person shall acquit the employer.

(c) Payment of death benefits by an employer in good faith to a dependent subsequent in right to another or other dependents shall protect and discharge the employer, unless and until such dependent or dependents prior in right shall have given notice of his or their claims. In case the employer is in doubt as to the respective rights of rival claimants, he may apply to the Industrial Commission to decide between them.

(d) A minor employee under the age of 18 years may sign agreements and receipts for payments of compensation for temporary total disability, and such agreements and receipts executed by such minor shall acquit the employer. Where the injury results in a permanent disability and the sum to be paid does not exceed five hundred dollars ($500.00) the minor employee may execute agreements and sign receipts and such agreements and receipts shall acquit the employer; provided, that when deemed necessary the Commission may require the signature of a parent or person standing in place of a parent. (1929, c. 120, s. 47; 1931, c. 274, s. 7; 1945, c. 766.)

§ 97-49. Benefits of mentally incompetent or minor employees under 18 may be paid to a trustee, etc.

If an injured employee is mentally incompetent or is under 18 years of age at the time when any right or privilege accrues to him under this Article, his guardian, trustee or committee may in his behalf claim and exercise such right or privilege. (1929, c. 120, s. 48.)

§ 97-50. Limitation as against minors or mentally incompetent.

No limitation of time provided in this Article for the giving of notice or making claim under this Article shall run against any person who is mentally incompetent, or a minor dependent, as long as he has no guardian, trustee, or committee. (1929, c. 120, s. 49.)

§ 97-51. Joint employment; liabilities.

Whenever an employee, for whose injury or death compensation is payable under this Article, shall at the time of the injury be in joint service of two or more employers subject to this Article, such employers shall contribute to the payment of such compensation in proportion to their wages liability to such employee; provided, however, that nothing in this section shall prevent any reasonable arrangement between such employers for a different distribution as between themselves of the ultimate burden of compensation. (1929, c. 120, s. 50.)

§ 97-52. Occupational disease made compensable; "accident" defined.

Disablement or death of an employee resulting from an occupational disease described in G.S. 97-53 shall be treated as the happening of an injury by accident within the meaning of the North Carolina Workers' Compensation Act and the procedure and practice and compensation and other benefits provided by said act shall apply in all such cases except as hereinafter otherwise provided. The word "accident," as used in the Workers' Compensation Act, shall not be construed to mean a series of events in employment, of a similar or like nature, occurring regularly, continuously or at frequent intervals in the course of such employment, over extended periods of time, whether such events may or may not be attributable to fault of the employer and disease attributable to such causes shall be compensable only if culminating in an occupational disease mentioned in and compensable under this Article: Provided, however, no compensation shall be payable for asbestosis and/or silicosis as hereinafter defined if the employee, at the time of entering into the employment of the employer by whom compensation would otherwise be payable, falsely represented himself in writing as not having previously been disabled or laid off because of asbestosis or silicosis. (1935, c. 123; 1979, c. 714, s. 2.)

§ 97-53. (See editor's note on condition precedent) Occupational diseases enumerated; when due to exposure to chemicals.

The following diseases and conditions only shall be deemed to be occupational diseases within the meaning of this Article:

(1)   Anthrax.

(2)   Arsenic poisoning.

(3)   Brass poisoning.

(4)   Zinc poisoning.

(5) Manganese poisoning.

(6) Lead poisoning. Provided the employee shall have been exposed to the hazard of lead poisoning for at least 30 days in the preceding 12 months' period; and, provided further, only the employer in whose employment such employee was last injuriously exposed shall be liable.

(7) Mercury poisoning.

(8) Phosphorus poisoning.

(9) Poisoning by carbon bisulphide, menthanol, naphtha or volatile halogenated hydrocarbons.

(10) Chrome ulceration.

(11) Compressed-air illness.

(12) Poisoning by benzol, or by nitro and amido derivatives of benzol (dinitrolbenzol, anilin, and others).

(13) Any disease, other than hearing loss covered in another subdivision of this section, which is proven to be due to causes and conditions which are characteristic of and peculiar to a particular trade, occupation or employment, but excluding all ordinary diseases of life to which the general public is equally exposed outside of the employment.

(14) Epitheliomatous cancer or ulceration of the skin or of the corneal surface of the eye due to tar, pitch, bitumen, mineral oil, or paraffin, or any compound, product, or residue of any of these substances.

(15) Radium poisoning or disability or death due to radioactive properties of substances or to roentgen rays, X rays or exposure to any other source of radiation; provided, however, that the disease under this subdivision shall be deemed to have occurred on the date that disability or death shall occur by reason of such disease.

(16) Blisters due to use of tools or appliances in the employment.

(17) Bursitis due to intermittent pressure in the employment.

(18) Miner's nystagmus.

(19) Bone felon due to constant or intermittent pressure in employment.

(20) Synovitis, caused by trauma in employment.

(21) Tenosynovitis, caused by trauma in employment.

(22) Carbon monoxide poisoning.

(23) Poisoning by sulphuric, hydrochloric or hydrofluoric acid.

(24) Asbestosis.

(25) Silicosis.

(26) Psittacosis.

(27) Undulant fever.

(28) Loss of hearing caused by harmful noise in the employment. The following rules shall be applicable in determining eligibility for compensation and the period during which compensation shall be payable:

a. The term "harmful noise" means sound in employment capable of producing occupational loss of hearing as hereinafter defined. Sound of an intensity of less than 90 decibels, A scale, shall be deemed incapable of producing occupational loss of hearing as defined in this section.

b. "Occupational loss of hearing" shall mean a permanent sensorineural loss of hearing in both ears caused by prolonged exposure to harmful noise in employment. Except in instances of preexisting loss of hearing due to disease, trauma, or congenital deafness in one ear, no compensation shall be payable under this subdivision unless prolonged exposure to harmful noise in employment has caused loss of hearing in both ears as hereinafter provided.

c. No compensation benefits shall be payable for temporary total or temporary partial disability under this subdivision and there shall be no award for tinnitus or a psychogenic hearing loss.

d. An employer shall become liable for the entire occupational hearing loss to which his employment has contributed, but if previous deafness is established by a hearing test or other competent evidence, whether or not the employee was exposed to harmful noise within six months preceding such test, the employer shall not be liable for previous loss so established, nor shall he be liable for any loss for which compensation has previously been paid or awarded and the employer shall be liable only for the difference between the percent of occupational hearing loss determined as of the date of disability as herein defined and the percentage of loss established by the preemployment and audiometric examination excluding, in any event, hearing losses arising from nonoccupational causes.

e. In the evaluation of occupational hearing loss, only the hearing levels at the frequencies of 500, 1,000, 2,000, and 3,000 cycles per second shall be considered. Hearing losses for frequencies below 500 and above 3,000 cycles per second are not to be considered as constituting compensable hearing disability.

f. The employer liable for the compensation in this section shall be the employer in whose employment the employee was last exposed to harmful noise in North Carolina during a period of 90 working days or parts thereof, and an exposure during a period of less than 90 working days or parts thereof shall be held not to be an injurious exposure; provided, however, that in the event an insurance carrier has been on the risk for a period of time during which an employee has been injuriously exposed to harmful noise, and if after insurance carrier goes off the risk said employee has been further exposed to harmful noise, although not exposed for 90 working days or parts thereof so as to constitute an injurious exposure, such carrier shall, nevertheless, be liable.

g. The percentage of hearing loss shall be calculated as the average, in decibels, of the thresholds of hearing for the frequencies of 500, 1,000, 2,000, and 3,000 cycles per second. Pure tone air conduction audiometric instruments, properly calibrated according to accepted national standards such as American Standards Association, Inc., (ASA), International Standards Organization (ISO), or American National Standards Institute, Inc., (ANSI), shall be used for measuring hearing loss. If more than one audiogram is taken, the audiogram having the lowest threshold will be used to calculate occupational hearing loss. If the losses of hearing average 15 decibels (26 db if ANSI or ISO) or less in the four frequencies, such losses of hearing shall not constitute any compensable hearing disability. If the losses of hearing average 82 decibels (93 db if ANSI or ISO) or more in the four frequencies, then the same shall constitute and be total or one hundred percent (100%) compensable hearing loss. In measuring hearing impairment, the lowest measured losses in each of the four frequencies shall be added together and divided by four to determine the average decibel loss. For each decibel of loss exceeding 15 decibels (26 db if ANSI or ISO) an allowance of one and one-half percent (1 1/2%) shall be made up to the maximum of one hundred percent (100%) which is reached at 82 decibels (93 db if ANSI or ISO). In determining the binaural percentage of loss, the percentage of impairment in the better ear shall be multiplied by five. The resulting figure shall be added to the percentage of impairment in the poorer ear, and the sum of the two divided by six. The final percentage shall represent the binaural hearing impairment.

h. There shall be payable for total occupational loss of hearing in both ears 150 weeks of compensation, and for partial occupational loss of hearing in both ears such proportion of these periods of payment as such partial loss bears to total loss.

i. No claim for compensation for occupational hearing loss shall be filed until after six months have elapsed since exposure to harmful noise with the last employer. The last day of such exposure shall be the date of disability. The regular use of employer-provided protective devices capable of preventing loss of hearing from the particular harmful noise where the employee works shall constitute removal from exposure to such particular harmful noise.

j. No consideration shall be given to the question of whether or not the ability of an employee to understand speech is improved by the use of a hearing aid. The North Carolina Industrial Commission may order the employer to provide the employee with an original hearing aid if it will materially improve the employee's ability to hear.

k. No compensation benefits shall be payable for the loss of hearing caused by harmful noise after October 1, 1971, if employee fails to regularly utilize employer-provided protection device or devices, capable of preventing loss of hearing from the particular harmful noise where the employee works.

(29) (See editor's note on condition precedent) Infection with smallpox, infection with vaccinia, or any adverse medical reaction when the infection or adverse reaction is due to the employee receiving in employment vaccination against smallpox incident to the Administration of Smallpox Countermeasures by Health Professionals, section 304 of the Homeland Security Act, Pub. L. No. 107-296 (Nov. 25, 2002) (to be codified at 42 U.S.C. § 233(p)), or when the

infection or adverse medical reaction is due to the employee being exposed to another employee vaccinated as described in this subdivision.

Occupational diseases caused by chemicals shall be deemed to be due to exposure of an employee to the chemicals herein mentioned only when as a part of the employment such employee is exposed to such chemicals in such form and quantity, and used with such frequency as to cause the occupational disease mentioned in connection with such chemicals. (1935, c. 123; 1949, c. 1078; 1953, c. 1112; 1955, c. 1026, s. 10; 1957, c. 1396, s. 6; 1963, c. 553, s. 1; c. 965; 1971, c. 547, s. 1; c. 1108, s. 1; 1973, c. 760, ss. 1, 2; 1975, c. 718, s. 4; 1987, c. 729, ss. 11, 12; 1991, c. 703, s. 10; 2003-169, s. 2.)

§ 97-54. "Disablement" defined.

The term "disablement" as used in this Article as applied to cases of asbestosis and silicosis means the event of becoming actually incapacitated because of asbestosis or silicosis to earn, in the same or any other employment, the wages which the employee was receiving at the time of his last injurious exposure to asbestosis or silicosis; but in all other cases of occupational disease "disablement" shall be equivalent to "disability" as defined in G.S. 97-2(9). (1935, c. 123; 1955, c. 525, s. 1.)

§ 97-55. "Disability" defined.

The term "disability" as used in this Article means the state of being incapacitated as the term is used in defining "disablement" in G.S. 97-54. (1935, c. 123.)

§ 97-56. Limitation on compensable diseases.

The provisions of this Article shall apply only to cases of occupational disease in which the last exposure in an occupation subject to the hazards of such diseases occurred on or after March 26, 1935. (1935, c. 123.)

§ 97-57. Employer liable.

In any case where compensation is payable for an occupational disease, the employer in whose employment the employee was last injuriously exposed to the hazards of such disease, and the insurance carrier, if any, which was on the risk when the employee was so last exposed under such employer, shall be liable.

For the purpose of this section when an employee has been exposed to the hazards of asbestosis or silicosis for as much as 30 working days, or parts thereof, within seven consecutive calendar months, such exposure shall be deemed injurious but any less exposure shall not be deemed injurious; provided, however, that in the event an insurance carrier has been on the risk for a period of time during which an employee has been injuriously exposed to the hazards of asbestosis or silicosis, and if after insurance carrier goes off the risk said employee is further exposed to the hazards of asbestosis or silicosis, although not so exposed for a period of 30 days or parts thereof so as to constitute a further injurious exposure, such carrier shall, nevertheless, be liable. (1935, c. 123; 1945, c. 762; 1957, c. 1396, s. 7.)

§ 97-58. Time limit for filing claims.

(a) Repealed by Session Laws 1987, c. 729, s. 13.

(b) The report and notice to the employer as required by G.S. 97-22 shall apply in all cases of occupational disease except in case of asbestosis, silicosis, or lead poisoning. The time of notice of an occupational disease shall run from the date that the employee has been advised by competent medical authority that he has same.

(c) The right to compensation for occupational disease shall be barred unless a claim be filed with the Industrial Commission within two years after death, disability, or disablement as the case may be. Provided, however, that the right to compensation for radiation injury, disability or death shall be barred unless a claim is filed within two years after the date upon which the employee first suffered incapacity from the exposure to radiation and either knew or in the exercise of reasonable diligence should have known that the occupational disease was caused by his present or prior employment. (1935, c. 123; 1945, c.

762; 1955, c. 525, s. 6; 1963, c. 553, s. 2; 1973, c. 1060, s. 3; 1981, c. 734, s. 1; 1987, c. 729, s. 13.)

§ 97-59. Employer to pay for treatment.

Medical compensation shall be paid by the employer in cases in which awards are made for disability or damage to organs as a result of an occupational disease after bills for same have been approved by the Industrial Commission.

In case of a controversy arising between the employer and employee relative to the continuance of medical, surgical, hospital or other treatment, the Industrial Commission may order such further treatments as may in the discretion of the Commission be necessary. (1935, c. 123; 1945, c. 762; 1973, c. 1061; 1981, c. 339; 1991, c. 703, s. 5.)

§ 97-60: Repealed by Session Laws 2003-284, s. 10.33(a), effective July 1, 2003.

§ 97-61. Rewritten as §§ 97-61.1 to 97-61.7.

§ 97-61.1. First examination of and report on employee having asbestosis or silicosis.

When the Industrial Commission is advised by an employer or employee that an employee has or allegedly has asbestosis or silicosis, the employee, when ordered by the Industrial Commission, shall submit to X rays and a physical examination by the advisory medical committee or other designated qualified physician who is not a member of the advisory medical committee. The employer shall pay the expenses connected with the examination by the advisory medical committee or other designated qualified physician who is not a member of the advisory medical committee in such amounts as shall be directed by the Industrial Commission. Within 30 days after the completion of the examination, the advisory medical committee or other designated qualified physician shall submit a written report to the Industrial Commission setting forth:

(1)   The X rays and clinical procedures used.

(2) Whether or not the claimant has contracted asbestosis or silicosis.

(3) The advisory medical committee's or designated qualified physician's opinion expressed in percentages of the impairment of the employee's ability to perform normal labor in the same or any other employment.

(4) Any other matter deemed pertinent.

When a competent physician certifies to the Industrial Commission that the employee's physical condition is such that his movement to the place of examination ordered by the Industrial Commission as herein provided in G.S. 97-61.1, 97-61.3 and 97-61.4 would be harmful or injurious to the health of the employee, the Industrial Commission shall cause the examination of the employee to be made by the advisory medical committee or other designated qualified physician as herein provided at some place in the vicinity of the residence of the employee suitable for the purposes of making such examination. (1935, c. 123; 1945, c. 762; 1955, c. 525, s. 2; 1973, c. 476, s. 128; 1989, c. 727, s. 219(15); 1997-443, s. 11A.37; 2003-284, s. 10.33(b).)

§ 97-61.2. Filing of first report; right of hearing; effect of report as testimony.

The advisory medical committee shall file its report in triplicate with the Industrial Commission, which shall send one copy thereof to the claimant and one copy thereof to the employer by registered mail or certified mail. Unless within 30 days from receipt of the copy of said report the claimant and employer, or either of them, shall request the Industrial Commission in writing to set the case for hearing for the purpose of examining and cross-examining the members of the advisory medical committee respecting the report of said committee, and for the purpose of introducing additional testimony, said report shall become a part of the record of the case and shall be accepted by the Industrial Commission as expert medical testimony to be considered as such and in connection with all the evidence in the case in arriving at its decision. (1935, c. 123; 1945, c. 762; 1955, c. 525, s. 2; 1963, c. 450, s. 5.)

§ 97-61.3. Second examination and report.

As soon as practicable after the expiration of one year following the initial examination by the advisory medical committee and when ordered by the Industrial Commission, the employee shall again appear before the advisory medical committee, at least one of whom shall conduct the examination, and the member or members of the advisory medical committee conducting the examination shall forward the X rays and findings to the member or members of the committee not present for the physical examination. Within 30 days after the completion of the examination, the advisory medical committee shall make a written report to the Industrial Commission signed by all of its members, setting forth any change since the first report in the employee's condition which is due to asbestosis or silicosis, said report to be filed in triplicate with the Industrial Commission, which shall send one copy thereof to the claimant, and one copy to the employer by registered mail or certified mail. The claimant and employer, or either of them, shall have the right only at the final hearing provided for in G.S. 97-61.4 to examine or cross-examine the members of the advisory medical committee respecting the second report of the committee. (1935, c. 123; 1945, c. 762; 1955, c. 525, s. 2; 1959, c. 863, s. 2.)

§ 97-61.4. Third examination and report.

As soon as practicable after the expiration of two years from the first examination and when ordered by the Industrial Commission, the employee shall appear before the advisory medical committee, or at least two of them, for final X rays and physical examination. Upon completion of this examination and within 30 days, the advisory medical committee shall make a written report setting forth:

(1)   The X rays and clinical procedures used by the committee.

(2)   To what extent, if any, has the damage to the employee's lungs due to asbestosis or silicosis changed since the first examination.

(3)   The opinion of the committee, expressed in percentages, with respect to the extent of impairment of the employee's ability to earn in the same or any other employment the wages which the employee was receiving at the time of his last injurious exposure to asbestosis or silicosis.

(4)   Any other matter deemed pertinent by the committee.

Said report shall be filed in triplicate with the Industrial Commission which shall send one copy thereof to the claimant and one copy to the employer by registered mail or certified mail. (1935, c. 123; 1945, c. 762; 1955, c. 525, s. 2; 1959, c. 863, s. 3.)

§ 97-61.5. Hearing after first examination and report; removal of employee from hazardous occupation; compensation upon removal from hazardous occupation.

(a) After the employer and employee have received notice of the first committee report, the Industrial Commission, unless it has already approved an agreement between the employer and employee, shall set the matter for hearing at a time and place to be decided by it, to hear any controverted questions, determine if and to whom liability attaches, and where appropriate, file a written opinion with its findings of fact and conclusions of law and cause its award to be issued thereon, all of which shall be subject to modification as provided in G.S. 97-61.6.

(b) If the Industrial Commission finds at the first hearing that the employee has either asbestosis or silicosis or if the parties enter into an agreement to the effect that the employee has silicosis or asbestosis, it shall by order remove the employee from any occupation which exposes him to the hazards of asbestosis or silicosis, and if the employee thereafter engages in any occupation which exposes him to the hazards of asbestosis or silicosis without having obtained the written approval of the Industrial Commission as provided in G.S. 97-61.7, neither he, his dependents, personal representative nor any other person shall be entitled to any compensation for disablement or death resulting from asbestosis or silicosis; provided, that if the employee is removed from the industry the employer shall pay or cause to be paid as in this subsection provided to the employee affected by such asbestosis or silicosis a weekly compensation equal to sixty-six and two-thirds percent (66 2/3%) of his average weekly wages before removal from the industry, but not more than the amount established annually to be effective October 1 as provided in G.S. 97-29 or less than thirty dollars ($30.00) a week, which compensation shall continue for a period of 104 weeks. Payments made under this subsection shall be credited on the amounts payable under any final award in the cause entered under G.S. 97-61.6. (1935, c. 123; 1945, c. 762; 1955, c. 525, s. 2; c. 1354; 1957, c. 1217; c. 1396, s. 8; 1963, c. 604, s. 6; 1967, c. 84, s. 7; 1969, c. 143, s. 6; 1971, c. 281, s. 5; 1973, c. 515, s. 6; c. 759, s. 5; 1981, c. 276, s. 1; c. 378, s. 1.)

§ 97-61.6. Hearing after third examination and report; compensation for disability and death from asbestosis or silicosis.

After receipt by the employer and employee of the advisory medical committee's third report, the Industrial Commission, unless it has approved an agreement between the employee and employer, shall set a final hearing in the cause, at which it shall receive all competent evidence bearing on the cause, and shall make a final disposition of the case, determining what compensation, if any, the employee is entitled to receive in addition to the 104 weeks already received.

Where the incapacity for work resulting from asbestosis or silicosis is found to be total, the employer shall pay, or cause to be paid, to the injured employee during such total disability a weekly compensation in accordance with G.S. 97-29.

When the incapacity for work resulting from asbestosis or silicosis is partial, the employer shall pay, or cause to be paid, to the affected employee, a weekly compensation equal to sixty-six and two-thirds percent (66 2/3%) of the difference between his average weekly wages at the time of his last injurious exposure, and the average weekly wages which he is able to earn thereafter, but not more than the amount established annually to be effective October 1 as provided in G.S. 97-29, a week, and provided that the total compensation so paid shall not exceed a period of 196 weeks, in addition to the 104 weeks for which the employee has already been compensated.

Provided, however, should death result from asbestosis or silicosis within two years from the date of last exposure, or should death result from asbestosis or silicosis, or from a secondary infection or diseases developing from asbestosis or silicosis within 350 weeks from the date of last exposure and while the employee is entitled to compensation for disablement due to asbestosis or silicosis, either partial or total, then in either of these events, the employer shall pay, or cause to be paid compensation in accordance with G.S. 97-38.

Provided further that if the employee has asbestosis or silicosis and dies from any other cause, the employer shall pay, or cause to be paid by one of the methods set forth in G.S. 97-38 compensation for any remaining portion of the 104 weeks specified in G.S. 97-61.5 for which the employee has not previously been paid compensation, and in addition shall pay compensation for such number of weeks as the percentage of disability of the employee bears to 196 weeks. If the employee was totally disabled as a result of asbestosis or silicosis, compensation shall be paid for any remaining portion of the 104 weeks specified in G.S. 97-61.5 for which the employee has not previously been paid compensation, and in addition shall be paid for an additional 300 weeks. (1935, c. 123; 1945, c. 762; 1955, c. 525, s. 2; c. 1354; 1957, c. 1271; 1963, c. 604, s. 7; 1965, c. 907; 1967, c. 84, s. 8; 1969, c. 143, s. 7; 1971, c. 281, s. 6; c. 631; 1973, c. 515, s. 7; c. 759, s. 6; c. 1308, ss. 6, 7; 1979, c. 246; 1981, c. 276, s. 1.)

§ 97-61.7. Waiver of right to compensation as alternative to forced change of occupation.

An employee who has been compensated under the terms of G.S. 97-61.5(b) as an alternative to forced change of occupation, may, subject to the approval of the Industrial Commission, waive in writing his right to further compensation for any aggravation of his condition that may result from his continuing in an occupation exposing him to the hazards of asbestosis or silicosis, in which case payment of all compensation awarded previous to the date of the waiver as approved by the Industrial Commission shall bar any further claims by the employee, or anyone claiming through him, provided, that in the event of total disablement or death as a result of asbestosis or silicosis with which the employee was so affected, compensation shall nevertheless be payable, but in no case, whether for disability or death or both, for a longer period than 100 weeks in addition to the 104 weeks already paid. Such written waiver must be filed with the Industrial Commission, and the Commission shall keep a record of each waiver, which record shall be open to the inspection of any interested person. (1935, c. 123; 1945, c. 762; 1955, c. 525, s. 2.)

§ 97-62. "Silicosis" and "asbestosis" defined.

The word "silicosis" shall mean the characteristic fibrotic condition of the lungs caused by the inhalation of dust of silica or silicates. "Asbestosis" shall mean a characteristic fibrotic condition of the lungs caused by the inhalation of asbestos dust. (1935, c. 123.)

§ 97-63. Period necessary for employee to be exposed.

Compensation shall not be payable for disability or death due to silicosis and/or asbestosis unless the employee shall have been exposed to the inhalation of dust of silica or silicates or asbestos dust in employment for a period of not less than two years in this State, provided no part of such period of two years shall have been more than 10 years prior to the last exposure. (1935, c. 123.)

§ 97-64. General provisions of act to control as regards benefits.

Except as herein otherwise provided, in case of disablement or death from silicosis and/or asbestosis, compensation shall be payable in accordance with the provisions of the North Carolina Workers' Compensation Act. (1935, c. 123; 1979, c. 714, s. 2.)

§ 97-65. Reduction of rate where tuberculosis develops.

In case of disablement or death due primarily from silicosis and/or asbestosis and complicated with tuberculosis of the lungs compensation shall be payable as hereinbefore provided, except that the rate of payments may be reduced one sixth. (1935, c. 123.)

§ 97-66. Claim where benefits are discontinued.

Where compensation payments have been made and discontinued, and further compensation is claimed, the claim for further compensation shall be made within two years after the last payment in all cases of occupational disease, provided, that claims for further compensation for asbestosis or silicosis shall be governed by the final award as set forth in G.S. 97-61.6. (1935, c. 123; 1945, c. 762; 1955, c. 525, s. 3; 1987, c. 729, s. 14.)

§ 97-67. Postmortem examinations; notice to next of kin and insurance carrier.

Upon the filing of a claim for death from an occupational disease where in the opinion of the Industrial Commission a postmortem examination is necessary to accurately ascertain the cause of death, such examination shall be ordered by the Industrial Commission. A full report of such examination shall be certified to the Industrial Commission. The surviving spouse or next kin and the employer or his insurance carrier, if their identity and whereabouts can be reasonably ascertained, shall be given reasonable notice of the time and place of such postmortem examination, and, if present at such examination, shall be given an opportunity to witness the same. Any such person may be present at and witness such examination either in person or through a duly authorized representative. If such examination is not consented to by the surviving husband or wife or next of kin, all right to compensation shall cease. (1935, c. 123.)

§ 97-68. Controverted medical questions.

The Industrial Commission may at its discretion refer to the advisory medical committee controverted medical questions arising out of occupational disease claims other than asbestosis or silicosis. (1935, c. 123; 1955, c. 525, s. 4.)

§ 97-69. Examination by advisory medical committee; inspection of medical reports.

The advisory medical committee, upon reference to it of a case of occupational disease shall notify the employee, or, in case he is dead, his dependents or personal representative, and his employer to appear before the advisory medical committee at a time and place stated in the notice. If the employee be living, he shall appear before the advisory medical committee at the time and place specified then or thereafter and he shall submit to such examinations including clinical and X-ray examinations as the advisory medical committee may require. The employee, or, if he be dead, the claimant and the employer shall be entitled to have present at all such examinations, a physician admitted to practice medicine in the State who shall be given every reasonable facility for observing every such examination whose services shall be paid for by the claimant or by the employer who engaged his services. If a physician admitted to practice medicine in the State shall certify that the employee is physically unable to appear at the time and place designated by the advisory medical committee, such committee may, upon the advice of the Industrial Commission, and on notice to the employer, change the place and/or time of the examination so as to reasonably facilitate the examination of the employee, and in any such case the employer shall furnish transportation and provide for other reasonably necessary expenses incidental to necessary travel. The claimant and the employer shall produce to the advisory medical committee all reports of medical and X-ray examinations which may be in their respective possession or control showing the past or present condition of the employee to assist the advisory medical committee in reaching its conclusions. Provided that this section shall not apply to a living employee who has contracted asbestosis or silicosis. (1935, c. 123; 1955, c. 525, s. 5.)

§ 97-70. Report of committee to Industrial Commission.

The advisory medical committee, shall, as soon as practicable after it has completed its consideration of a case, report to the Industrial Commission its opinion regarding all medical questions involved in the case. The advisory medical committee shall include in its report a statement of what, if any, physician or physicians were present at the examination on behalf of the claimant or employer and what, if any, medical reports and X rays were produced by or on behalf of the claimant or employer. (1935, c. 123.)

§ 97-71. Filing report; right of hearing on report.

The advisory medical committee shall file its report in triplicate with the Industrial Commission, which shall send one copy thereof to the claimant and one copy to the employer by registered mail. Unless within 30 days from receipt of the copy of said report the claimant and/or employer shall request the Industrial Commission in writing to set the case for further hearing for the purpose of examining and/or cross-examining the members of the advisory medical committee respecting the report of said committee, said report shall become a part of the record of the case and shall be accepted by the Industrial Commission as expert medical testimony to be considered as such in connection with all the evidence in the case in arriving at its decision. (1935, c. 123.)

§ 97-72. Appointment of advisory medical committee; terms of office; duties and functions; salaries and expenses.

(a)   There shall be an advisory medical committee consisting of three members, who shall be licensed physicians in good professional standing and peculiarly qualified in the diagnosis or treatment of occupational diseases. They shall be appointed by the Industrial Commission with the approval of the Governor, and one of them shall be designated as chairman of the committee by the Industrial Commission. The members of committee shall be appointed to serve terms as follows: one for a term of two years, one for a term of four years, and one for a term of six years. Upon the expiration of each term as above mentioned the Industrial Commission shall appoint a successor for a term of six years. The function of the committee shall be to conduct examinations and make reports as required by G.S. 97-61.1 through 97-61.6 and 97-68 through 97-71, and to assist in any postmortem examinations provided for in G.S. 97-67 when so directed by the Industrial Commission. Members of the committee shall devote to the duties of the office so much of their time as may be required in the conducting of examinations with reasonable promptness, and they shall attend hearings as scheduled by the Industrial Commission when their attendance is desired for the purpose of examining and cross-examining them respecting any report or reports made by them.

(b)   Repealed by Session Laws 2003-284, s. 10.33(c), effective July 1, 2003.

(c)   Notwithstanding any other provision of this Article, the Industrial Commission, in its discretion, may designate a qualified physician who is not a member of the advisory medical committee to perform an examination of an employee who has filed a claim for benefits for asbestosis or silicosis. This physician shall file his reports in the same manner a member of the advisory medical committee files reports; and these reports shall be deemed reports of the advisory medical committee. (1935, c. 123; 1955, c. 525, s. 7; 1981, c. 562, s. 2; 1989, c. 439; 1991, c. 481, s. 1; 1997-443, s. 11A.38; 1997-508, s. 1; 2003-284, s. 10.33(c).)

§ 97-73. Fees.

(a)   Claims. - The Industrial Commission may establish by rule a schedule of fees for examinations conducted, reports made, documents filed, and agreements reviewed under this Article. The fees shall be collected in accordance with rules adopted by the Industrial Commission.

(b), (c) Repealed by Session Laws 2003-284, s. 10.33(d), effective July 1, 2003.

(d) Safety. - A fee in the amount set by the Industrial Commission is imposed on an employer for whom the Industrial Commission provides an educational training program on how to prevent or reduce accidents or injuries that result in workers' compensation claims or a person for whom the Industrial Commission provides other educational services. The fees are departmental receipts. (1935, c. 123; 1955, c. 525, s. 8; 1991, c. 481, s. 2; 1991 (Reg. Sess., 1992), c. 1039, s. 2; 1997-443, s. 11A.39; 2003-284, s. 10.33(d); 2005-276, s. 45.1(a); 2009-451, s. 14.16(a).)

§ 97-74. Expense of hearings taxed as costs in compensation cases; fees collected directed to general fund.

In hearings arising out of claims for disability and/or death resulting from occupational diseases the Industrial Commission shall tax as a part of the costs in cases in which compensation is awarded a reasonable allowance for the services of members of the advisory medical committee attending such hearings and reasonable allowances for the services of members of the advisory medical committee for making investigations in connection with all claims for compensation on account of occupational diseases, including uncontested cases, as well as contested cases, and whether or not hearings shall have been conducted in connection therewith. All such charges, fees and allowances to be collected by the Industrial Commission shall be paid into the general fund of the State treasury to constitute a fund out of which to pay the expenses of the advisory medical committee. (1935, c. 123.)

§§ 97-75, 97-76: Repealed by Session Laws 2003-284, s. 10.33(f), effective July 1, 2003.

§ 97-77. North Carolina Industrial Commission created; members appointed by Governor; terms of office; chairman.

(a) There is hereby created a commission to be known as the North Carolina Industrial Commission, consisting of six commissioners who shall devote their entire time to the duties of the Commission. The Governor shall appoint the members of the Commission for terms of six years. Three commissioners shall be persons who, on account of their previous vocations, employment or affiliations, can be classed as representatives of employers. Three commissioners shall be persons who, on account of their previous vocations, employment or affiliations, can be classed as representatives of employees. No person may serve more than two terms on the Commission, including any term served prior to the effective date of this section. In calculating the number of terms served, a partial term that is less than three years in length shall not be included.

(a1) Appointments of commissioners are subject to confirmation by the General Assembly by joint resolution. The names of commissioners to be appointed by the Governor shall be submitted by the Governor to the General Assembly for confirmation by the General Assembly on or before March 1 of the year of expiration of the term. If the Governor fails to timely submit nominations, the General Assembly shall appoint to fill the succeeding term upon the joint recommendation of the President Pro Tempore of the Senate and the Speaker of the House of Representatives in accordance with G.S. 120-121 not inconsistent with this section.

In case of death, incapacity, resignation, or any other vacancy in the office of any commissioner prior to the expiration of the term of office, a nomination to fill the vacancy for the remainder of the unexpired term shall be submitted by the Governor within four weeks after the vacancy arises to the General Assembly for confirmation by the General Assembly. If the Governor fails to timely nominate a person to fill the vacancy, the General Assembly shall appoint a person to fill the remainder of the unexpired term upon the joint recommendation of the President Pro Tempore of the Senate and the Speaker of the House of Representatives in accordance with G.S. 120-121 not inconsistent with this section. If a vacancy arises or exists pursuant to this subsection when the General Assembly is not in session, and the appointment is deemed urgent by the Governor, the commissioner may be appointed and serve on an interim basis pending confirmation by the General Assembly. For the purpose of this subsection, the General Assembly is not in session only (i) prior to convening of the Regular Session, (ii) during any adjournment of the Regular Session for more than 10 days, and (iii) after sine die adjournment of the Regular Session.

No person while in office as a commissioner may be nominated or appointed on an interim basis to fill the remainder of an unexpired term, or to a full term that commences prior to the expiration of the term that the commissioner is serving.

(b) One member, to be designated by the Governor, shall act as chairman. The chairman shall be the chief judicial officer and the chief executive officer of the Industrial Commission; such authority shall be exercised pursuant to the provisions of Chapter 126 of the General Statutes and the rules and policies of the State Human Resources Commission. Notwithstanding the provisions of this Chapter, the chairman shall have such authority as is necessary to direct and oversee the Commission. The chairman may delegate any duties and responsibilities as may be necessary to ensure the proper management of the Industrial Commission. Notwithstanding the provisions of this Chapter, Chapter 143A, and Chapter 143B of the General Statutes, the chairman may hire or fire personnel and transfer personnel within the Industrial Commission.

The Governor may designate one vice-chairman from the remaining commissioners. The vice-chairman shall assume the powers of the chairman upon request of the chairman or when the chairman is absent for 24 hours or more. The authority delegated to the vice-chairman shall be relinquished immediately upon the return of the chairman or at the request of the chairman. (1929, c. 120, s. 51; 1931, c. 274, s. 8; 1991, c. 264, s. 1; 1993, c. 399, s. 3; 1993 (Reg. Sess., 1994), c. 769, s. 28.15(a); 2011-287, ss. 16, 17; 2013-382, s. 9.1(c).)

§ 97-77.1. Expired.

§ 97-78. Salaries and expenses; administrator, executive secretary, deputy commissioners, and other staff assistance; annual report.

(a) The salary of each commissioner shall be the same as that fixed from time to time for district attorneys except that the commissioner designated as chair shall receive one thousand five hundred dollars ($1,500) additional per annum.

(b) (Effective until July 1, 2015) The Commission may appoint an administrator whose duties shall be prescribed by the Commission, and who shall be subject to the State Personnel System. The Commission may appoint an executive secretary whose duties shall be prescribed by the Commission, and who shall be subject to the State Personnel System and who, upon entering upon his duties, shall give bond in such sum as may be fixed by the Commission. The Commission may also employ such clerical or other assistance as it may deem necessary, and fix the compensation of its staff, except that the salaries of the administrator and the executive secretary shall be fixed by subsection (b1) of this section. The compensation of Commission staff shall be in keeping with the compensation paid to the persons employed to do similar work in other State departments.

(b) (Effective July 1, 2015) The Commission may appoint an administrator whose duties shall be prescribed by the Commission. The Commission may appoint an executive secretary whose duties shall be prescribed by the Commission, and who, upon entering upon his duties, shall give bond in such sum as may be fixed by the Commission. The Commission may also employ such clerical or other assistance as it may deem necessary, and fix the compensation of its staff, except that the salaries of the administrator and the executive secretary shall be fixed by subsection (b1) of this section. The compensation of Commission staff shall be in keeping with the compensation paid to the persons employed to do similar work in other State departments.

(b1) The salary of the administrator shall be ninety percent (90%) of the salary of a commissioner. The salary of the executive secretary shall be ninety percent (90%) of the salary of a commissioner.

(b2) The Chairman of the Industrial Commission shall designate one deputy commissioner as chief deputy commissioner. The salary of the chief deputy commissioner shall be ninety percent (90%) of the salary of a commissioner.

(b3) The salary of deputy commissioners shall be based upon years of experience as a deputy commissioner as follows:

(1) Seventy-five percent (75%) of the salary of a commissioner, with three years of experience or less.

(2) Seventy-seven percent (77%) of the salary of a commissioner, with more than three but less than seven years of experience.

(3) Eighty percent (80%) of the salary of a commissioner, with seven or more but less than 10 years of experience.

(4) Eighty-three percent (83%) of the salary of a commissioner, with 10 or more but less than 12 years of experience.

(5) Eighty-five percent (85%) of the salary of a commissioner, with 12 or more years experience.

(b4) In lieu of merit and other incremental raises, the administrator, executive secretary, chief deputy commissioner, and deputy commissioners shall receive longevity pay on the same basis as is provided to other employees subject to the North Carolina Human Resources Act.

(c) The members of the Commission and its assistants shall be entitled to receive from the State their actual and necessary expenses while traveling on the business of the Commission, but such expenses shall be certified by the person who incurred the same, and shall be approved by the chairman of the Commission before payment is made.

(d) All salaries and expenses of the Commission shall be audited and paid out of the State treasury, in the manner prescribed for similar expenses in other departments or branches of the State service, and to defray such salaries and expenses a sufficient appropriation shall be made under the General Appropriation Act as made to other departments, commissions and agencies of the State government.

(e) No later than October 1 of each year, the Commission shall publish annually for free distribution a report of the administration of this Article, together with such recommendations as the Commission deems advisable. No later than October 1 of each year, the Commission shall submit this report to the Joint Legislative Commission on Governmental Operations.

(f) No later than April 1, 2008, the Commission shall prepare and implement a strategic plan for accomplishing all of the following:

(1) Tracking compliance with the provisions of G.S. 97-18(b), (c), and (d), and establishing a procedure to enforce compliance with the requirements of these subsections.

(2) Expeditiously resolving requests for, or disputes involving, medical compensation under G.S. 97-25, including selection of a physician, change of physician, the specific treatment involved, and the provider of such treatment.

(g) The Commission shall demonstrate its success in implementing its strategic plan under subsection (f) of this section by including all of the following in its annual report under subsection (e) of this section:

(1) The total number of claims made during the preceding calendar year, the total number of claims in which compliance was not timely made, and, for each claim, the date the claim was filed, the date by which compliance was required, the date of actual compliance, and any sanctions or other remedial action imposed by the Commission.

(2) The total number of requests for, and disputes involving, medical compensation under G.S. 97-25 in which final disposition was not made within 45 days of the filing of the motion with the Commission, and, for each such request or dispute, the date the motion or other initial pleading was filed, the date on which final disposition was made and, where reasonably ascertainable, the date on which any ordered medical treatment was actually provided. (1929, c. 120, s. 52; 1931, c. 274, s. 9; 1941, c. 358, s. 2; 1947, c. 823; 1957, c. 541, s. 6; 1971, c. 527, s. 1; c. 1147, s. 1; 1983, c. 717, s. 20; 1983 (Reg. Sess., 1984), c. 1034, s. 164; 1997-443, s. 33.4; 1998-212, s. 28.18(a); 2005-276, s. 29.20(b); 2007-323, ss. 13.4A(a), (b); 2013-382, s. 9.1(c); 2013-413, s. 60(a).)

§ 97-78.1. Standards of judicial conduct to apply to commissioners and deputy commissioners.

The Code of Judicial Conduct for judges of the General Court of Justice and the procedure for discipline of judges in Article 30 of Chapter 7A of the General Statutes shall apply to commissioners and deputy commissioners. Commissioners and deputy commissioners shall be liable for impeachment for the causes and in the manner provided for judges of the General Court of Justice in Chapter 123 of the General Statutes. (2011-287, s. 18.)

§ 97-79. Offices and supplies; deputies with power to subpoena witnesses and to take testimony; meetings; hearings.

(a) The Commission shall be provided with adequate offices in which the records shall be kept and its official business transacted during regular business hours; it shall also be provided with necessary office furniture, stationery, and other supplies.

(b) (Effective until July 1, 2015) The Commission may appoint deputies who shall have the same power as members of the Commission pursuant to G.S. 97-80 and the same power to take evidence, and enter orders, opinions, and awards based thereon as is possessed by the members of the Commission. The deputies shall be subject to the State Personnel System.

(b) (Effective July 1, 2015) The Commission may appoint deputies who shall have the same power as members of the Commission pursuant to G.S. 97-80 and the same power to take evidence, and enter orders, opinions, and awards based thereon as is possessed by the members of the Commission. Deputies appointed pursuant to this subsection shall not be considered hearing officers within the meaning of G.S. 126-5(d)(7).

(c) The Commission or any member thereof may hold sessions at any place within the State as may be deemed necessary by the Commission.

(d) Hearings before the Commission shall be open to the public and shall be stenographically reported, and the Commission is authorized to contract for the reporting of such hearings. The Commission shall by regulation provide for the preparation of a record of the hearings and other proceedings. Notwithstanding the provisions of this subsection, informal hearings conducted pursuant to the provisions of G.S. 97-18.1, whether by telephone or in person, shall not be open to the public nor stenographically reported unless the Commission orders otherwise.

(e) The Commission, or any member thereof, or any deputy is authorized by appropriate order, to make additional parties plaintiff or defendant in any proceeding pending before the Commission when it is made to appear that such new party is either a necessary party or a proper party to a final determination of the proceeding.

(f) The Commission shall create an ombudsman program to assist unrepresented claimants, employers, and other parties, to enable them to protect their rights under this Article. In addition to other duties assigned by the Commission, the ombudsman shall meet with, or otherwise provide information to, injured employees, investigate complaints, and communicate with employers' insurance carriers and physicians at the request of the claimant. Assistance provided under this subsection shall not include representing the claimant in a compensation hearing.

(g) The Commission shall adopt rules, in accordance with Article 2A of Chapter 150B of the General Statutes, for administrative motions, including practices and procedures for carrying out the provisions of this Article. (1929, c. 120, s. 53; 1931, c. 274, s. 10; 1951, c. 1059, s. 7; 1955, c. 1026, s. 11; 1971, c. 527, s. 2; c. 1147, s. 2; 1981 (Reg. Sess., 1982), c. 1243, s. 1; 1993 (Reg. Sess., 1994), c. 679, s. 5.2; 2013-294, s. 5; 2013-413, s. 60(b).)

§ 97-80. Rules and regulations; subpoena of witnesses; examination of books and records; depositions; costs.

(a) The Commission shall adopt rules, in accordance with Article 2A of Chapter 150B of the General Statutes and not inconsistent with this Article, for carrying out the provisions of this Article.

The Commission shall adopt rules establishing processes and procedure to be used under this Article.

Processes, procedure, and discovery under this Article shall be as summary and simple as reasonably may be.

(b) The Commission or any member thereof, or any person deputized by it, shall have the power, for the purpose of this Article, to tax costs against the parties, to administer or cause to have administered oaths, to preserve order at hearings, to compel the attendance and testimony of witnesses, and to compel the production of books, papers, records, and other tangible things.

(c) The Commission may order parties to participate in mediation, under rules substantially similar to those approved by the Supreme Court for use in the Superior Court division, except the Commission shall determine the manner in which payment of the costs of the mediated settlement conference is assessed.

(d) The Commission may order testimony to be taken by deposition and any party to a proceeding under this Article may, upon application to the Commission, which application shall set forth the materiality of the evidence to be given, cause the depositions of witnesses residing within or without the State to be taken, the costs to be taxed as other costs by Commission. Depositions ordered by the Commission upon application of a party shall be taken after giving the notice and in the manner prescribed by law for depositions in action at law, except that they shall be directed to the Commission, the commissioner, or the deputy commissioner before whom the proceedings may be pending.

(e)   A subpoena may be issued by the Commission and served in accordance with G.S. 1A-1, Rule 45. A party shall not issue a subpoena duces tecum less than 30 days prior to the hearing date except upon prior approval of the Commission. Upon a motion, the Commission may quash a subpoena if it finds that the evidence the production of which is required does not relate to a matter in issue, the subpoena does not describe with sufficient particularity the evidence the production of which is required, or for any other reason sufficient in law the subpoena may be quashed. Each witness who appears in obedience to such subpoena of the Commission shall receive for attendance the fees and mileage for witnesses in civil cases in courts of the county where the hearing is held.

(f)   The Commission may by rule provide for and limit the use of interrogatories and other forms of discovery, including production of books, papers, records, and other tangible things, and it may provide reasonable sanctions for failure to comply with a Commission order compelling discovery.

(g)   The Commission or any member or deputy thereof shall have the same power as a judicial officer pursuant to Chapter 5A of the General Statutes to hold a person in civil contempt, as provided thereunder, for failure to comply with an order of the Commission, Commission member, or deputy. A person held in civil contempt may appeal in the manner provided for appeals pursuant to G.S. 97-85 and G.S. 97-86. The provisions of G.S. 5A-24 shall not apply to appeals pursuant to this subsection.

(h)   The Commission or any member or deputy thereof shall also have the same power as a judicial officer pursuant to Chapter 5A of the General Statutes to punish for criminal contempt, subject to the limitations thereunder, (i) for willful behavior committed during the sitting of the commissioner or deputy commissioner and directly tending to interrupt the proceedings; (ii) for willful disobedience of a lawful order of the Commission or a member or deputy thereof; or (iii) for willful refusal to be sworn or affirmed as a witness, or, when so sworn or affirmed, willful refusal to answer any legal and proper question when refusal is not legally justified. The Commission or any member or deputy thereof may issue an order of arrest as provided by G.S. 15A-305 when authorized by G.S. 5A-16 in connection with contempt proceedings. When the commissioner or deputy commissioner chooses not to proceed summarily pursuant to G.S. 5A-14, the proceedings shall be before a district court judge, and venue lies throughout the district where the order was issued directing the person charged to appear. A person found in criminal contempt may appeal in the manner provided for appeals in criminal actions to the superior court of the district in which the order of contempt was issued, and the appeal is by hearing de novo before a superior court judge. (1929, c. 120, s. 54; 1977, cc. 456, 505; 1981 (Reg. Sess., 1982), c. 1243, s. 2; 1993, c. 321, s. 25(b); c. 399, s. 1; 1993 (Reg. Sess., 1994), c. 679, ss. 5.3, 5.4; 1995, c. 358, s. 8(a), (b); c. 437, s. 6(a), (b); c. 467, s. 5(a), (b); c. 507, ss. 25.13, 27.8(o); c. 509, s. 48; 2000-140, s. 93.1(a); 2001-424, s. 12.2(b); 2011-287, s. 19; 2013-294, s. 6.)

§ 97-81. Blank forms and literature; statistics; safety provisions; accident reports; studies and investigations and recommendations to General Assembly; to cooperate with other agencies for prevention of injury.

(a)   The Commission shall prepare and cause to be printed, and upon request furnish, free of charge to any employee or employer, such blank forms and literature as it shall deem requisite to facilitate or prompt the efficient administration of this Article. Notwithstanding G.S. 150B-2(8a)d., any new forms or substantive amendments to old forms adopted after July 1, 2013, shall be adopted in accordance with Article 2A of Chapter 150B of the General Statutes. The Commission may authorize the use of electronic submission of forms and other means of transmittal of forms and notices when it deems appropriate.

(b)   The Commission shall tabulate the accident reports received from employers in accordance with G.S. 97-92 and shall publish the same in the annual report of the Commission and as often as it may deem advisable, in such detailed or aggregate form as it may deem best. The name of the employer or employee shall not appear in such publications, and the employers' reports shall be private records of the Commission, and shall not be open for public inspection except for the inspection of the parties directly involved, and only to the extent of such interest, and except for inspection by the Department of Labor and other State or federal agencies pursuant to subsections (d) and (e) of this section. These reports shall not be used as evidence against any employer in any suit at law brought by any employee for the recovery of damages.

(c)   The Commission shall make studies and investigations with respect to safety provisions and the causes of injuries in employments covered by this

Article, and shall from time to time make to the General Assembly and to employers and carriers such recommendations as it may deem proper as to the best means of preventing such injuries.

(d)   In making such studies and investigations the Commission shall:

(1)   Cooperate with any agency of the United States charged with the duty of enforcing any law securing safety against injury in any employment covered by this Article, or with any State agency engaged in enforcing any laws to assure safety for employees, and

(2)   Permit any such agency to have access to the records of the Commission.

In carrying out the provisions of this section the Commission or any officer or employee of the Commission is authorized to enter at any reasonable time upon any premises, tracks, wharf, dock, or other landing place, or to enter any building, where an employment covered by this Article is being carried on, and to examine any tool, appliance, or machinery used in such employment.

(e)   The Commission shall, upon written request from the Commissioner of Labor, provide from the Commission's records the following information from claims filed by employees, and from employer reports of injury to an employee required by G.S. 97-92:

(1)   Name and business address of the employer;

(2)   Type of business of the employer;

(3)   Date the accident, illness, or injury occurred;

(4)   Nature of the injury or disease reported; and

(5)   Whether compensation for disability or medical expenses was paid to the injured employee.

Information provided to the Commissioner of Labor pursuant to this subsection, and to other State and federal agencies pursuant to subsection (d) of this section, shall be private and exempt from public inspection to the same extent that records of the Commission are so exempt. (1929, c. 120, s. 55; 1991 (Reg.

Sess., 1992), c. 894, s. 2; 1993 (Reg. Sess., 1994), c. 679, s. 10.2; 2013-294, s. 7.)

§ 97-82. Memorandum of agreement between employer and employee to be submitted to Commission on prescribed forms for approval; direct payment as award.

(a)   If the employer and the injured employee or his dependents reach an agreement in regard to compensation under this Article, they may enter into a memorandum of the agreement in the form prescribed by the Commission.

An agreement, however, shall be incorporated into a memorandum of agreement in regard to compensation: (i) for loss or permanent injury, disfigurement, or permanent and total disability under G.S. 97-31, (ii) for death from a compensable injury or occupational disease under G.S. 97-38, or (iii) when compensation under this Article is paid or payable to an employee who is incompetent or under 18 years of age.

The memorandum of agreement, accompanied by the material medical and vocational records, shall be filed with and approved by the Commission; otherwise such agreement shall be voidable by the employee or his dependents.

(b)   If approved by the Commission, a memorandum of agreement shall for all purposes be enforceable by the court's decree as hereinafter specified. Payment pursuant to G.S. 97-18(b), or payment pursuant to G.S. 97-18(d) when compensability and liability are not contested prior to expiration of the period for payment without prejudice, shall constitute an award of the Commission on the question of compensability of and the insurer's liability for the injury for which payment was made. Compensation paid in these circumstances shall constitute payment of compensation pursuant to an award under this Article. (1929, c. 120, s. 56; 1993 (Reg. Sess., 1994), c. 679, s. 3.2; 2005-448, s. 7.)

§ 97-83. Commission is to make award after hearing.

If the employer and the injured employee or his dependents fail to reach an agreement in regard to benefits under this Article within 14 days after the employer has written or actual notice of the injury or death, or upon the arising of a dispute under this Article, either party may make application to the Commission for a hearing in regard to the matters at issue, and for a ruling thereon.

Immediately after such application has been received the Commission shall set the date of a hearing, which shall be held as soon as practicable and shall notify the parties at issue of the time and place of such hearing. The hearing or hearings shall be held in the city or county where the injury occurred, unless otherwise authorized by the Commission. (1929, c. 120, s. 57; 1955, c. 1026, s. 121/2; 1977, c. 743; 1993 (Reg. Sess., 1994), c. 679, s. 3.3.)

§ 97-83.1. Facilities for hearings; security.

The senior resident superior court judge shall provide suitable facilities for the conduct of hearings under this Article in the county or counties within the judge's district at the time the Commission schedules hearings therein. The senior resident superior court judge shall, to the extent the judge determines necessary and practicable, provide or arrange for security at Commission hearings upon the request of a member or deputy of the Commission. (1993 (Reg. Sess., 1994), c. 679, s. 5.7.)

§ 97-84. Determination of disputes by Commission or deputy.

The Commission or any of its members shall hear the parties at issue and their representatives and witnesses, and shall determine the dispute in a summary manner. The Commission shall decide the case and issue findings of fact based upon the preponderance of the evidence in view of the entire record. The award, together with a statement of the findings of fact, rulings of law, and other matters pertinent to the questions at issue shall be filed with the record of the proceedings, within 180 days of the close of the hearing record unless time is extended for good cause by the Commission, and a copy of the award shall immediately be sent to the parties in dispute. The parties may be heard by a deputy, in which event the hearing shall be conducted in the same way and manner prescribed for hearings which are conducted by a member of the Industrial Commission, and said deputy shall proceed to a complete determination of the matters in dispute, file his written opinion within 180 days of the close of the hearing record unless time is extended for good cause by the Commission, and the deputy shall cause to be issued an award pursuant to such determination. (1929, c. 120, s. 58; 1951, c. 1059, s. 7; 1987, c. 729, s. 15; 2011-287, s. 20.)

§ 97-85. Review of award.

(a) If application is made to the Commission within 15 days from the date when notice of the award shall have been given, the full Commission shall review the award, and, if good ground be shown therefor, reconsider the evidence, receive further evidence, rehear the parties or their representatives, and, if proper, amend the award: Provided, however, when application is made for review of an award, and such an award has been heard and determined by a commissioner of the North Carolina Industrial Commission, the commissioner who heard and determined the dispute in the first instance, as specified by G.S. 97-84, shall be disqualified from sitting with the full Commission on the review of such award, and the chairman of the Industrial Commission shall designate a deputy commissioner to take such commissioner's place in the review of the particular award. The deputy commissioner so designated, along with the two other commissioners, shall compose the full Commission upon review. Provided further, the chairman of the Industrial Commission shall have the authority to designate a deputy commissioner to take the place of a commissioner on the review of any case, in which event the deputy commissioner so designated shall have the same authority and duty as does the commissioner whose place he occupies on such review.

(b) Unless waived by consent of the parties, all hearings of the full Commission shall be recorded. Court reporters, transcription personnel, or electronic or other mechanical devices may be utilized. If an electronic or other mechanical device is utilized, it shall be the duty of some person designated by the Commission to operate the device while a hearing is in progress, and the recording shall be preserved and may be transcribed, as required. If stenotype, shorthand, or stenomask equipment is used, the original tapes, notes, discs, or other records are the property of the State and the Commission shall keep them in its custody. The compensation and allowances of reporters shall be fixed by the Commission in a manner that is consistent with policies set by the Administrative Office of the Courts for the General Court of Justice. (1929, c. 120, s. 59; 1963, c. 402; 1977, cc. 390, 431; 2013-163, s. 1.)

§ 97-86. Award conclusive as to facts; appeal; certified questions of law.

The award of the Industrial Commission, as provided in G.S. 97-84, if not reviewed in due time, or an award of the Commission upon such review, as provided in G.S. 97-85, shall be conclusive and binding as to all questions of fact; but either party to the dispute may, within 30 days from the date of such award or within 30 days after receipt of notice to be sent by registered mail or certified mail of such award, but not thereafter, appeal from the decision of said Commission to the Court of Appeals for errors of law under the same terms and conditions as govern appeals from the superior court to the Court of Appeals in ordinary civil actions. The procedure for the appeal shall be as provided by the rules of appellate procedure.

The Industrial Commission of its own motion may certify questions of law to the Court of Appeals for decision and determination by said Court. In case of an appeal from the decision of the Commission, or of a certification by said Commission of questions of law, to the Court of Appeals, said appeal or certification shall operate on a supersedeas except as provided in G.S. 97-86.1, and no employer shall be required to make payment of the award involved in said appeal or certification until the questions at issue therein shall have been fully determined in accordance with the provisions of this Article. If the employer is a noninsurer, then the appeal of such employer shall not act as a supersedeas and the plaintiff in such case shall have the same right to issue execution or to satisfy the award from the property of the employer pending the appeal as obtains to the successful party in an action in the superior court.

When any party to an appeal from an award of the Commission is unable, by reason of his poverty, to make the deposit or to give the security required by law for said appeal, any member of the Commission or any deputy commissioner shall enter an order allowing said party to appeal from the award of the Commission without giving security therefor. The party appealing from the judgment shall, within 30 days from the filing of the appeal from the award, make an affidavit that he is unable by reason of his poverty to give the security required by law. The request shall be passed upon and granted or denied by a member of the Commission or deputy commissioner within 20 days from receipt of the affidavit specified above. (1929, c. 120, s. 60; 1947, c. 823; 1957, c. 1396, s. 9; 1959, c. 863, s. 4; 1967, c. 669; 1971, c. 1189; 1975, c. 391, s. 15; 1977, c. 521, s. 1; 1993 (Reg. Sess., 1994), c. 679, s. 10.5; 1995 (Reg. Sess., 1996), c. 552, s. 1.)

§ 97-86.1. Payment of award pending appeal in certain cases.

(a) When any appeal or certification to the Court of Appeals is pending, and it appears to the Commission that any part of the award appealed from is not appealed by the issues raised by such appeal, the Commission may, on action or of its own motion, render a judgment directing compliance with any portion of such award not affected by such appeal; or, if the only issue raised by such appeal is the amount of the average weekly wage, the Commission shall, on motion of the claimant, direct the payment of such portion of the compensation payable under its award as is not in dispute, if any, pending final adjudication of the undisputed portion thereof.

(b) In any claim under the provisions of this Chapter where it is conceded by all parties that the employee's claim is a compensable one and the amount is not disputed and where the only issue is which employer or employers, carrier or carriers are liable, the Commission may, where an appeal from a hearing commissioner or the full Commission is taken by one or more parties, order payment made to the employee pending outcome of the case on appeal. The order of payment shall contain the provision that if the employer or carrier ordered to pay is not ultimately liable for the amount paid, the employer or carrier will be reimbursed by the employer or carrier ultimately held liable.

(c) No payment made pursuant to the provisions of this section shall in any manner operate as an admission of liability or estoppel to deny liability by an employer or carrier.

(d) In any claim under the provisions of this Chapter wherein one employer or carrier has made payments to the employee or his dependents pending a final disposition of the claim and it is determined that different or additional employers or carriers are liable, the Commission may order any employers or carriers determined liable to make repayment in full or in part to any employer or carrier which has made payments to the employee or his dependents. (1977, c. 521, s. 2.)

§ 97-86.2. Interest on awards after hearing.

In any workers' compensation case in which an order is issued either granting or denying an award to the employee and where there is an appeal resulting in an ultimate award to the employee, the insurance carrier or employer shall pay interest on the final award or unpaid portion thereof from the date of the initial hearing on the claim, until paid at the legal rate of interest provided in G.S. 24-1. If interest is paid it shall not be a part of, or in any way increase attorneys' fees, but shall be paid in full to the claimant. (1981, c. 242, s. 1; 1985, c. 598; 1987, c. 729, s. 16.)

§ 97-87. Judgments on awards.

(a)   As used in this section, "award" includes the following:

(1)   A form filed, or an award arising, under G.S. 97-18(b), 97-18(d), or 97-82(b).

(2)   A memorandum of agreement approved by the Commission.

(3)   An order or decision of the Commission.

(4)   An award of the Commission from which there has been no appeal.

(5)   An award of the Commission affirmed on appeal.

(b)   When an award or portion of an award provides for a sum certain or for a sum that can by computation be made certain, and that sum is due and payable as of the date of the award, a judgment may be docketed as provided in subsection (d) of this section, in an amount equal to that sum.

(c)   When an award or portion of an award provides for periodic payments to be made on or after the date of the award, a judgment may be docketed as provided in subsection (d) of this section, in an amount equal to the sum stated in any Certificate of Accrued Arrearages that is issued by the Commission under this subsection. If any payment that has accrued after the date of the award, or after the date specified in the most recent Certificate of Accrued Arrearages issued under this subsection, is not received by the claimant when due, the following procedure is available for obtaining a Certificate of Accrued Arrearages:

(1)   The claimant may file with the Commission a Statement of Accrued Arrearages, on a form approved by the Commission, and shall serve a copy on all parties against whom judgment is sought and their attorney of record.

(2) Any party against whom judgment is sought may, within 15 days of the date of service of a Statement of Accrued Arrearages, file with the Commission proof of any payments that have been made or other responsive pleadings.

(3) If no proof or other responsive pleading is filed within 15 days of the date of service of the Statement, the Commission shall immediately issue a Certificate of Accrued Arrearages.

(4) If proof of payment or other responsive pleading is filed, the Commission shall, within seven days, either issue a Certificate of Accrued Arrearages that shall state the sum of payments due or decline to issue a Certificate of Accrued Arrearages. The Commission shall notify the claimant, the party against whom judgment is sought, and their attorney of record of the Commission's decision.

(5) If any party disputes the decision of the Commission entered under subdivision (c)(4) of this section, the party may appeal to the full Commission within 10 days of the entry of the decision of the Commission. The nonappealing party may file a response within 10 days of receiving notice of appeal. The notice of appeal shall request one of the following:

a. The Commission reconsider the decision entered based on the record and any additional evidence that parties submit with the notice and response.

b. A de novo evidentiary hearing before the full Commission.

(6) The Commission shall grant the request for an evidentiary hearing under sub-subdivision (c)(5)b. of this section if a material issue of fact exists whose resolution is necessary to determine the appeal.

(7) If a notice of appeal is given under sub-subdivision (c)(5)a. of this section, the Commission shall issue its decision within 10 days of the filing of the response under subdivision (c)(5)b. of this section. If a notice of appeal is given under sub-subdivision (c)(5) of this section, the Commission shall either conduct an evidentiary hearing and issue its decision on the appeal within 90 days of the filing of the response under subdivision (c)(5) of this section or deny the request for the evidentiary hearing and issue its decision within 10 days of the filing of the response under subdivision (c)(5) of this section. Further appeals are governed by G.S. 97-86.

(8) Each award and each Certificate of Accrued Arrearages shall include the following information:

a. The names and addresses of the parties.

b. The sum of all principal amounts that have accrued and remain unpaid since the date of the award or since the date of the most recent prior Certificate of Accrued Arrearages.

c. The total of any interest that has accrued on the award, as of the date of the Certificate of Accrued Arrearages, since the date of the award or since the date of the most recent prior Certificate of Accrued Arrearages.

d. Any costs, penalties, or monetary sanctions included in the award.

(d) Any party in interest may file a certified copy of an award described in subsection (b) of this section, or of a Certificate of Accrued Arrearages, in the office of the clerk of superior court of the county in which the defendant has a place of business or has property, or in which an injury occurred, or in Wake County. An award shall be accompanied by the party's affidavit stating that the award has become final and the time for making the first payment under the award has expired.

(e) Promptly after a certified copy of an award or of a Certificate of Accrued Arrearages is filed, the clerk shall docket and index a judgment as provided in Chapter 1 of the General Statutes. The principal amount in the award or in the Certificate of Accrued Arrearages shall bear interest at the judgment rate from the date the judgment is docketed. The judgment may be enforced in the same manner as a judgment docketed under Chapter 1 of the General Statutes.

(f) The filing of an award, or of a Certificate of Accrued Arrearages, for docketing as a judgment under this section shall be treated as a civil action for record-keeping purposes. The amount in which the judgment is docketed shall determine the amount of the costs to be collected at the time of filing and assessed pursuant to G.S. 7A-305.

(g) Nothing in this section shall be construed to limit the Commission's authority to impose any other remedy provided by law. (1929, c. 120, s. 61; 2001-477, s. 1.)

§ 97-88. Expenses of appeals brought by insurers.

If the Industrial Commission at a hearing on review or any court before which any proceedings are brought on appeal under this Article, shall find that such hearing or proceedings were brought by the insurer and the Commission or court by its decision orders the insurer to make, or to continue payments of benefits, including compensation for medical expenses, to the injured employee, the Commission or court may further order that the cost to the injured employee of such hearing or proceedings including therein reasonable attorney's fee to be determined by the Commission shall be paid by the insurer as a part of the bill of costs. (1929, c. 120, s. 62; 1931, c. 274, s. 11; 1971, c. 500.)

§ 97-88.1. Attorney's fees at original hearing.

If the Industrial Commission shall determine that any hearing has been brought, prosecuted, or defended without reasonable ground, it may assess the whole cost of the proceedings including reasonable fees for defendant's attorney or plaintiff's attorney upon the party who has brought or defended them. (1979, c. 268, s. 1.)

§ 97-88.2. Penalty for fraud.

(a)   Any person who willfully makes a false statement or representation of a material fact for the purpose of obtaining or denying any benefit or payment, or assisting another to obtain or deny any benefit or payment under this Article, shall be guilty of a Class 1 misdemeanor if the amount at issue is less than one thousand dollars ($1,000). Violation of this section is a Class H felony if the amount at issue is one thousand dollars ($1,000) or more. The court may order restitution.

(a1)   When a person is convicted under subsection (a) of this section, the Commission may enter such orders as necessary to ensure that the person convicted does not benefit from the unlawful conduct.

(b)   The Commission shall:

(1)   Perform investigations regarding all cases of suspected fraud and all violations related to workers' compensation claims, by or against insurers or

self-funded employers, and refer possible criminal violations to the appropriate prosecutorial authorities;

(2) Conduct administrative violation proceedings; and

(3) Assess and collect civil penalties and restitution.

The Commission may employ sworn law enforcement officers duly appointed and certified through the North Carolina Criminal Justice Education and Training Standards Commission to conduct the investigations mandated by this subsection.

(c) Any person who threatens an employee with criminal prosecution under the provisions of subsection (a) of this section for the purpose of coercing or attempting to coerce the employee into agreeing to compensation or agreeing to forgo compensation under this Article shall be guilty of a Class H felony.

(d) The Commission shall not be liable in a civil action for any action made in good faith under this section, including the identification and referral of a person for investigation and prosecution for an alleged administrative violation or criminal offense. Any person, including, but not limited to, an attorney, an employee, an employer, an insurer, and an employee of an insurer, who in good faith comes forward with information under this section, shall not be liable in a civil action.

(e) The Commission shall report annually to the General Assembly on the number and disposition of investigations involving claimants, employers, insurance company officials, officials of third-party administrators, insurance agents, attorneys, health care providers, and vocational rehabilitation providers. (1993 (Reg. Sess., 1994), c. 679, s. 7.1; 1995, c. 507, s. 25(a); 1997-353, s. 1; 2005-448, s. 8; 2007-358, s. 1.)

§ 97-88.3. Penalty for health care providers.

(a) In addition to any liability under G.S. 97-88.2, any health care provider who willfully or intentionally undertakes the following acts is subject to an administrative penalty, assessed by the Commission, not to exceed ten thousand dollars ($10,000):

(1) Submitting charges for health care that was not furnished;

(2) Fraudulently administering, providing, and attempting to collect for inappropriate or unnecessary treatment or services; or

(3) Violating the provisions of Article 28 of Chapter 90 of the General Statutes.

A penalty assessed by the Commission for a violation of subdivision (3) of this subsection is in addition to penalties assessed under G.S. 90-407.

(b) In addition to any liability under G.S. 97-88.2, any health care provider who willfully or intentionally undertakes the following acts is subject to an administrative penalty, assessed by the Commission, not to exceed one thousand dollars ($1,000):

(1) Failing or refusing to timely file required reports or records;

(2) Making unnecessary referrals; and

(3) Knowingly violating this Article or rules promulgated hereunder, including treatment guidelines, with intention to deceive or to gain improper advantage of a patient, employee, insurer, or the Commission.

(c) A health care provider who knowingly charges or otherwise holds an employee financially responsible for the cost of any services provided for a compensable injury under this Article is guilty of a Class 1 misdemeanor.

(d) Any person, including, but not limited to, an employer, an insurer, and an employee of an insurer, who in good faith comes forward with information under this section, shall not be liable in a civil action.

(e) Information relating to possible violations under this section shall be reported to the Commission which shall refer the same to the appropriate licensing or regulatory board or authority for the health care provider involved.

(f) A hospital that relies in good faith on a written order of a physician in performing health care services shall not be subject to an administrative penalty in violation of this section. (1993 (Reg. Sess., 1994), c. 679, s. 7.2.)

§ 97-89. Commission may appoint qualified physician to make necessary examinations; expenses; fees.

The Commission or any member thereof may, upon the application of either party, or upon its own motion, appoint a disinterested and duly qualified physician or surgeon to make any necessary medical examination of the employee, and to testify in respect thereto. Said physician or surgeon shall be allowed traveling expenses and a reasonable fee to be fixed by the Commission. The fees and expenses of such physician or surgeon shall be paid by the employer. (1929, c. 120, s. 63; 1931, c. 274, s. 12; 1973, c. 520, s. 3.)

§ 97-90. Legal and medical fees to be approved by Commission; misdemeanor to receive fees unapproved by Commission, or to solicit employment in adjusting claims; agreement for fee or compensation.

(a) Fees for attorneys and charges of health care providers for medical compensation under this Article shall be subject to the approval of the Commission; but no physician or hospital or other medical facilities shall be entitled to collect fees from an employer or insurance carrier until he has made the reports required by the Commission in connection with the case. Except as provided in G.S. 97-26(g), a request for a specific prior approval to charge shall be submitted to the Commission for each such fee or charge.

(b) Any person (i) who receives any fee, other consideration, or any gratuity on account of services so rendered, unless such consideration or gratuity is approved by the Commission or the court, as provided in subsection (c), or (ii) who makes it a business to solicit employment for a lawyer or for himself in respect of any claim or award for compensation, shall be guilty of a Class 1 misdemeanor.

(c) If an attorney has an agreement for fee or compensation under this Article, he shall file a copy or memorandum thereof with the hearing officer or Commission prior to the conclusion of the hearing. If the agreement is not considered unreasonable, the hearing officer or Commission shall approve it at the time of rendering decision. If the agreement is found to be unreasonable by the hearing officer or Commission, the reasons therefor shall be given and what is considered to be reasonable fee allowed. If within five days after receipt of notice of such fee allowance, the attorney shall file notice of appeal to the full Commission, the full Commission shall hear the matter and determine whether or not the attorney's agreement as to a fee or the fee allowed is unreasonable. If the full Commission is of the opinion that such agreement or fee allowance is unreasonable and so finds, then the attorney may, by filing written notice of appeal within 10 days after receipt of such action by the full Commission, appeal to the senior resident judge of the superior court in the county in which the cause of action arose or in which the claimant resides; and upon such appeal said judge shall consider the matter and determine in his discretion the reasonableness of said agreement or fix the fee and direct an order to the Commission following his determination therein. The Commission shall, within 20 days after receipt of notice of appeal from its action concerning said agreement or allowance, transmit its findings and reasons as to its action concerning such agreement or allowance to the judge of the superior court designated in the notice of appeal. In all other cases where there is no agreement for fee or compensation, the attorney or claimant may, by filing written notice of appeal within five days after receipt of notice of action of the full Commission with respect to attorneys' fees, appeal to the senior resident judge of the superior court of the district of the county in which the cause arose or in which the claimant resides; and upon such appeal said judge shall consider the matter of such fee and determine in his discretion the attorneys' fees to be allowed in the cause. The Commission shall, within 20 days after notice of appeal has been filed, transmit its findings and reasons as to its action concerning such fee or compensation to the judge of the superior court designated in the notice of appeal; provided that the Commission shall in no event have any jurisdiction over any attorneys' fees in any third-party action. In any case in which an attorney appeals to the superior court on the question of attorneys' fees, the appealing attorney shall notify the Commission and the employee of any and all proceedings before the superior court on the appeal, and either or both may appear and be represented at such proceedings.

The Commission, in determining an allowance of attorneys' fees, shall examine the record to determine the services rendered. The factors which may be considered by the Commission in allowing a reasonable fee include, but are not limited to, the time invested, the amount involved, the results achieved, whether the fee is fixed or contingent, the customary fee for similar services, the experience and skill level of the attorney, and the nature of the attorney's services.

In making the allowance of attorneys' fees, the Commission shall, upon its own motion or that of an interested party, set forth findings sufficient to support the amount approved.

The Commission may deny or reduce an attorney's fees upon proof of solicitation of employment in violation of the Rules of Professional Conduct of the North Carolina State Bar.

(d) Provided, that nothing contained in this section shall prevent the collection of such reasonable fees of physicians and charges for hospitalization as may be recovered in an action, or embraced in settlement of a claim, against a third-party tort-feasor as described in G.S. 97-10.2.

(e) A health care provider shall not pursue a private claim against an employee for all or part of the costs of medical treatment provided to the employee by the provider unless the employee's claim or the treatment is finally adjudicated not to be compensable or the employee fails to request a hearing after denial of liability by the employer. Notwithstanding subsequent denial of liability or adjudication that the condition treated was not compensable, the insurer shall be liable as provided in G.S. 97-26 to providers whose services have been authorized by the insurer or employer. The statute of limitations applicable to a provider's claim for payment shall be tolled during the period the compensability of a claim or liability for particular treatment remains an issue in a compensation case.

(f) The Commission shall hear and determine any dispute between an employee's current and past attorney or attorneys regarding the division of a fee as approved by the Commission pursuant to this section. An attorney who is a party to an action under this subsection shall have the same rights of appeal as outlined in subsection (c) of this section. (1929, c. 120, s. 64; 1955, c. 1026, s. 4; 1959, cc. 1268, 1307; 1973, c. 520, s. 4; 1981, c. 521, s. 4; 1991, c. 703, s. 6; 1993, c. 539, s. 680; 1994, Ex. Sess., c. 24, s. 14(c); 1993 (Reg. Sess., 1994), c. 679, s. 9.1; 2013-278, s. 1.)

§ 97-90.1. Insurers that provide employee's health benefit plans, disability income plans, or any other health insurance plans as real parties in interest; reimbursement.

An insurer that covers an employee under a health benefit plan as defined in G.S. 58-3-167, a disability income plan, or any other health insurance plan is not a real party in interest and shall not intervene or participate in any proceeding or settlement agreement under this Article to determine whether a claim is compensable under this Article or to seek reimbursement for medical payments under its plan. The insurer that covers an employee under a health benefit plan as defined in G.S. 58-3-167 or any other health insurance plan may seek reimbursement from the employee, employer, or carrier that is liable or responsible for the specific medical charge according to a final adjudication of the claim under this Article or an order of the Commission approving a settlement agreement entered into under this Article for health plan payments for that specific medical charge. Upon the admission or adjudication that a claim is compensable, the party or parties liable shall notify in writing any known health benefit plan covering the employee of the admission or adjudication. (2001-216, s. 1; 2001-487, s. 102(b).)

§ 97-91. Commission to determine all questions.

All questions arising under this Article if not settled by agreements of the parties interested therein, with the approval of the Commission, shall be determined by the Commission, except as otherwise herein provided. (1929, c. 120, s. 65.)

§ 97-92. Employer's record and report of accidents; records of Commission not open to public; supplementary report upon termination of disability; penalty for refusal to make report; when insurance carrier liable.

(a) Every employer shall hereafter keep a record of all injuries, fatal or otherwise, received by his employees in the course of their employment on blanks approved by the Commission. Within five days after the occurrence and knowledge thereof as provided in G.S. 97-22 of an injury to an employee, causing his absence from work for more than one day or charges for medical compensation exceeding the amount set by the Commission, a report thereof shall be made in writing and mailed or transmitted to the Commission in the form approved by the Commission for this purpose.

(b) The records of the Commission that are not awards under G.S. 97-84 and that are not reviews of awards under G.S. 97-85, insofar as they refer to accidents, injuries, and settlements are not public records under G.S. 132-1 and shall not be open to the public, but only to the parties satisfying the Commission of their interest in such records and the right to inspect them, and to State and federal agencies pursuant to G.S. 97-81.

(c) Upon the termination of the disability of the injured employee, or if the disability extends beyond a period of 60 days, then, also, at the expiration of such period the employer shall make a supplementary report to the Commission on blanks to be procured from the Commission for the purpose.

(d) The said report shall contain the name, nature, and location of the business of the employer and name, age, sex, and wages and occupation of the injured employee, and shall state the date and hour of the accident causing injury, the nature and cause of the injury, and such other information as may be required by the Commission.

(e) Any employer who refuses or neglects to make the report required by this section shall be liable for a penalty of not less than five dollars ($5.00) and not more than twenty-five dollars ($25.00) for each refusal or neglect. The fine herein provided may be assessed by the Commission in an open hearing, with the right of review and appeal as in other cases. In the event the employer has transmitted the report to the insurance carrier for transmission by such insurance carrier to the Industrial Commission, the insurance carrier willfully neglecting or failing to transmit the report shall be liable for the said penalty.

(f) Any bill, report, application, and document of every nature and kind, which is required or permitted by Commission rules to be transmitted to the Commission by electronic media or is recorded among the Commission records on computer disk, optical disk, microfilm, or similar media and which is produced or reproduced in written form in the normal course of business or is certified as a true and accurate copy of the data recorded at the Commission in the normal course of its business shall be treated as a signed original in all uses before the Commission and as a duplicate within the meaning of Rule 1003 of the North Carolina Rules of Evidence. (1929, c. 120, s. 66; 1945, c. 766; 1991, c. 703, s. 9; 1991 (Reg. Sess., 1992), c. 894, s. 3; 1993 (Reg. Sess., 1994), c. 679, s. 10.8; 2001-216, s. 3; 2001-487, s. 102(b).)

§ 97-93. Employers required to carry insurance or prove financial ability to pay for benefits; employers required to post notice; self-insured employers regulated by Commissioner of Insurance.

(a) Every employer subject to the provisions of this Article relative to the payment of compensation shall either:

(1) Insure and keep insured his liability under this Article in any authorized corporation, association, organization, or in any mutual insurance association formed by a group of employers so authorized; or

(2) Repealed by Session Laws 1997-362, s. 5.

(3) Obtain a license from the Commissioner of Insurance under Article 5 of this Chapter or under Article 47 of Chapter 58 of the General Statutes.

(b) through (d) Repealed by Session Laws 1997-362, s. 5.

(e) Every employer who is in compliance with the provisions of subsection (a) of this section shall post in a conspicuous place in places of employment a notice stating that employment by this employer is subject to the North Carolina Workers' Compensation Act and stating whether the employer has a policy of insurance against liability or qualifies as a self-insured employer. In the event the employer allows its insurance to lapse or ceases to qualify as a self-insured employer, the employer shall, within five working days of this occurrence, remove any notices indicating otherwise. (1929, c. 120, s. 67; 1943, c. 543; 1973, c. 1291, s. 12; 1979, c. 345; 1983, c. 728; 1985, c. 119, s. 1; 1993, c. 120, ss. 1, 2; 1993 (Reg. Sess., 1994), c. 679, s. 8.2; 1995, c. 193, s. 64; c. 471, s. 1; 1997-362, s. 5.)

§ 97-94. Employers required to give proof that they have complied with preceding section; penalty for not keeping liability insured; review; liability for compensation; criminal penalties for failure to secure payment of compensation.

(a) Every employer subject to the compensation provisions of this Article shall file with the Commission, in form prescribed by it, as often as the Commission determines to be necessary, evidence of its compliance with the provisions of G.S. 97-93 and all other provisions relating thereto.

(b) Any employer required to secure the payment of compensation under this Article who refuses or neglects to secure such compensation shall be punished by a penalty of one dollar ($1.00) for each employee, but not less than fifty dollars ($50.00) nor more than one hundred dollars ($100.00) for each day of such refusal or neglect, and until the same ceases; and the employer shall be liable during continuance of such refusal or neglect to an employee either for compensation under this Article or at law at the election of the injured employee.

The penalty herein provided may be assessed by the Industrial Commission administratively, with the right to a hearing if requested within 30 days after notice of the assessment of the penalty and the right of review and appeal as in other cases. Enforcement of the penalty shall be made by the Office of the Attorney General. The clear proceeds of penalties provided for in this subsection shall be remitted to the Civil Penalty and Forfeiture Fund in accordance with G.S. 115C-457.2.

(c)   Any employer required to secure the payment of compensation under this Article who willfully fails to secure such compensation shall be guilty of a Class H felony. Any employer required to secure the payment of compensation under this Article who neglects to secure the payment of compensation shall be guilty of a Class 1 misdemeanor.

(d)   Any person who, with the ability and authority to bring an employer in compliance with G.S. 97-93, willfully fails to bring the employer in compliance, shall be guilty of a Class H felony. Any person who, with the ability and authority to bring an employer in compliance with G.S. 97-93, neglects to bring the employer in compliance, shall be guilty of a Class 1 misdemeanor. Any person who violates this subsection may be assessed a civil penalty by the Commission in an amount up to one hundred percent (100%) of the amount of any compensation due the employer's employees injured during the time the employer failed to comply with G.S. 97-93.

(e)   Notwithstanding the provisions of G.S. 97-101, the Commission may suspend collection or remit all or part of any civil penalty imposed under this section on condition that the employer or person pays the compensation due and complies with G.S. 97-93. (1929, c. 120, s. 68; 1945, c. 766; 1963, c. 499; 1973, c. 1291, s. 13; 1985, c. 119, s. 4; 1985 (Reg. Sess., 1986), c. 1027, s. 54; 1987, c. 729, s. 17; 1993, c. 539, s. 681; 1994, Ex. Sess., c. 24, s. 14(c); 1993 (Reg. Sess., 1994), c. 679, s. 8.1; 1997-353, s. 2; 1998-215, s. 115.)

§ 97-95. Actions against employers failing to effect insurance or qualify as self-insurer.

As to every employer subject to the provisions of this Article who shall fail or neglect to keep in effect a policy of insurance against compensation liability arising hereunder with some insurance carrier as provided in G.S. 97-93, or who shall fail to qualify as a self-insurer as provided in the Article, in addition to other penalties provided by this Article, such employer shall be liable in a civil action which may be instituted by the claimant for all such compensation as may be awarded by the Industrial Commission in a proceeding properly instituted before said Commission, and such action may be brought by the claimant in the county of his residence or in any county in which the defendant has any property in this State; and in said civil action, ancillary remedies provided by law in civil actions of attachment, receivership, and other appropriate ancillary remedies shall be available to plaintiff therein. Said action may be instituted before the award shall be made by the Industrial Commission in such case for the purpose of preventing the defendant from disposing of or removing from the State of North Carolina for the purpose of defeating the payment of compensation any property which the defendant may own in this State. In said action, after being instituted, the court may, after proper amendment to the pleadings therein, permit the recovery of a judgment against the defendant for the amount of compensation duly awarded by the North Carolina Industrial Commission and subject any property seized in said action for payment of the judgment so awarded. The institution of said action shall in no wise interfere with the jurisdiction of said Industrial Commission in hearing and determining the claim for compensation in full accord with the provisions of this Article. Nothing in this section shall be construed to limit or abridge the rights of an employee as provided in subsection (b) of G.S. 97-94. (1941, c. 352.)

§ 97-96: Repealed by Session Laws 1997-362, s. 7.

§ 97-97. Insurance policies must contain clause that notice to employer is notice to insurer, etc.

All policies insuring the payment of compensation under this Article must contain a clause to the effect that, as between the employer and the insurer the notice to or acknowledgment of the occurrence of the injury on the part of the insured employer shall be deemed notice or knowledge as the case may be, on the part of the insurer; that jurisdiction of the insured for the purposes of this Article shall be jurisdiction of the insurer, that the insurer shall in all things be bound by and subject to the awards, judgments, or decrees rendered against such insured employer, and that insolvency or bankruptcy of the employer and/or discharge therein shall not relieve the insurer from the payment of compensation for disability or death sustained by an employee during the life of such policy or contract. (1929, c. 120, s. 70.)

§ 97-98. Policy must contain agreement promptly to pay benefits; continuance of obligation of insurer in event of default.

No policy of insurance against liability arising under this Article shall be issued unless it contains the agreement of the insurer that it will promptly pay to the person entitled to same all benefits conferred by this Article, and all installments of the compensation that may be awarded or agreed upon, and that the obligation shall not be affected by any default of the insured after the injury or by any default in giving notice required by such policy or otherwise. Such agreement shall be construed to be a direct promise by the insurer to the person entitled to compensation enforceable in his name. (1929, c. 120, s. 71.)

§ 97-99. Law written into each insurance policy; form of policy to be approved by Commissioner of Insurance; single catastrophe hazards.

(a)   Every policy for the insurance of the compensation in this Article, or against liability therefor, shall be deemed to be made subject to the provisions of this Article. No corporation, association or organization shall enter into any such policy of insurance unless its form has been approved by the Commissioner of Insurance.

(b)   This Article shall not apply to policies of insurance against loss from explosion of boilers or flywheels or other similar single catastrophe hazards: Provided, that nothing in this Article relieves an employer from liability for injury or death of an employee as a result of such an explosion or catastrophe. (1929, c. 120, s. 72; 1943, c. 170; 1945, c. 381, s. 1; 1959, c. 863, s. 5; 1967, c. 1218; 1993, c. 504, s. 31; 2001-241, s. 1.)

§ 97-100. Rates for insurance; carrier to make reports for determination of solvency; tax upon premium; wrongful or fraudulent representation of carrier punishable as misdemeanor; notices.

(a)   The rates charged by all carriers of insurance, including the parties to any mutual insurance association writing insurance against the liability for compensation under this Article, shall be fair, reasonable, and adequate.

(b) Each insurance carrier shall report to the Commissioner of Insurance, in accordance with rules adopted by the Commissioner of Insurance, for the purpose of determining the solvency of the carrier and the adequacy of its rates; for this purpose the Commissioner of Insurance may inspect the books and records of any insurance carrier, and examine its agents, officers, and directors under oath.

(c) Every insurer under this Article, every employer carrying its own risk under G.S. 97-93, and every group of employers that has pooled the employers' liabilities under G.S. 97-93 is subject to the premiums tax levied in Article 8B of Chapter 105 of the General Statutes.

(d) through (f). Repealed by Session Laws 1995, c. 360, s. 1.

(g) Any person who acts or assumes to act as agent for any insurance carrier whose authority to do business in this State has been suspended, while the suspension remains in force, who neglects or refuses to comply with any of the provisions of this section, or who willfully makes a false or fraudulent statement of the business or condition of any insurance carrier, is guilty of a Class 2 misdemeanor.

(h) Whenever by this Article, or the terms of any policy contract, any officer is required to give any notice to an insurance carrier, the notice may be given by delivery, or by mailing by registered letter properly addressed and stamped, to the principal office or general agent of the insurance carrier within this State, or to its home office, or to the secretary, general agent, or chief officer of the carrier in the United States, or to the Commissioner of Insurance.

(i) through (k). Repealed by Session Laws 1995, c. 360, s. 1. (1929, c. 120, s. 73; 1931, c. 274, s. 13; 1947, c. 574; 1961, c. 833, s. 13; 1977, c. 828, s. 7; 1985, c. 119, s. 2; 1985 (Reg. Sess., 1986), c. 928, s. 13; 1989, c. 647, s. 1; 1993, c. 539, s. 682; 1994, Ex. Sess., c. 24, s. 14(c); 1995, c. 360, s. 1(h).)

§ 97-101. Collection of fines and penalties.

The Industrial Commission shall have the power by civil action brought in its own name to enforce the collection of any fines or penalties provided by this Article, and fines or penalties collected by the Commission shall become a part of the maintenance fund referred to in subsection (j) of G.S. 97-100. (1931, c. 274, s. 14.)

Vision Books Order Form

Fax Orders:	1-980-299-5965
Phone Orders:	1-704-898-0770
E-mail Orders:	www.visionbooks.org
Mail Orders:	Vision Books, LLC P.O. Box 42406 Charlotte, NC 28215

Shipp To:
Name_____
Address_____
City_____State_____Zip_____
Phone_____Fax_____
Email_____@_____

Bill To: We can bill a third party on your behalf.
Name_____
Address_____
City_____State_____Zip_____
Phone___(_____)_____Fax_____
Email_____@_____

Pamphlet Number ($15.00 Each)	Qty	Total Cost
_____	_____	_____
_____	_____	_____
_____	_____	_____
_____	_____	_____
_____	_____	_____
_____	_____	_____
_____	_____	_____
Full Volume Set 1-92	**92 Pamphlets**	**1,380.00**

Free Shipping Shipping & Handling on Full Volume Orders
Add $1.00 Shipping & Handling per pamphlet $_____

Total Cost $_____

Thank you for your support. Management!

DID YOU ENJOY THIS BOOK?

Vision Books, LLC would like to hear from you! If you or someone you know has been fasely imprisoned, we would like to hear your story. If the 'North Carolina Criminal Law and Procedure' has had an effect in your life or if you have suggestions, we would like to hear from you. Send your letters to:

Vision Books, LLC
Attn: Staff Writers
P.O. Box 42406
Charlotte, NC 28215
Email: staff@visionbooks.org

Order Additional Copies:

Fax Orders:	1-980-299-5965
Phone Orders:	1-704-898-0770
E-mail Orders:	www.visionbooks.org
Mail Orders:	Vision Books, LLC P.O. Box 42406 Charlotte, NC 28215

www.ingramcontent.com/pod-product-compliance
Lightning Source LLC
Chambersburg PA
CBHW051628170526
45167CB00001B/107